A LAW AND ECONOMICS APPROACH TO CRIMINAL GANGS

Special thanks to Ilan and Patricia Vertinsky and to Jeff Evanseck for their encouragement and support throughout my academic endeavors.

Thanks also to Professor Oliver Hart, from whose teaching and guidance I benefited immensely.

A Law and Economics Approach to Criminal Gangs

LIZA VERTINSKY, Ph.D., J.D.
Hill & Barlow, A Professional Corporation

Ashgate
Aldershot • Brookfield USA • Singapore • Sydney

Published by
Ashgate Publishing Ltd
Gower House
Croft Road
Aldershot
Hants GU11 3HR
England

Ashgate Publishing Company
Old Post Road
Brookfield
Vermont 05036
USA

British Library Cataloguing in Publication Data
Vertinsky, Liza
A law and economics approach to criminal gangs
1. Gangs 2. Gangs - Social aspects 3. Gang members - Psychology 4. Gang members - Legal status, laws, etc.
I. Title
364.1'066

Library of Congress Catalog Card Number: 98-74512

ISBN 1 84014 898 5

Printed and bound by
Antony Rowe Ltd, Chippenham, Wiltshire

Contents

Preface

The increase in number, size and level of sophistication of criminal gangs has generated concern in political and law enforcement circles. This concern has fueled interest in expanding the scope and the use of "group based" criminal laws which apply to multiple offender crimes or patterns of related crimes and which allow for affiliative and compound liability. While the current legal system provides for deviations from the traditional framework of isolated prosecution and punishment for specific events, it fails to incorporate the organizational structure of the criminal group into rule design. Chapter one examines the state of the law regarding group based criminal activities in general and criminal street gang activities in particular, and evaluates the current approach from an economic perspective. A simple economic model is used to demonstrate some of the ways in which policy variables might impact upon the activities of a criminal gang. The model shows that under certain circumstances group based sanctions may actually increase rather than decrease a gang's criminal capabilities. This result highlights the need for a closer integration of legal and economic analysis in the design of group based criminal laws.

The range of functions that the gang structure performs and the diverse set of factors which operate either to constrain or enhance its operations make the criminal street gang an interesting case study in collective action. Chapter two begins by reviewing some of the economic approaches which have been taken towards modeling joint production and/or decision making and suggests ways in which these approaches can be applied to better understand the structure and behavior of criminal street gangs. Part two of the chapter presents a model of the criminal street gang as an agreement enforcing institution. Gang membership provides participants in illegal markets with the ability to make agreements which will be self-enforcing. In the absence of third party enforcement, the development of an alternative commitment device based on repeated interaction plays a key role in sustaining efficient trade. The model is used to explain certain stylized features of criminal street gangs and to suggest ways in which cooperative relationships can be sustained in illegal markets.

The third chapter provides a framework for examining the economic organization of American gangs involved in the illegal narcotics market. The chapter is based on the premise that gangs adopt organizational structures which are effective at exploiting the income opportunities and minimizing the risks in territories which they currently occupy or plan to control in the future. A model is developed which suggests that different organizational structures will emerge as efficient responses to economic conditions. In this model drug dealing street gangs face a basic choice between two forms of organization, a vertical form of organization in which the quantity of drugs which each gang member has to sell is selected by a gang leader, and a horizontal form of organization in which individuals make their own quantity and effort choices. This model is then used to map features of the market environment onto a basic set of determinants of organizational choice, and to explain observed differences in the organization of drug dealing street gangs in different geographic locations, across different ethnic groups, and in different product markets.

The author wishes to express her thanks to Oliver Hart and Judge Stanley Marcus, who both contributed greatly to her understanding of law and economics. She also wishes to thank her parents for their help and support during the writing of this book.

1 A Law and Economics Approach to Group-based Criminal Laws and Criminal Street Gangs

Introduction

Criminal gangs are forming a new and increasingly powerful level of organized crime in America, and law enforcement efforts have been ineffective at controlling their growth, proliferation and development.[1] Many of these organized criminal gangs start out as loosely structured, ethnically homogenous social groups whose primarily teen-age and young adult members face few if any alternative income earning prospects and little economic or geographic mobility.[2] The gang structure provides the vehicle for successful entry into illegal income generating activities and allows for more sophisticated responses to illegal market opportunities and law enforcement strategies. The legal system has not been designed to address the special problems created by these new criminal groups,[3] and recognition of this inadequacy has prompted both federal and state governments to increase the scope and the use of older group-based criminal statutes and to enact new statutes targeted explicitly at criminal organizations.[4] Major changes at the federal and state level include the use of racketeering and criminal enterprise statutes that allow for an expanded range of evidentiary and sentencing options, joint trials, affiliative and compound liability. Some states have tried to address the problem of gang-related crimes even more directly through the enactment of anti-gang statutes and carefully tailored loitering and nuisance laws.[5]

While policy makers have made a concerted effort to address criminal groups, little attention has been paid to the organization of these groups in rule design. This chapter employs an economic model of a criminal street gang to illustrate the potential dangers of adopting group-based liability without consideration of the organization and incentive structure of the criminal group. It is based on the premise that when dealing with criminal groups, efficient legal rules and strategies must incorporate information about the economic structures of the target criminal organizations. The first part of the chapter provides an overview of the current statutory framework governing group-based crimes, including recent developments in statutory approaches towards criminal street gangs. The second part develops a simple economic model of a criminal street gang that is used to demonstrate some of the ways in which policy variables might impact upon the activities of a criminal group. The model shows that under certain circumstances group-based sanctions may actually increase rather than decrease a gang's criminal capabilities. Selected applications of this model to specific criminal law provisions and law enforcement problems are considered in the third part. The chapter concludes with a discussion of the need for a closer integration of legal and economic analysis in the design of effective group-based criminal laws.

I. The American Criminal Law Approach to Group-based Crimes

American criminal law has developed around the paradigm of an individual wrongdoer who is held responsible for a single event attributable to his own intentional or reckless conduct, the severity of the punishment tailored to the reprehensibility and harmfulness of the act. In this "transaction-based" model of criminality, prosecution of a specific individual for a specific event is carried out using evidence which is restricted to information concerning the individual's conduct and liability which is proportional to the magnitude of the harm which he causes or attempts to cause. The shortcomings of this approach have been most evident in its application to the activities of sophisticated criminal organizations. When there are multiple actors involved to varying degrees in multiple criminal activities it will generally be more difficult to pin point the primary actors, establish proof of act (actus reus) and intent (mens rea), and allocate individual liability for a specific crime. Law enforcement strategies which are effective at addressing individual crimes may not be effective at controlling organized activities, particularly since the most culpable participants are often the least directly connected to the commission of the crime and the most difficult to prosecute under an individualized act and intent based legal system. Organizations will have their own incentive system in place, and in the case of sophisticated organizations this system will be designed to diffuse responsibility for criminal acts and to offset the deterrent effects of enforcement policies. Indeed, criminal organizations may be more effective than law enforcement at deterring acts by their members which they regard as harmful because of the relative closeness of the relationships between participants and the absence of legal constraints on the types of penalties available for those who break the organization's rules. More importantly, measures which leave the control structure and the economic base of the organization in place are unlikely to make more than a temporary dent in the organization's activities.

The transaction-based approach can be contrasted with an enterprise-based approach that focuses on a group of related actors who share a common underlying objective and jointly engage in activities which are conducted in pursuit of this objective. Under an enterprise-based approach the law enforcer and policy maker are encouraged to look at ongoing patterns of crimes committed by members of a group as opposed to single events committed by individuals. The criminal enterprise, defined as an ongoing series of criminal transactions conducted by repeat players, replaces the individual transaction as the unit of analysis. Criminal investigations, methods of prosecution, and penalties are targeted at patterns of events. Examples include the use of racketeering statutes, which enhance the penalties attached to crimes occurring in clusters within a particular time frame and in furtherance of group objectives, and the use of conspiracy charges, which penalize agreements made by multiple persons to commit crimes. The demonstrated ability of criminal street gangs to transform themselves into sophisticated business enterprises has led to a new policy focus on the control structure and economic foundation of criminal groups. Asset forfeiture and money laundering statutes have been applied with increasing frequency to attack the economic foundation and structure of criminal organizations. Judges have expanded the attention devoted to the organizational aspects of criminal enterprises during the course of trial and sentencing, and trends towards more expansive application of racketeering and conspiracy theories in conviction and sentencing are evident.[6] The Federal Sentencing Commission has explicitly incorporated size of transactions and degree of control over criminal organization into sentencing guidelines, and criminal penalties are now more reflective of degree of involvement in and control over high profit criminal activities.

While there has been a policy shift away from the simple transaction-based approach to certain types of criminal activities, particularly those involving illegal drug trafficking, too little attention has been paid to the economic organization of criminal enterprises. Rather than designing a new set of substantive laws, the predominant legal approach towards group crimes has been to superimpose additional provisions onto the existing set of individual based crimes and to allow for an increased flexibility in the application of act and intent requirements of existing group-based statutes.

Those new group-based statutes which have been developed are the products of attempts to fit enterprise liability into the traditional "transaction-based" model by treating participation in patterns of criminal activities and associations as a unified crime with individualized act and intent requirements. "Agreement" to participate in a criminal group and "knowledge" of conspiracy activities become substitutes for traditional "act" and "intent" requirements used to determine liability. Charges of conspiracy and racketeering are stretched to encompass conspiracy members by construing the requirements of "direct involvement," "overt act," and "apparent knowledge of the criminal purposes of the conspiracy" extremely broadly. This approach can lead to uncertainty and disparity in convictions and sentencing and is not amenable to adjustment based on organizational roles and profit shares. The use of plea bargaining and other such discretionary measures to obtain information from key players further distorts the process of matching penalty to culpability. Moreover, relying upon the same basic guidelines for conspiratorial charges, different courts have reached very different conclusions as to the scope of individual liability for the crimes committed by a criminal conspiracy, and every aspect of these group-based rules have been the subject of substantial litigation. While an organization-based approach has been employed to a limited extent in the context of civil liability and criminal liability for legitimate enterprises through, for example, the use of respondeat superior liability, it has not been applied to criminal enterprises. Ad hoc insertion of group-based provisions into the existing transaction-based system has led to the implementation of criminal laws that in many cases are inefficient and ineffective at addressing organized criminal activity.

This chapter is based on the central premise that efficient and effective criminal rules and enforcement strategies must take into account the economic motivation and organization of criminal groups involved in money generating crimes. The rules and procedures they employ must reflect the control and incentive structures of the entities they seek to regulate. This change in approach must be translated into tangible changes in the structure of legal rules and enforcement strategies. Key areas of divergence between individual and group-based statutes should include the unit of analysis upon which criminal prosecution is based, the information available to the prosecutor, the charges applicable to the same set of facts, scope for consolidated trials, and the penalty structure.[7] An organization-based statute should allow the prosecutor and the jury to consider a pattern of related events, past criminal activities, and criminal membership when assessing guilt for a particular activity and harm associated with this activity. This will include a more flexible application of rules of evidence to allow for additional information sources, such as hearsay testimony by co-conspirators, and a broader range of background information, such as gang affiliation. An organization-based statute should allow for consolidated trials of criminal group members. As well as conferring economies of scale, consolidated trials increase the range of evidence presented at trial and allow for guilt by association and inferences from a related pattern of events. The jury is allowed information about a broader range of factors when assessing individual guilt for alleged misconduct. Organization-based statutes also provide for higher penalties for group-based criminal activities through sentence enhancement, compound liability and forfeiture of assets which are derived from or invested in the illegal enterprise. The additional bargaining tools conferred by wider prosecutorial discretion, consolidated trials and more severe penalties can be employed to induce plea bargaining and cooperation by members of a criminal group, increasing the scope for implicating upper level members of criminal organizations. Asset forfeiture provisions will allow law enforcers to attack and remove the economic foundation of the enterprise and may lead to a reduction in the cost of enforcement through asset recoupment. See Appendix Five for a more detailed discussion of the structure of legal rules.

Special Dangers Posed by Criminal Groups

The design of enterprise-based criminal rules is motivated by the notion that group activity is different from, and more dangerous than, individual activity. But while there has been a recognition of the increased dangers associated with criminal groups, insufficient attention has been devoted to identifying how the behavior of a criminal group diverges from that of individual criminals. Criminal organizations serve as substitute market structures, as vehicles for exploiting economies to scale in production of crimes and specialization of labor, and as mechanisms for spreading and/or reducing the cost of protection from both law enforcement and competitors. They provide an underground system of trade, information transfer and contract enforcement which substitutes for the services performed by legitimate markets and the legal system. Transaction costs are lowered through coordination of illegal activities and methods of risk reduction and diversification, and group reputations prove more effective at sustaining a system of contractual agreements than individual reputations. Bargaining power and limits on the rate of increase in risk increase the expected profitability of large scale transactions, particularly those involving activities such as drug trafficking or money laundering.

In addition to its role as a proxy for legitimate market structures, a criminal organization can provide a vehicle for increasing the crime production capacity of individual contributors. Participation in a criminal group allows individuals to exploit scale economies in production and protection of resources for use in crime production. It also offers expanded opportunities for investment of criminal proceeds. The greater size and longevity of the gang allows members to invest in a gang reputation in situations where individual reputations would be ineffective. Larger groups can exploit the benefits of specialization by delegating specific job functions to different group members. Group interaction during the planning and commission of crimes can also alter the incentives facing individual participants, changing the nature of the choices available to each participant and the perceived costs and benefits associated with these choices. Crimes which, taken on their own, might have little effect on future criminal opportunities, can have longer term effects on criminal opportunities via impact on group reputation, individual status within the group, and opportunities for re-investment in larger projects. Understanding the roles that these organizations play in the illegal economy can facilitate law enforcement efforts to regulate and suppress illegal market activities.

A central benefit of group activity is the ability to share the cost of protection of criminal actors and their assets from apprehension by law enforcement. Individual criminals can be provided with incentives to warn each other of approaching danger and can take advantage of economies to scale in surveillance and other defensive activities. In the more sophisticated organizations, criminal activities can be organized to minimize the overall impact of law enforcement activity on the volume and profitability of criminal activities. Where the enforcement mechanisms are strong, the effect on criminal participants may dominate the deterrent effect from law enforcement penalties. Proceeds from investments in a criminal enterprise can be used to obstruct law enforcement, to make jail-time more comfortable, and to diversify into legitimate activities. The ongoing nature of the criminal street gang creates opportunities for members who spend time in jail to continue their gang related activities both during and after their jail sentences, and incarceration can have important feed-back effects on gang membership.[8]

A sophisticated organization may even be able to utilize law enforcement schemes to enhance its internal operations.[9] Threats from rival gangs and pressure from law enforcement can sometimes be deployed to increase gang cohesion and the level of cooperation between gang members, as illustrated by the model presented in section two of the chapter. Where the organization is able to amass sufficient financial resources, it can expand its illegal network to encompass those involved in law enforcement. The involvement of banks in illegal money laundering ventures provides a good example of the role that money can play in undermining law enforcement efforts. Expansion of illegal organizations into legitimate businesses is of particular concern to policy makers, since this provides gangs with a flow of legitimate income and a broader range of contacts that can be used to facilitate illegal activities.[10]

Criminal Street Gangs

Criminal street gangs have a distinctive form of organization that has been adapted to a variety of different and inhospitable environments. They are distinguishable from other types of criminal gangs by their reliance on and close association with a particular geographic territory and the visibility of gang membership. They rely heavily on group identity to sustain cooperation among gang members. The gang structure performs multiple services for its members, including both economic and non-economic functions. The presence of an identifiable and ongoing organization lends a continuity to the activities of individual members which facilitates criminal transactions and enables gangs to engage in networking in ways which are unavailable to criminals who operate independently. Gangs are able to establish market reputations in situations where individuals are unable to do so. Repeated interaction between gang members increases the scope for internal cooperation, and internal incentive schemes can be employed to induce further cooperation. Geographic concentration of crime can lead to positive feed-back effects on gang membership by reducing legitimate opportunities and increasing the benefits from illegitimate ones. Concentrated activity reduces the costs of information transfer and increases the ability of illegal market participants to identify focal points of market activity.

Well-known street gangs such as the El Rukns and the Black Gangster Disciples provide examples of the extent to which the gang structure can facilitate the development of powerful illegal organizations. These gangs have been able to establish a group identity and an internal system of governance paralleling that of a mini-state, with a written constitution, a membership numbering in the thousands, informal systems of taxation and investment, and large revenues from illegal market activities.[11] Gang identity plays an important role in the structure and functioning of these groups. While affiliation is not essential to conduct locally based illegal activities, many of the smaller and more loosely organized gangs affiliate themselves with larger umbrella groups, highlighting the importance of gang identity (and reputation) in facilitating criminal activities. The way in which gang identity is established and the ways in which it is employed, will influence the structure of the criminal group.

Understanding the basis of relationships between gang members and the ability to identify factors that influence gang cohesiveness form important parts of anti-gang law enforcement strategies. Methods of developing and sustaining group cohesiveness differ across different ethnic groups, varying in response to factors such as cultural values and relationships with the surrounding community. Gangs tend to be racially and ethnically homogenous, due at least in part to lower communication costs and enhanced ability to develop visible group identities. Hispanic street gangs tend to be more territorial than African-American street gangs, for example, and have closer ties to the neighborhoods in which their activities are based. They also tend to be more loosely structured and less hierarchical. The relative importance of community and reliance on extended family ties makes it easier for these groups to sustain close ties to each other without highly structured internal incentive systems.

An effective group-based criminal law will be one that takes into account the special capacities and incentive structures of different criminal organizations. Group-based statutes which are insensitive to the special characteristics of criminal groups and the ways in which these groups vary are likely to be less efficient at achieving enforcement objectives and, in the extreme, run the risk of enhancing rather than deterring the operations of the group. The model developed in section two is designed to highlight these dangers and to suggest ways in which an economic framework can be employed to assess the potential effects of alternative group-based statutes.

II. An Economic Model of a Criminal Street Gang

Economic Approaches Towards Crime and Crime Prevention

The literature on crime and crime prevention has focused largely on the decision problem of the individual criminal, with little attention paid to the ways in which decision making might differ for members of a criminal group. Becker (1968) provides a starting point for the economic analysis of individual crimes by modeling the level of crime as the outcome of a cost-benefit optimization problem by a profit maximizing criminal.[12] The standard law enforcement problem is framed as one of selecting policy variables such as magnitude of penalty and probability of detection in order to minimize social loss for a simple model of criminal decision making, where social loss includes both the cost of crime and the cost of law enforcement. Subsequent work has focused on alternative types of penalties and methods of allocating law enforcement resources. Topics of analysis have included the choice between probability of capture and magnitude of punishment, use of fines versus imprisonment, and general versus specific enforcement. More recently, attention has been focused on the secondary effects of law enforcement strategies on expectations about the probability of apprehension, perceptions of the magnitude of punishment, and possible feed-back effects on the level of crime and number of criminals.[13] The possibilities of privatization of law enforcement and penal facilities have added additional considerations to the debate over alternative methods of law enforcement. In this section I suggest ways in which the traditional law enforcement framework can be adapted to a group context and investigate the robustness of some of the standard results to a shift from an individual to a group-based context. The section focuses on the scope for cooperation by gang members who are faced with individual and group penalties for engaging in criminal activities.[14] The results suggest that different law enforcement strategies may be required when criminals are engaged in group crimes.

The ability to sustain cooperation is a key determinant of the success of a criminal organization. Where cooperation breaks down, gang membership can be turned into a liability. The ability to exploit the benefits of the gang structure will depend on the gang's ability to control the divergence of individual and group interests in the absence of legally enforceable agreements and well-defined property rights.[15] The model presented in this section examines a situation in which individuals can expand their criminal capabilities by operating as a criminal gang. A criminal gang can be loosely defined as a group of individuals with a shared objective who interact on a repeated basis to commit crimes using common guidelines and shared resources. A criminal street gang is distinguished by its association with and reliance on a physical territory to conduct its activities and by the importance accorded to group identity and reputation. The decision problem faced by gang members is complicated by two characteristics of gang activities. First, cooperation must be self-enforceable since members of a criminal organization do not have access to legally enforceable contracts and do not have legally enforceable or clearly established property rights over the group's shared resources. Second, members are subject to external penalties for their criminal activities and potentially for their gang membership. Members of a criminal organization use group resources, such as gang protected territory and group reputation, to generate private benefits and to perform income producing crimes.

Gang members must sustain a cooperative, collusive relationship with each other in the absence of legally enforceable contracts and property rights and in the presence of high information costs and limited information transfer. Where effort levels cannot be directly observed and contracted upon and the benefits of individual investments are dispersed among gang members, the criminal organization faces a team production problem in which gang members have incentives to under-invest in group resources. This moral hazard problem is likely to play a central role in limiting the production possibilities of a criminal street gang. Several different ways of analyzing this type of team production problem have been suggested. Static principal-agent models of moral hazard arising from joint production have been developed by Alchian and Demsetz (1972) and Holmstrom (1982).[16] Grossman and Hart (1983) present a standard agency model with hidden action, and Itoh (1991) utilizes this structure in a multi-agent setting where team production is endogenous.[17] In Itoh's model agents can increase the outcome of the tasks of other agents by "helping" i.e. contributing effort to the tasks of others. The principal can select a task structure by selecting appropriate wage schedules. Itoh looks at the optimal wage structure in a hidden action principal agent model with two risk averse agents who select effort levels to devote to their own task and to helping other members with their tasks. This section employs a similar notion of "helping effort" in a different context, focusing attention on the potential effects of external penalties on the moral hazard problems faced by a criminal street gang. It highlights the role that external penalties can play in enhancing cooperation between self-interested criminals who operate as a group.

The Model

Criminals have the option of operating individually or forming a gang. The ways in which group penalties will affect the criminal activity level of gang members will depend in part upon how gang members can influence each other's activity choices and upon how their own activity choices affect others. This model focuses on a situation in which gang members can help each other to evade detection by law enforcement, where help might include engaging in surveillance and cover-up activities. While the gang as a whole will be better off if gang members exert effort in protecting each other, individuals do not derive a direct benefit from their efforts. The absence of legally enforceable contracts and problems in observing and monitoring effort levels makes it difficult to sustain cooperative agreements. By imposing a cost on those gang members who do not behave cooperatively, group penalties provide the impetus for helping fellow gang members. Under the assumptions of this model, positive effort is devoted to helping other criminals evade capture for committing crimes when and only when there are group penalties.

Law Enforcement when Criminals Operate Independently

A criminal who operates independently will decide how may crimes to commit based on the expected payoff, given by a revenue of R dollars per crime, and the expected penalty, given by the product of the probability of detection (p(x)) and the penalty if caught (a number Z of days in jail). The criminal must decide how many crimes to commit given the revenue, detection technology, and penalty size. The policy-maker must decide the level at which to set the penalty given the detection technology and the relative costs of crime and punishment.

Define:

	x	= number of crimes, $0 \leq x \leq \bar{x}$
	R	= revenue per crime, $0 < R < \infty$
	$p(x)$	= probability of being caught committing a crime
	Z	= level of penalty, measured by number of days in jail
	β	= social cost of keeping a person in jail for one day, $0 < \beta < 1$

Assumption 1.1: p(x) is a continuous, differentiable function which has the following properties: (i) $p(0)=0$ and $p(\bar{x})=1$; (ii) $p'(x)>0$, (iii) $p''(x)>0$.

The Criminal's Optimization Problem The criminal chooses the number of crimes he will commit to maximize his expected profit. Since the probability of punishment is increasing in the number of crimes, the criminal balances the increase in revenue against the higher expected penalty when making his decision. The criminal faces the following optimization problem:

(1) $\text{Maximize } \{x\}\ Rx - p(x)Z$

See Appendix One for a characterization of the solution.

The Policy-maker's Optimization Problem The policy-maker faces the task of selecting the penalty level to minimize social loss, which is a function of the revenue lost from crimes committed and the cost of keeping the criminal in jail for Z days if caught. Taking the detection technology as given, the policy-maker will select a penalty size which minimizes social loss. The social loss function is given by the sum of revenue lost and cost of punishment. For a population of N criminals, this is given by:

(2) $L = NRx + N\beta p(x)Z$

Note that the optimal penalty level (Z) in this model will be independent of the number of criminals. Thus, for ease of calculation, it is assumed that N=2. In a more realistic setting the number of criminals would affect the cost of detection and punishment, and additional factors such as capacity constraints and scale economies or diseconomies in enforcement would influence the choice of penalties.[18] The social problem is to minimize social loss by choosing Z to solve:

(3) $\text{Minimize } \{Z\}\ 2Rx(Z) + 2\beta\, p(x(Z))\, Z$

Solving for the optimal level of punishment and the social loss yields a penalty level given by:

$$Z^* = [R^2(1+\beta) / \beta p''(x)\, p(x)]^{1/2}$$

where Z* is increasing in the revenue lost to crime (R) and decreasing in the cost of jail (β). Social loss is given by:

$$L^* = 2Rx + 2\beta p(x)[R^2(1+\beta) / \beta p''(x)\, p(x)]^{1/2}$$

See Appendix One for first-order conditions.

A change in Z has two competing effects on social loss. The level of crime is decreasing in the penalty level (i.e. $x'(Z) < 0$), and an increase in Z thus has a crime deterrence effect which results in a lower measure of social loss. An increase in Z also has a cost increasing effect, since the cost of punishment increases as the penalty increases.[19] The policy-maker balances these effects to arrive at the optimal level of the penalty Z.

Law Enforcement when Criminals Operate as a Gang

Instead of operating individually, two individuals (person 1 and person 2) may decide to form a gang. Once part of a gang, each gang member can take steps to reduce the probability that his fellow members will be caught. Making the necessary effort is costly, however, and in the absence of additional incentives gang members will have no incentive to help each other.

The Criminal's Optimization Problem Each individual has two choice variables, the first being the number of crimes which he will commit, given by x_1 for person 1 and x_2 for person 2, and the second being the level of effort which each will devote to helping the other to evade detection. Let e_1 equal the effort that person 1 devotes to helping person 2, and e_2 denote the effort that person 2 devotes to helping person 1. The probability that person 1 gets caught is given by the function $p(x_1,e_2)$, and the probability that person 2 gets caught is given by the function $p(x_2,e_1)$.

The policy-maker can observe whether criminals operate individually or as members of a gang, and can impose two different kinds of penalties on gang members. The first is a standard penalty of Z days in jail which is imposed on an individual who is caught committing a crime. The second is a group-based penalty of Y days in jail for each of the remaining gang members if one of the members is caught committing a crime. β denotes the social cost of keeping a person in jail for a day.

Define:		
	R	= revenue per crime, $0 < R < \infty$
	x_1	= number of crimes committed by person 1, $0 \leq x_1 \leq \bar{x}$
	x_2	= number of crimes committed by person 2, $0 \leq x_2 \leq \bar{x}$
	e_1	= effort exerted by person 1 to help person 2, $0 \leq e_1 \leq \bar{e}$
	e_2	= effort exerted by person 2 to help person 1, $0 \leq e_2 \leq \bar{e}$
	$p(x_1,e_2)$	= probability that person 1 is caught committing crime
	$p(x_2,e_1)$	= probability that person 2 is caught committing crime
	Z	= individual penalty level, given by the number of days in jail for person caught committing a crime
	Y	= group penalty level, given by number of days in jail for each of the remaining gang members if one of the members is caught committing a crime
	β	= social cost per day of keeping someone in jail, $0 < \beta < 1$

Assumption 2.1: p(.) is a continuous, differentiable function which has the following properties: (i) $p(\bar{x},e_2) = 1$ and $p(\bar{x},e_1) = 1$, $p(0,e_1) = p(0,e_2) = 0$; (ii) $p_x(x_1,e_2) > 0$ and $p_x(x_2,e_1) > 0$; (iii) $p_e(x_1,e_2) < 0$ and $p_e(x_2,e_1) < 0$; (iv) $p_{xx}(x_1,e_2) > 0$ and $p_{xx}(x_2,e_1) > 0$; (v) $p_{ee}(x_1,e_2) > 0$ and $p_{ee}(x_2,e_1) > 0$; (vi) $p_{ex}(x_1,e_2) < 0$ and $p_{ex}(x_2,e_1) < 0$.

The individual decision problems faced by the two gang members are as follows. Individual 1 chooses x_1 and e_1 to solve:

(1) Maximize $\{x_1,e_1\}$ $Rx_1 - p(x_1,e_2)Z - p(x_2,e_1)Y - e_1$

and individual 2 chooses x_2 and e_2 to solve:

(2) Maximize $\{x_2,e_2\}$ $Rx_2 - p(x_2,e_1)Z - p(x_1,e_2)Y - e_2$

The optimization problem for each individual is separable in crime level and effort choices, taking penalties as fixed. The problem can be viewed in terms of two non-cooperative simultaneous moves games, the first involving choice of x_1 and e_2, the second involving choice of x_2 and e_1. The following assumption ensures that the game as described is stable.

Assumption 2.2: $p_{xx}(x_1,e_2)p_{ee}(x_1,e_2) > p_{xe}^2(x_1,e_2)$

Proposition 1: Gang members will help each other to commit crimes only when there is a positive group-based penalty, and the help offered is an increasing function of the group-based penalty. i.e. $e_1 > 0$ and $e_2 > 0$ if and only if $Y > 0$, and $e_1'(Y) > 0$, $e_2'(Y) > 0$.

Proposition 2: The level of crime increases when the group penalty is increased. i.e. $x_1'(Y) > 0$ and $x_2'(Y) > 0$ for $Y > 0$.

See Appendix Two for the proofs to Proposition 1 and 2.

The Policy-maker's Optimization Problem The social loss function is given by:

$$L=R(x_1+x_2) + \beta[p(x_1,e_2)+ p(x_2,e_1)] (Y+ Z)$$

The policy-maker must select Y and Z to minimize social loss, taking the detection technology as given and taking into account the effects that changes in the individual penalty (Z) and group penalty (Y) will have on the level of crime and the level of cooperation between gang members. The policy-maker's problem is given by:

(3) Minimize $\{Y,Z\}$ $L=R(x_1+x_2) + \beta[p(x_1,e_2)+ p(x_2,e_1)] (Y+Z)$

The group penalty has two different and offsetting effects on social loss. The first is a crime enhancing effect that increases social loss. The group penalty functions as a mechanism for inducing cooperation among gang members, providing gang members with incentives to help each other to evade capture. The resulting decrease in the probability of being caught leads to an increase in the level of crime. The second effect is a reduction in the expenditure on punishment due to the decrease in the probability of capture, which reduces the number of individuals who are caught for any given level of criminal activity.[20] It can be shown that when the probability of detection is separable in effort and the number of crimes, social loss will always be minimized by setting group-based penalties equal to zero.

Proposition 3: Using group-based penalties will increase the level of social loss where the probability of detection is separable in the number of crimes and effort devoted to evading detection. i.e. when $p(x,e)$ is separable in x and e, social loss is minimized by setting $Y^* = 0$.

See Appendix Two for the proof. The result can be easily demonstrated by considering a situation in which $Y>0$ and $Z>0$. The cost of law enforcement can be reduced by reducing Y and increasing Z by the off-setting amount necessary to prevent an increase in criminal activity. When a positive group penalty is used in combination with an individual penalty, the policy-maker will always be able to reduce social loss by reducing the group penalty to zero and increasing the individual penalty to the level necessary to maintain the same level of deterrence. Under the assumptions of the model, use of group penalties is never an efficient method of deterring crime, and individual penalties always provide a cheaper way of obtaining a given level of deterrence.

Robustness to Assumptions about Gang Structure

These results are significant primarily because they demonstrate the potential danger of imposing group-based penalties without consideration of organizational structure. The model highlights the fact that group penalties which are designed without regard to economic organization could have unintended side-effects on the operations of a criminal group which make the penalties less efficient at deterring crime. The results are not intended to suggest that group penalties will, as a general rule, be ineffective, and situations in which group penalties reduce criminal activity are easy to identify. As shown in the following examples, changes in the structure of the model, representing different assumptions about the gang, can generate results in which group penalties have either no effect on criminal activity or a crime reducing effect.

Case 1: Group Penalties Have No Effect on Criminal Activity

Consider the same two person framework as used above, with the difference that gang members no longer make explicit decisions about how much effort to devote to helping each other. Instead, they effect each other indirectly through their individual decisions about how many crimes to commit. By joining the gang, each member can earn a larger return from his crimes (due, for example, to scale economies, an increase in criminal opportunities, or complementarities between crimes), but also faces a risk of being penalized for gang membership.

Each individual selects the number of crimes that he will commit, taking the other individual's quantity decision as given. Let x_1 equal the number of crimes that person 1 chooses to commit and x_2 denote the number of crimes that person 2 commits. The probability that person 1 gets caught is given by the function $p(x_1)$, and the probability that person 2 gets caught is given by the function $p(x_2)$. Each gang member receives a revenue given by the function $R(x_1,x_2)$, where individual returns are increasing in the number of crimes committed by the gang as a whole. The policy-maker can observe whether criminals operate individually or as members of a gang, and can impose two different kinds of penalties on gang members. The first is a standard penalty of Z days in jail that is imposed on an individual who is caught committing a crime. The second is a group-based penalty of Y days in jail for each of the remaining gang members if one of the members is caught committing a crime. β denotes the social cost of keeping a person in jail for a day.

Define: $R(x_1,x_2)$ = revenue received by each gang member
- x_1 = number of crimes committed by person 1, $0 \le x_1 \le \bar{x}$
- x_2 = number of crimes committed by person 2, $0 \le x_2 \le \bar{x}$
- e_1 = effort exerted by person 1 to help person 2, $0 \le e_1 \le \bar{e}$
- e_2 = effort exerted by person 2 to help person 1, $0 \le e_2 \le \bar{e}$
- $p(x_1)$ = probability that person 1 is caught committing crime
- $p(x_2)$ = probability that person 2 is caught committing crime
- Z = individual penalty (number of days in jail)
- Y = group penalty (number of days in jail)
- β = social cost per day of keeping someone in jail

Assumption 3.1: p(x) is a continuous, differentiable function which has the following properties: (i) p(0)=0 and $p(\bar{x})=1$; (ii) $p'(x)>0$, (iii) $p''(x)>0$.

Assumption 3:2: $R(x_1,x_2)$ is a continuous, differentiable function which has the following properties: (i) $R(0,0) = 0$, $R(\bar{x},\bar{x})<\infty$; (ii) $R_1(x_1,x_2)>0$, $R_2(x_1,x_2)>0$; (iii) $R_{11}(x_1,x_2)<0$, $R_{22}(x_1, x_2)<0$; (iv) $R_{12}(x_1, x_2)=R_{21}(x_1, x_2)<0$.

Criminal's Optimization Problem Each individual selects his own level of criminal activity taking the other individual's actions as given. The number of crimes which each individual engages in can be determined as the Nash Equilibrium outcomes of a non-co-operative simultaneous moves game. Individual 1 chooses x_1 to solve:

$$\text{Maximize } \{x_1,e_1\}\ R(x_1,x_2) - p(x_1)Z - p(x_2)Y$$

and individual 2 chooses x_2 to solve:

$$\text{Maximize } \{x_2,e_2\}\ R(x_1,x_2) - p(x_2)Z - p(x_1)Y$$

Proposition 4: The level of criminal activity is not affected by the level of the group penalty as long as the penalty is not high enough to drive both gang members out of the illegal market. i.e. for $x_1 > 0$ and $x_2 > 0$, $x_1'(Y) = x_2'(Y) = 0$.

See Appendix Three for the proof. Note that if individual 1 and 2 were to choose their criminal activity levels jointly, then the choices of x_1 and x_2 would depend upon the group penalty level. In a co-operative game, each individual would be forced to take into account the effect of his criminal activity level on the expected penalty for his fellow gang member, and would internalize the negative effect when making his quantity choice. Interestingly, this result suggests that in some instances, closer co-operation between gang members will make group penalties more rather than less effective. For example, if individual 1 and 2 were to choose their criminal activity levels jointly (i.e. choosing quantities to maximize $2\,R(x_1, x_2) + \beta[p(x_1) + p(x_2)](Y+Z)$), then the choices of x_1 and x_2 would vary negatively with the group penalty level.

The Policy-maker's Optimization Problem The social loss function is given by:

$$L = 2R(x_1, x_2) + \beta[p(x_1)+ p(x_2)] (Y+ Z)$$

The policy-maker must select Z and Y to minimize social loss, taking the detection technology as given and taking into account the effects that changes in the individual penalty (Z) and group penalty (Y) will have on the level of crime. The 's problem is given by:

$$\text{Minimize } \{Y,Z\}\ L = 2R(x_1, x_2) + \beta[p(x_1)+ p(x_2)] (Y+Z)$$

Proposition 5a: It is socially efficient to set the group penalty equal to zero. i.e. $Y^* = 0$.

See Appendix Three. Although in this model group penalties do not have the perverse effect of increasing the level of criminal activity, it remains more efficient to impose an individual penalty than to impose a group penalty. In comparison, group penalties will be efficient if the gang members cooperate and select quantities to maximize joint profits.

Proposition 5b: Where the gang members cooperate and select drug quantities to maximize joint profits, $Y^*>0$ and $Z^*>0$ when the loss function is a convex function of Y and Z. When the loss function is a concave function of Y and Z, either $Y^*>0$ and $Z^*=0$ or $Y^*=0$ and $Z^*>0$.

In this model, the group penalty has the same effects as the individual penalty and the two can be used interchangeably. See Appendix Three.

Case 2: Group Penalties Have a Negative Effect on Criminal Activity

In this model, as in the original two person model, each gang member chooses both the number of crimes to commit and the level of effort to exert in controlling the actions of his fellow gang member. In this case, however, instead of exerting effort to help each other, gang members exert effort to disassociate themselves from the criminal activities of other gang members and to shift the blame for crimes committed by the gang. Thus, the effort exerted by person 1 has a negative effect on the probability of punishment by person two, and vice versa. Here, $p(x_i,e_j)$ gives the probability that person i is caught committing a crime, and $q(x_j, e_i)$ gives the probability that person i is penalized when person j is caught committing a crime.

Define:

R	=	revenue per crime, $0 < R < \infty$
x_1	=	number of crimes committed by person 1, $0 \leq x_1 \leq \bar{x}$
x_2	=	number of crimes committed by person 2, $0 \leq x_2 \leq \bar{x}$
e_1	=	effort exerted by person 1 to help person 2, $0 \leq e_1 \leq \bar{e}$
e_2	=	effort exerted by person 2 to help person 1, $0 \leq e_2 \leq \bar{e}$
$p(x_1,e_2)$	=	probability that person 1 is caught committing crime
$p(x_2,e_1)$	=	probability that person 2 is caught committing crime
$q(x_2,e_1)$	=	probability person 1 penalized when person 2 caught
$q(x_1,e_2)$	=	probability person 2 penalized when person 1 caught
Z	=	individual penalty (number of days in jail)
Y	=	group penalty (number of days in jail)
β	=	social cost incurred per day in jail, $0 < \beta < 1$

Each individual selects the number of crimes that he will commit and the effort that he will exert, taking the other individual's quantity and effort decisions as given. The policy-maker can observe whether criminals operate individually or as members of a gang, and can impose two different kinds of penalties on gang members, a standard penalty of Z days in jail that is imposed on an individual who is caught committing a crime, and a group-based penalty of Y days in jail for each of the remaining gang members if one of the members is caught committing a crime.

Assumption 4.1: $p(x_i, e_j)$ is a continuous, differentiable function which has the following properties: (i) $p(0,e_j) = 0$, $0<p(\bar{x},e_i) \leq 1$; (ii) $p_x(x_i, e_j) > 0$, $p_e(x_i, e_j)>0$; (iii) $p_{xx}(x_i, e_j) > 0$, $p_{ee}(x_i, e_j) > 0$; (iv) $p_{xe}(x_i, e_j) = p_{ex}(x_i, e_j) > 0$.

Assumption 4.2: $q(x_i, e_j)$ is a continuous, differentiable function which has the following properties: (i) $q(0,e_j) = 0$, $0<q(\bar{x}, e_j) \leq 1$; (ii) $q_x(x_i, e_j) > 0$, $q_e(x_i, e_j)<0$; (iii) $q_{xx}(x_i, e_j) > 0$, $q_{ee}(x_i, e_j) > 0$; (iv) $q_{xe}(x_i, e_j) = q_{ex}(x_i, e_j) < 0$.

Criminal's Optimization Problem Individual 1 chooses x_1 and e_1 to solve:

$$\text{Maximize } \{x_1,e_1\}\ Rx_1 - p(x_1,e_2)Z - q(x_2,e_1)Y - e_1$$

and individual 2 chooses x_2 to solve:

$$\text{Maximize } \{x_2\}\ Rx_2 - p(x_2,e_1)Z - q(x_1,e_2)Y - e_2$$

The optimization problem for each individual is separable in crime level and effort choices, taking penalties as fixed. The problem can be viewed in terms of two non-cooperative simultaneous moves games, the first involving choice of x_1 and e_2, the second involving choice of x_2 and e_1.

Proposition 6: The level of crime is a decreasing function of the group penalty. i.e. $x_1'(Y) < 0$ and $x_2'(Y) < 0$.

See Appendix Three for the proof

The Policy-maker's Optimization Problem The social loss function is given by:

$$L = R(x_1+x_2) + \beta[p(x_1,e_2)+p(x_2,e_1)]\,Z + \beta[q(x_1,e_2)+ q(x_2,e_1)]Y$$

The policy-maker must select Z and Y to minimize social loss, taking the detection technology as given and taking into account the effects that changes in the individual penalty (Z) and group penalty (Y) will have on the level of crime. The policy-maker's problem is given by:

$$\text{Min } \{Y,Z\}\ R(x_1+x_2)+\beta[p(x_1,e_2)+p(x_2,e_1)]Z+\beta[q(x_1,e_2)+ q(x_2,e_1)]Y$$

Proposition 7: It is socially efficient to have a group penalty when the beneficial effect of group penalties on the level of crime outweighs the expected increase in the frequency, and therefore the cost of punishment. i.e. $Y^*>0$ when

$$-[2R+2\beta p_x(x_1,e_2)Z]x_1'(Y)>2\beta Z p_e(x_1,e_2)e_2'(Y)+2\beta q(x_1,e_2)$$

See Appendix Three for the proof.

III. Applications to Common Group-based Criminal Statutes

Overview of Relevant Statutes

The crimes of complicity, solicitation and conspiracy provide a foundation for both state and federal group-based criminal laws. The most basic approach to group criminality has been to extend liability for a crime to individuals who are substantial contributors. Complicity doctrine has developed around the idea that individuals who share the primary offender's guilty intent and take deliberate facilitating acts are equally culpable and therefore deserving of the same treatment as primary offenders. Individuals who substantially aid in the commission of a crime (accomplices) are treated as principles of the crime, with act and intent requirements designed to match those of the substantive crime.[21] Criminal solicitation is based on a similar principle of derivative liability. A person is guilty of "criminal solicitation" if "with the purpose of promoting or facilitating its commission he commands, encourages or requests another person to engage in specific conduct which would constitute such crime or an attempt to commit such crime or which would establish his complicity in its commission or attempted commission."[22] Actual communication is not required as long as the individual engages in conduct "designed to effect such communication."[23] The person is punished as if he performed the crime that he solicited someone else to perform, the rationale being that the solicitor possesses the same criminal intent and undertakes the same sort of direct action intended to bring about a crime, the difference being that he or she attempts to cause the crime via the use of another person. Only recently has attention been focused on the role that solicitation plays in expanding the number of criminals and increasing the interdependence between them. Some states have enacted special rules that increase the penalties and lower the act requirements associated with criminal solicitation of individuals who are below a certain age in an attempt to dampen gang recruitment.

Conspiracy doctrine has developed around the idea that groups who share a criminal objective and agree to participate in a criminal venture pose a special danger that needs to be addressed at the earliest possible stage. Multi-party involvement and shared criminal purpose are introduced for the first time as an independent basis for imposing criminal liability. Conspiracy departs from the traditional "transaction-based" approach by attaching additional liability to the act of combining to commit a crime and by allowing prosecutors to present jurors with information about activities and relationships extending beyond the specific criminal transaction. Criminal conspiracy is an agreement or combination by two or more persons to commit a crime. An individual can be charged with conspiracy if he agrees to engage or aid in the commission of a specified crime with the purpose of ensuring its successful completion and he takes some action to further this purpose. Authorities are mixed on the question of whether the agreement itself satisfies the overt act requirement. Conspiracy functions both as an inchoate crime designed to reach preparatory conduct and as a group-based crime designed to penalize combined criminal action. Unlike attempt and solicitation, the charge of conspiracy is not merged into other substantive offenses, and unlike complicity, conspiracy allows imposition of liability both for the crimes that the conspiracy produces and for the conspiracy itself. These differences are attributable to the role that it plays in addressing the "special dangers" of group crime.[24] Under the judicially created Pinkerton Rule each member of the conspiracy can be held responsible for all of the acts performed by other members in furtherance of the agreed upon conspiracy. The consequences of involvement in the conspiracy (particularly a drug conspiracy) can extend beyond periods of individual involvement where the activities of the conspiracy are "reasonably foreseeable" and are consistent with the overall objective(s) of the conspiracy. Liability for involvement ceases when a member of the conspiracy renounces the criminal purposes of the enterprise and provides evidence of a complete withdrawal from the group's criminal activities. Providing substantial assistance to law enforcement is regarded as one way of satisfying the exit requirement and also provides an avenue for sentence reduction.

A set of statutes targeted at particular forms and levels of organized crime have been added to this foundation, the best known being the federal Racketeering Influenced and Corrupt Organizations Act (RICO) and state-based RICO imitations. These statutes depart from the transaction-based framework by focusing on patterns of crimes which are related in a specified way and which are designed to further shared criminal objectives. Attempts are made to tailor liability to reflect degree of control over and benefit from ongoing criminal operations. Attempts are also made to exploit the structure of the organization through the use of informants and information obtained through plea bargaining. Complex criminal statutes such as the federal RICO statute and Continuing Criminal Enterprise (CCE) statute are based on a set of predicate crimes selected from existing substantive crimes and an additional set of conditions designed to identify connections between criminal participants and crimes. Statutes of this sort employ a limited organizational approach, introducing a form of enterprise liability for crimes that take place in the context of an organization. RICO targets crimes committed by, or in the context of, an "enterprise," where "enterprise" is construed broadly to include any form of continuous organized activity.[25] It imposes additional liability where predicate crimes are related to each other in a particular kind of causal nexus.[26] The statute creates three substantive crimes and the crime of RICO conspiracy.[27] The substantive crimes require that a "person" use the collection of unlawful debt or a "pattern of racketeering activity," or two of the listed predicate crimes within a ten year period, in order to: (i) acquire an interest in, establish, or operate an enterprise; (ii) acquire or maintain an interest in or control of an enterprise; and/or (iii) conduct or participate in conducting an enterprise.[28] The Continuing Criminal Enterprise (CCE) statute provides a method by which the leadership and key players, or "kingpins," of a sufficiently large drug-trafficking criminal organization can be severely punished and the enterprise dismantled through asset forfeiture.[29] Ideally, this type of statute will channel law enforcement resources at those participants and resources that are most essential to the operations of the criminal enterprise. The statute includes a mandatory minimum sentencing provision of 10 years for first time offenders, 20 years for second offenders and life sentences for principal leaders or organizers of a particularly large drug ring, and fines and forfeiture of property obtained from or used in a CCE.[30] It has been applied both to kingpins and, more recently, to third party aiders and abettors of kingpins.[31] Like RICO, CCE is a compound offense committed by perpetrating predicate crimes, but unlike RICO these predicate crimes are limited to drug crimes and CCE creates only one offense, which the Supreme Court has construed as resembling conspiracy more than a substantive offense.

While federal and state provisions concerning complicity and conspiracy tend to be relatively similar, the federal and state governments have diverged in their statutory responses to the new wave of crime by criminal gangs (and, in particular, criminal street gangs), with clusters of states occupying different positions along the spectrum of organizational-based versus individual-based liability. State and federal governments have introduced a number of anti-gang statutes designed to combat gang-related criminal activities. Although sharing the same objective, these statutes vary in their targets and the nature of their penalty structures. Federal statutes have focused on the leadership of criminal organizations that have achieved a certain size and complexity, although more recent proposals have sought to extend the coverage of federal criminal law to include a broader range of gang participants and activities. State statutes have been targeted more broadly at gang participants and at the resources used and activities engaged in by gangs (such as loitering and intimidating others in public spaces). A variety of enforcement methods have been employed, including enhanced sentencing for gang related crimes, making new crimes out of participation in gang activities, and injunctions for loitering and other activities held to constitute a threat to public safety. An overview of the statutory framework currently in place is contained in Appendix Six.

Effect of Group-based Criminal Laws on Level of Criminal Activity

Complicity, conspiracy and racketeering statutes form the basis of the current approach towards criminal groups. The same rules are applied indiscriminately to situations in which there are multiple participants involved in a crime or series of crimes, with little attention paid to the nature of the criminal group or the ways in which group members and their activities are related. Informed applications of existing rules, or modifications of these rules, can be used to increase the effectiveness of law enforcement efforts. Blind application of group-based rules can sometimes generate unexpected and counter-productive results. The basic framework employed in this chapter can be used to explore the possible consequences of some of the more commonly used group-based criminal laws. Stylized versions of these laws can be characterized in terms of differences in the penalty structure and detection technology.[32]

Complicity

Complicity provides a natural starting point for analysis since it involves the smallest deviation from the individual paradigm. The crime of complicity establishes a form of derivative liability that involves holding people responsible for crimes that they help to participate in. The group penalty kicks in for contributions which rise above a certain level of effort or involve certain kinds of help. This form of liability can be approximated as follows. The expected profit function for person 1 is given by:

$$E\Pi_1 = Rx_1 - p(x_1,e_2)Z - p(x_2,e_1)f(e_1)Z - e_1$$

Person 2 has a symmetrical profit function. The penalty structure for person 1, who is considering whether to devote effort to helping person 2 commit crimes, is given by $f(e_1)Z$, where

$$f(e_1) = \begin{cases} 1 & \text{for } e_1 > \bar{e} \\ 0 & \text{for } e_1 \leq \bar{e} \end{cases}$$

This penalty scheme is designed to hold individuals liable as primary offenders if they exert a sufficient level of effort or perform certain kinds of facilitating acts. The potential effects of this penalty structure are examined below. The impact that it will have on participation in criminal activities and, in particular, gang related activities, will vary substantially depending upon the assumptions of the model. An analysis of the basic paradigm is followed by a brief examination of how the results would change if law enforcement identified complicitous behavior with some error (e.g. using guilt by association instead of basing guilt on actions taken) or if gang members earned a share of the revenue for their complicitous activities.

Proposition 8: Under the assumptions of the model, a complicity penalty structure has no effect on the level of crime or social loss.

See Appendix Four for the proof. Under the assumptions of the model, a complicity penalty structure is an improvement over a fixed group-based penalty but offers no improvement over an individual based fixed penalty scheme. Indeed, adding a penalty for complicity to an individual based penalty scheme will leave the level of crime and social loss unchanged. Imposing a penalty for complicity may actually increase the level of criminal activity and the magnitude of social loss, however, where law enforcement is imperfect and individuals face a positive risk of being incorrectly punished as accomplices. On the other hand, complicity may be used to reduce the level of criminal activity and the magnitude of social loss where gang members have a strong incentive to help each other in the absence of group penalties.

Mistakes by Law Enforcement If law enforcers make mistakes in imposing liability, then individuals who are not participating in the crimes of others may nevertheless be held liable. When law enforcers overestimate the participation levels of non-participants and low level participants with some positive probability, individuals are unable to avoid the risk of group penalties even when they do not participate in a gang. Consider the following example. Suppose there is an error rate of $0<\beta<1$, and the effective penalty is βZ for all individuals who select $e_i \leq \bar{e}$ and Z for individuals who select $e_i > \bar{e}$.

Proposition 9: Imposing a penalty for complicity will lead to an increase in crime and an increase in social loss where there is a positive probability β of error in identifying accomplices.

See Appendix Four for the proof.

In contrast, where gang members receive substantial benefits from helping each other, such as a share of profits, a penalty for complicity could have a crime reducing effect by deterring such help. To see this, consider the following modification of the standard model. Person 1's expected profit function (which is the same as Person 2's) is given by the following:

$$E\Pi_1 = Rx_1 + g(e_1)Rx_2 - p(x_1,e_2)Z - p(x_2,e_1)f(e_1)Z - e_1$$

The penalty structure is given by $Y = f(e_1)Z$ such that:

$$f(e_1) = 0 \quad \text{if } e_1 \leq \bar{e}$$
$$\quad = 1 \quad \text{if } e_1 > \bar{e}$$

Assumption 5.1: $g(e_i)$ is a continuous, differentiable function which satisfies the following properties: (i) $g(0)=0$ and $g(e_i)>0$ fore $e_i>0$; (ii) $g'(e_i)>0$; (iii) $g''(e_i)<0$.

Without a penalty for complicity, the profit maximizing level of effort for person 1 to expend in helping fellow gang members is given by $e_1^*>0$. Where there is a penalty for complicity, and the unconstrained effort choice e_1^* is larger than $\bar{e}$, a significantly large penalty for complicity will have a deterrent effect on helping effort. When the effect of this penalty is to push $e_i<\bar{e}$, then the complicity penalty structure improves upon an individualized penalty structure. When $e_i \geq \bar{e}$ even under a penalty for complicity, this penalty structure may not be an efficient method of crime deterrence. In this case the policy-maker must select $\bar{e}$ to minimize social loss, given by:

$$L=R(x_1+x_2) + \beta[p(x_1,e_2)+ p(x_2,e_1)]\ (Z+f(e_i)Z)$$

This problem is analogous to that faced by a law enforcer who must rely on general deterrence measures when specific deterrence is not available. The policy-maker must balance competing effects of a change in $\bar{e}$ on the level of crime and the cost of punishment when setting this policy parameter, and must consider the potential danger of imposing uniform penalties on criminals who may have very different decision problems.

Proposition 10: Imposing a penalty for complicity will be efficient when the penalty fully deters gang members from helping each other.

Note that a penalty for complicity may also be efficient when it partially deters gang members from helping each other and the positive impact of the penalty on crime level outweighs the higher cost of punishment. See Appendix Four for the proof.

Conspiracy

The crime of complicity is applicable to group endeavors only when there is sufficient evidence of direct involvement in criminal activities. Conspiracy imposes much broader liability for group activities, and both conspiracy and racketeering statutes have been applied with increasing frequency and expansiveness in the context of group crimes. Conspiracy introduces both affiliative and compound liability, where affiliative liability involves punishment based on group membership and compound liability involves additional charges and higher sentencing for the same activity if it is part of a series of connected activities. Criminals are punished for making an agreement to commit a crime, and sentences may be enhanced if the crimes committed are part of a conspiracy. Liability can be extended to encompass all of the crimes that are committed by members of the conspiracy as long as they are reasonably foreseeable and are performed in furtherance of the general objectives of the conspiracy. While different courts have established different boundaries for assessing the degree of liability, the general effects of this rule can be captured by treating liability as an increasing function of effort contributed towards helping group members.

Let the group penalty be given by an increasing function of helping effort such that, when person i exerts effort e_i in helping person j, the penalty imposed on person i is given by $Y_i = f(e_i)Y$.

Assumption 6.1: The function $f(e_i)$ is continuous and differentiable and has the following properties: (i) $f(e_i)>0$ for $e_i \geq 0$; (ii) $f'(e_i)>0$; (iii) $f''(e_i)>0$.

The higher the effort level contributed to helping fellow gang members, the greater the magnitude of the penalty. Person 1's decision problem becomes:

$$\text{Maximize } \{x_1,e_1\}\ Rx_1 - p(x_1,e_2)Z - p(x_2,e_1)f(e_1)Y - e_1$$

Similarly, person 2's decision problem becomes:

$$\text{Maximize } \{x_2,e_2\}\ Rx_2 - p(x_2,e_1)Z - p(x_2,e_2)f(e_2)Y - e_2$$

Social loss is given by:

$$L = R(x_1+x_2) + \beta(p(x_1,e_2) + p(x_2,e_1))\, Z + \beta\, p(x_1,e_2)\, f(e_2)Y + \beta\, p(x_2,e_1)\, f(e_1)Y$$

Proposition 11: Where the probability of detection is separable in effort and number of crimes, imposing a penalty for conspiracy (i.e. a penalty which is an increasing function of effort) increases social loss, and conspiracy penalties should be set equal to zero.

See Appendix Four for the proof. The main benefits of applying this type of penalty structure take the form of a marginal reduction in effort contributions as compared to a flat penalty system and a deterrent effect on individuals who are thinking about joining a conspiracy. Under the assumptions of the model, once individuals are in a conspiracy, social loss will be minimized by setting group penalties equal to zero. There are situations in which the complicity penalty scheme will dominate a flat group penalty scheme, however, since it dampens the level of help offered by gang members.

Example: Let $h(e_1)$ be the inverse function of $f(e_1)$ and let $p(x_1,e_2)=h(e_2)g(x_1)$ and $p(x_2,e_1)=h(e_1)g(x_2)$. Person 1's problem becomes:

$$E\Pi_1 = Rx_1 - h(e_2)g(x_1)Z - h(e_1)g(x_2)f(e_1)Y - e_1$$
$$= Rx_1 - f(e_2)g(x)Z_1 - g(x_2)Y - e_1$$

Similarly, person 2's problem becomes:

$$E\Pi_2 = Rx_2 - h(e_1)g(x_2)Z - h(e_2)g(x_1)f(e_2)Y - e_2$$
$$= Rx_2 - f(e_1)g(x_2)Z - g(x_1)Y - e_1$$

Gang members maximize their profits by selecting $e_1=e_2=0$, and therefore x_1 and x_2 will be lower than they would under a flat group penalty scheme and will be the same as they would under an individualized penalty scheme. As in the case of a complicity penalty structure, relaxation of the assumptions of no error in measuring level of involvement and no direct benefit from involvement may change the above results.

RICO

RICO imposes substantially higher penalties for crimes that are related to each other in a particular way. It also allows for procedural measures such as consolidated trials that can decrease the cost of prosecution and increase the likelihood of conviction. The penalty is targeted at ongoing patterns of criminal activities which are used to further the objectives of an underlying criminal enterprise. RICO makes provisions for both affiliative liability (i.e. penalties for being involved in a criminal organization) and compound liability (i.e. higher sentencing for a crime if it is committed in connection with other crimes to further the purposes of a criminal organization). RICO also includes asset forfeiture provisions that allow law enforcers to reach the assets of the underlying criminal enterprise. The RICO penalty structure incorporates the basic features of conspiracy as well as providing for a charge of RICO conspiracy, and the results developed above can be generalized to include RICO penalties.

The asset forfeiture provision of RICO is important because it can be used to increase the effective penalty that can be imposed on a criminal who participates in a criminal enterprise. The two person framework could be modified to include asset forfeiture as follows. The individual now chooses quantity and effort to solve the following:

$$\text{Maximize } \{x_1,e_1\}\ (1-p(x_1,e_2))\ Rx_1 - p(x_1,e_2)Z - p(x_2,e_1)Y - e_1$$

And the social planner chooses Y and Z to minimize:

$$L = (1-p(x_1,e_2))Rx_1+(1-p(x_2,e_1))Rx_2+\beta(p(x_1,e_2)+ p(x_2,e_1))(Z+Y)$$

Where asset forfeiture is applied to the enterprise as a whole rather than to the individual's assets, the individual's problem becomes:

$$\text{Maximize } \{x_1,e_1\}\ (2-p(x_1,e_2)-p(x_2,e_1))\ Rx_1 - p(x_1,e_2)Z - p(x_2,e_1)Y - e_1$$

And social loss becomes:

$$L=(p(x_1,e_2)+ p(x_2,e_1))(Rx_1 + Rx_2)+ \beta\ (p(x_1,e_2) + p(x_2,e_1))\ (Z+ Y)$$

In a world in which both economic constraints (e.g. limited wealth, limited prison capacity) and non-economic constraints (e.g. constitutional prohibition against excessive punishment and requirement of proportionality) are imposed on penalty structures, group penalties can be used as an alternative method of increasing the magnitude of punishment when individual measures are limited. Asset forfeiture provisions which allow law enforcers to reach the assets of the enterprise as a whole have the added benefit of allowing law enforcers to recoup assets, thus lowering the net cost of law enforcement.

The enhanced sentencing provision provides a way of penalizing individuals for becoming involved in a large and/or highly profitable criminal enterprise. It provides a form of deterrence which increases with the volume of criminal activity. Ideally, where liability is based on the volume of criminal activity engaged in by the organization as a whole, participants in a criminal enterprise will have incentives to monitor and dampen the criminal activity level of their neighbors. This intended effect forms part of the foundation for the Continuing Criminal Enterprise (CCE) penalty structure.

Broader Impact of Alternative Statutes on Social Loss

The policy-maker is charged with the task of designing criminal penalties that will minimize the social cost of crime and punishment. This task is complicated by the fact that the effects of a particular penalty structure will vary depending upon the nature of the relationships between gang members and their activities. Although the discussion in this chapter has focused primarily on the effects of alternative criminal rules within a static framework, changes in penalty structure will affect decisions about entry into the gang and organizational decisions such as how to allocate control and how to structure criminal activities. One of the primary motivations behind the imposition of a RICO penalty structure, for example, is to make the cost of the same activity much higher when performed in the context of a group. While this chapter has emphasized the impact on level of criminal activity performed by a group and the expenditure on punishment, other important factors to consider include the impact on entry into and exit from a criminal organization. Trends towards decentralization of many previously highly structured criminal organizations can be attributed to changes in law enforcement strategies, and the proliferation of criminal gangs can be attributed in part to feed-back effects from enforcement policies. Criminal rules must also be selected with an eye to financial constraints on implementing penalties and technological constraints on the detection and apprehension of criminals.

Ideally, a simple economic framework can be used to evaluate the relative merits of different criminal rules in different contexts and to make a determination of how robust these rules will be to environmental changes and imperfect enforcement. By highlighting some of the competing effects associated with group-based criminal rules, such a framework can help to identify the trade-offs inherent in alternative strategies for combating organized crime. It can also be used to identify relationships between key variables such as group-based penalties and level of crime. The following examples suggest some applications of the economic framework developed in Part II. They are designed to illustrate the range of effects which group penalties might have on group-based criminal activity.

The Role of Anti-gang Statutes in Increasing Gang Cohesion

By focusing attention on gang membership, anti-gang law enforcement measures can have the effect of enhancing group identity. This type of reinforcing effect on gang identity was highlighted by Malcolm Klein in his studies of different types of gang control measures. Klein describes the results of experimental programs implemented in the Los Angeles area which involved assignment of case workers to specific gangs. He notes that these programs had the effect of reinforcing gang ties and enhancing the development of the gang's organizational structure. Gang patrols which have as their primary focus the monitoring of gang activities could have similar effects. Gang based investigation, enforcement and penalties may facilitate collusion by emphasizing the positive and negative externalities of individual actions and by highlighting the relationships between loosely defined and otherwise unconnected groups. Loose boundaries are reinforced through law enforcement activities, facilitating collusive group formation. In addition, the reputation of a gang may take on additional value in an environment which places a premium on group membership. External threats may operate to enhance the stability of a criminal street gang by increasing the costs of failing to cooperate. Indeed, criminal penalties may function as a mechanism for enforcing internal agreements. Proposition one in Part II can be applied to suggest that gang-based statutes which have the effect of criminalizing gang membership may lead to higher levels of gang activity.

Gang Mediation in Cabrini Green

The reverse logic of Proposition One can be applied to suggest ways in which criminal penalties can be employed to induce crime reducing behavior by criminal organizations. This can be achieved by designing rules which allow an internalization of negative externalities associated with criminal activity. Where a criminal gang is performing a variety of different activities, it may be possible to alter this pattern by altering the relative costs of the different activities either directly (through negotiations between gangs and law enforcers) or indirectly, through strategic use of penalties. The organizational structure can be utilized to achieve law enforcement objectives. Such an approach has been employed in innovative mediation programs designed to reduce the level of gang violence by establishing treaties between competitor gangs.

Eric Davis, a former gang member from Chicago's infamous Cabrini Green housing projects, returned to his former home as a police officer to practice a new form of community policing. He recognized that the larger Chicago gangs had well-developed organizational structures in place which could be utilized to produce benefits for rival gang members and the surrounding community. Based on the premise that escalating gang violence in areas such as Cabrini Green could be attributed in part to the absence of coordinating mechanisms and channels of communication between rival gangs, Eric Davis helped to set up a forum for the leaders of rival gangs to meet and explore mutually beneficial ways of reducing gang violence. He relied upon the business interests and enforcement structures of the dominant rival street gangs in Chicago, exploiting the mutual interest of rival gangs in maintaining stable and accessible drug markets and reducing the risks imposed on gang members to establish a gang truce in the face of escalating violence. The effect of these efforts on the level of violence in Cabrini Green was substantial.

The basic idea is that where gangs engage in a range of different activities, some of which are more harmful than others, it may be possible to exploit their interests in protecting one set of activities to reduce the level of other activities. The organizational structure can be employed to shift from more to less harmful criminal activities.

Feed-back Effects of Incarceration

The U.S. war on crime and, more recently, on drugs and gangs, has taken the form of a policy of incarceration which has resulted in a U.S. per capita incarceration rate which is higher than any other industrialized country. The strategy has had a number of perverse effects on criminal gang activity, including a dramatic increase in the number and influence of prison gangs both in and outside of prison. These prison gangs have swelled their ranks with gang and non-gang recruits and have established close connections with gangs operating on the street. In some cities released members of prison gangs have taken over the control of local drug markets, sometimes by regaining influence in a street gang they formerly belonged to, sometimes operating independently, and sometimes establishing their own branch of the prison gang. Crime participation and incarceration rates are highest in poor, crime-ridden neighborhoods, and noticeable correlation between the crime participation rate of certain groups and variables such as location (city vs. suburb vs. rural community), employment, age structure, and race and ethnicity (e.g. black vs. white, immigrant groups) remain even after controlling for economic and deterrence variables.[33] The local concentration of individuals who have spent time in jail and/or are likely to do so in poor, socially isolated neighborhoods has created fertile ground for further escalation in crime. Since these tend to be the same neighborhoods that spawn gang activity, the feed-back effects have a direct effect on gang participation and on the rate at which street gangs are transformed into drug gangs. The high concentration of individuals who have spent time in prison leads to a strengthening of the local criminal network in the neighborhood and a reduction in the stigma and other perceived costs associated with criminal penalties. These localized effects are reinforced by media stereotyping, social and economic immobility, and a strengthening of racial barriers through the disproportionate effects of sentencing structures on poor minorities (such as the disproportionate effect of heavy sentencing for sellers of crack cocaine on poor African-American males). The degree of social control exerted in the neighborhood continues to drop as criminal ties strengthen and those individuals who have jobs and other opportunities relocate. The pattern of exit and entry back into the same neighborhood creates regular openings for new entrants into the criminal scene and feeds the perception that spending time in jail is an unavoidable cost of doing business. A high recidivism rate is the product of a narrower set of legitimate opportunities and an increased range of criminal opportunities.

An evaluation of the effect of higher incarceration rates on street gang activity must take into account these feed-back effects, which include replacement effects and concentration effects such as reductions in the perceived cost of the penalty and the opportunity cost of committing crimes, and an increase in the opportunities for committing crime. These feed-back effects can be captured in a dynamic model which allows for adjustment of the expected costs and benefits of committing crimes in response to changes in the local crime participation and incarceration rates. Since the model presented in this chapter is a static model, incorporation of the feed-back effects would take the form primarily of a shift down in the expected disutility of punishment, a relaxation of the participation constraint, and/or a dependence of the costs and benefits of gang participation on the proportion of some locally defined population who had spent time in jail.

A number of economists have tried to formalize the role that an individual's environment might play in influencing his criminal propensity.[34] Sah (1991) examines the effect of endogenizing the perceived probability of punishment on the aggregate level of crime.[35] He presents a model in which individual perceptions (concerning probabilities of punishments) and decisions to commit crimes are determined endogenously based on the information made available to them. He uses the model to demonstrate how past crime may breed future crime and suggests how the magnitude of first-round effects of variable changes on crime participation rates may be amplified.[36] He also demonstrates how highly segregated groups within a society who face similar parameters can end up with different crime participation rates. Given U.S. estimates that fewer than one-third of crimes are reported, fewer than one-fifth of the reported crimes lead to arrest, and fewer than half of the arrests leading to incarceration, an individual in a high crime neighborhood is likely to observe a large number of people who are committing crimes and are not punished and a high rate of recidivism by those who have been arrested.[37] An alternative way of introducing feed-back effects into a model of crime is offered by Minnetti (1991), who demonstrates that the benefits of membership in a criminal mafia may depend upon the proportion of people in the region who are also members. In the context of this model, changes in the detection technology can be seen as incorporating the effects of community assessments of the risk of being caught. Alternatively, the effects may translate into a shift down in the individual penalty level due to factors which make the penalty seem less costly, such as reduced stigma associated with imprisonment.

Contemporary Applications of an Economic Organization Approach

The sophistication and size of some of the criminal enterprises operating in the illegal market place, coupled with a recognition of the ineffectiveness of traditional methods of crime fighting to control modern illegal business activities, has led to a shift in thinking and policy making relating to group-based crime. The introduction of the Federal Sentencing Guidelines can be seen as one such manifestation of the shift towards an economic organization approach to penalty design. Other examples include the strategic focus on money laundering and asset forfeiture as techniques for attacking drug cartels and the use of maxi-trials to disband mafia groups in Italy.

The Federal Sentencing Guidelines A Federal Sentencing Commission was established in 1984 and charged with the task of developing a more effective and less disparate set of guidelines for assigning criminal penalties. The scheme is based on a set of variables designed to reflect factors such as the profitability of the criminal activities and the importance of the role played by the criminal actor being charged. The guidelines provide a formula for calculating the sentence of a convicted criminal. The formula is based upon a series of factors which include previous criminal history, the nature of the crime, and the role played by the criminal in the crime. For drug crimes the type and amount of drugs are important determinants of sentence length. A number of disputes arise over the appropriate sentence for a member of a drug trafficking conspiracy. Even minor players in a conspiracy which deals in large quantities of drugs can face between thirty years and life in prison. Liability can be extended to include the acts of other members of the conspiracy performed both during and subsequent to periods of active membership. Moreover, since trials involving conspiracy charges are often consolidated and involve multiple defendants, minor players are more likely to be implicated in and charged for more substantial acts. There is an active ongoing debate surrounding the use of this formulaic approach and there is some dispute regarding the factors which are or should be included in the sentencing formula. An economic organization framework can be used to explore some of the potential consequences of the federal sentencing guidelines on the activities of members of drug dealing conspiracies.

Use of Asset and Organization-based Statutes to Attack the Cali Cartel Colombia supplies approximately eighty percent of the cocaine consumed in North America.[38] The combined assets of Colombia's ten biggest drug dealers are estimated to amount to $76 billion, which would rank them among the dozen largest companies in the world, and they own an estimated 9.9 million acres of Colombian land. The market is dominated by a small number of sophisticated cartels who have been able to coordinate their activities in order to exploit market opportunities and minimize government intervention. The Cali cartel was until recently the dominant player in the Colombian market, controlling about eighty percent of the Colombian cocaine production and earning about $20 billion dollars a year from its participation in the international cocaine trade.[39] Large cartels such as the Cali cartel employ sophisticated money laundering techniques to hide and legitimize the proceeds earned from drug trafficking. The Cali cartel also developed an illicit money trading market to help move illegally acquired funds out of the United States and into Colombia.[40] The laundered money is invested in legitimate businesses that are then used to produce legitimate earnings both for profit and to finance further criminal operations.[41] Investing in a wide range of industries has allowed the cartels to reduce investment risk and expand their economic bases.[42]

Money laundering and asset forfeiture statutes allow prosecutors to attack the economic foundation of the organization, reducing the asset base available to finance the running of the organization and the magnitude of the returns from participation in criminal activities. The flow of illicitly obtained money back into the economy serves as a useful "bottle neck" for law enforcement purposes, since the financial operations of the enterprise provide not only the rewards for criminal activities but also the means of maintaining control within the organization and circumventing legal procedures. The leadership of criminal organizations is also more likely to play a direct role in large money transactions than in the more basic criminal transactions which generate the revenue. Despite the fact that the Colombian drug cartels have developed into sophisticated criminal enterprises, the U.S. policy focus has only recently shifted towards more market-oriented strategies designed to reduce the profitability of criminal operations.[43] "Congress recently has recognized the influence of economics and implemented anti-drug legislation that targets the financial transactions connected with narcotics trafficking rather than the trafficking activity itself."[44] It has reacted by introducing and expanding the scope of criminal forfeiture statutes, including measures such as a "substitute asset" provision allowing forfeiture of substitute assets if the target assets were made unavailable.[45] It has also introduced more comprehensive money laundering statutes. In 1986, as part of the Anti-Drug Abuse Act of 1986, the United States enacted the Money Laundering Control Act as part of an attempt to increase the government's ability to identify and seize assets obtained from illegal activities and punish individuals for knowing participation in laundering of money.[46] This was followed by the Money Laundering Prosecution Improvements Act of 1988, which reduced reporting requirements, increased fines and privacy exceptions and provided for establishment of international currency control measures.[47] Current proposals include regulation of wire transfers. The Colombian government has followed suit by passing a new law allowing the seizure of assets gained through drug dealing, kidnapping or extortion.[48]

Maxi-trials Large scale investigations and procedures which allow for the prosecution of a criminal group as a group have also played a key role in breaking up sophisticated criminal organizations. A good example is provided by the recent use of "maxi-trials," consolidated trials involving multiple members and prosecution for patterns of criminal activities, to obtain the conviction of key members of the Italian Mafia. These types of group trials provide prosecutors with a number of advantages, including an increase in the range of evidence and penalties available, reduced costs of prosecuting, and the availability of strategic tools such as plea bargaining. A simple way of introducing the benefits of consolidated trials into the model would be to incorporate the effects into the probability and magnitude of punishment.

IV. Conclusion

The American approach to group criminality reflects a tension between concern about the special dangers associated with criminal organizations and a desire to fit group criminality into the traditional legal framework based on individual liability for harm directly caused by that individual.[49] Ideally, group criminality statutes should provide a more integrated set of tools with which to attack the organization, including penalties which target the leadership, incentive structure, and economic base of the enterprise. The current system reduces individual protections and increases the liability attached to multiple offender crimes without properly addressing the nature and structure of the criminal organization and the ways in which these changes might affect group activity. This chapter presents an alternative law and economics approach to group crime which is motivated by the belief that criminal laws should be based on an understanding of the nature and structure of the criminal organization. To the extent that organized groups pose special dangers or problems, the criminal rules which are targeted at these groups should be designed in light of principles of economic organization and a practical understanding of the realities of illegal markets.

An economic approach can be combined with a legal analysis of the criminal process and its limitations in order to identify criminal laws which are both feasible and efficient and to examine the practical consequences of these rules for economic-minded criminal decision makers. Difficulties in incorporating non-economic objectives and constraints (e.g. First Amendment concerns) into an economic framework, perceptions of criminal gangs as being different from (and less rational than) business enterprises, and a general reluctance on the part of law makers to apply an economic framework to criminal issues, have played major roles in inhibiting the development of an organization-based approach. Despite these difficulties, introducing an organization-based approach would enhance the coherency and effectiveness of the current legal treatment of criminal organizations.[50]

Appendix One

Individual Criminal

Define: x = number of crimes, $0 \leq x \leq \bar{X}$
R = revenue per crime, $0 < R < \infty$
$p(x)$ = probability of being caught committing a crime
Z = number of days in jail
β = social cost of keeping a person in jail for one day

Assumption 1.1: p(x) is a continuous, differentiable function which has the following properties: (i) $p(0)=0$ and $p(x)=1$; (ii) $p'(x)>0$, (iii) $p''(x)>0$.

The individual criminal chooses the number of crimes x to solve:

$$\text{Maximize } \{x\}\ Rx - p(x)\,Z$$

First-order condition:

$$(1) \quad R - p'(x)\,Z = 0$$

We know from the first-order condition (1) that:

$$p'(x)=R/Z > 0 \ \text{ for } x<\bar{x} \ \text{ and } x'(Z) = -R/\,Z^2p''(x) \ < 0$$

The social loss function is given by the sum of revenue lost and cost of punishment, which for a population of two identical criminals is given by:

$$L = 2\,R\,x + 2\,\beta\,p(x)\,Z$$

The social problem is to minimize social loss, choosing Z to solve:

$$\text{Minimize } \{Z\}\ 2\,R\,x(Z) + 2\beta p(x(Z))\,Z$$

First-order condition:

$$(2) \quad R\,x'(Z) + \beta p(x) + \beta p'(x)x'(Z)Z = 0$$

From (1) and (2) :

$$Z^* = [R^2(1+\beta)\,/\,\beta p''(x)p(x)]^{1/2}$$

$$L^* = 2Rx + 2\beta p(x)[R2(1+\beta)\,/\,p''(x)p(x)]^{1/2}$$

Appendix Two

Two Criminals Operating as a Gang

Define:

R	=	revenue per crime, $0 < R < \infty$
x_1	=	number of crimes committed by person 1, $0 \leq x_1 \leq \bar{x}$
x_2	=	number of crimes committed by person 2, $0 \leq x_2 \leq \bar{x}$
e_1	=	effort exerted by person 1 to help person 2, $0 \leq e_1 \leq \bar{e}$
e_2	=	effort exerted by person 2 to help person 1, $0 \leq e_2 \leq \bar{e}$
$p(x_1,e_2)$	=	probability that person 1 is caught committing crime
$p(x_2,e_1)$	=	probability that person 2 is caught committing crime
Z	=	individual penalty level, given by the number of days in jail for person caught committing a crime
Y	=	group penalty level, given by number of days in jail for each of the remaining gang members if one of the members is caught committing a crime
β	=	social cost per day of keeping someone in jail, $0 < \beta < 1$

Assumption 2.1: p(.) is a continuous, differentiable function which has the following properties: (i) $p(\bar{x},e_2) = 1$ and $p(\bar{x},e_1) = 1$, $p(0,e_1) = p(0,e_2) = 0$; (ii) $p_x(x_1,e_2) > 0$ and $p_x(x_2,e_1) > 0$; (iii) $p_e(x_1,e_2) < 0$ and $p_e(x_2,e_1) < 0$; (iv) $p_{xx}(x_1,e_2) > 0$ and $p_{xx}(x_2,e_1) > 0$; (v) $p_{ee}(x_1,e_2) > 0$ and $p_{ee}(x_2,e_1) > 0$; (vi) $p_{ex}(x_1,e_2) < 0$ and $p_{ex}(x_2,e_1) < 0$.

Individual 1 chooses x_1 and e_1 to solve:

$$\text{Maximize } \{x_1,e_1\}\ Rx_1 - p(x_1,e_2)Z - p(x_2,e_1)Y - e_1$$

Individual 2 chooses x_2 and e_2 to solve:

$$\text{Maximize } \{x_2,e_2\}\ Rx_2 - p(x_2,e_1)Z - p(x_1,e_2)Y - e_2$$

There are two non-cooperative simultaneous moves games going on, the first involving choice of x_1 and e_2, the second involving choice of x_2 and e_1. The optimization problem for each individual is separable in crime level and effort choices, taking penalties as fixed, and the problem is symmetrical, i.e. $x_1 = f(e_2,Z)$, $x_2 = f(e_1,Z)$, $e_1 = g(x_2,Y)$, $e_2 = g(x_1,Y)$

Consider Game 1 (person 1 chooses x_1, person 2 chooses e_2)

First-order conditions for x_1 and e_2 respectively, for interior solutions:

(1) $R- p_x(x_1,e_2)Z=0$
(2) $-p_e(x_1,e_2)Y-1=0$

Slope of reaction curve for person 1 in game 1 (choosing x_1 given e_2):

$$- p_{xx}(x_1,e_2)Z- p_{xe}(x_1,e_2)e_2'(x_1)Z = 0$$

(3) $e_2'(x_1) = - p_{xx}(x_1,e_2)/ p_{xe}(x_1,e_2)$

Slope of reaction curve for person 2 in game 1 (choosing e_2 given x_1):

$$-p_{ee}(x_1,e_2)e_2'(x_1)Y-p_{ex}(x_1,e_2)Y=0$$

(4) $e_2'(x) = -p_{ex}(x_1,e_2) / p_{ee}(x_1,e_2)$

Condition for stability of the game (x_1,e_2) is that person 1's reaction curve is steeper than person 2's, i.e. that $p_{xx}(x_1,e_2)p_{ee}(x_1,e_2) > p_{xe}^2(x_1,e_2)$.

Assumption 2.2: $p_{xx}(x_1,e_2)p_{ee}(x_1,e_2) > p_{xe}^2(x_1,e_2)$

Comparative Statics for Game 1:

Response of x to change in Z

$$x'(Z) = -p_x /[p_{xe}(x_1,e_2)\, e_2'(Z)+p_{xx}(x_1,e_2)]Z$$

Solving for $e_2'(Z)$

$$-p_{ee}(x_1,e_2)e_2'(x_1)x_1(Z)Y - p_{ex}(x_1,e_2)x_1'(Z)Y = 0$$
$$e_2'(Z) = - p_{ex}(x_1,e_2)x'(Z) / p_{ee}(x_1,e_2)$$

(5) $x'(Z) = - p_x (x_1,e_2)\, p_{ee}(x_1,e_2) / Z[p_{xx}(x_1,e_2)p_{ee}(x_1,e_2) - p_{xe}^2(x_1,e_2)] < 0$

$$e_2'(Z) = p_{ex}(x_1,e_2)\, p_x (x_1,e_2) / Z[p_{xx}(x_1,e_2)p_{ee}(x_1,e_2) - p_{xe}^2(x_1,e_2)] < 0$$

Response of x_1 and e_2 to change in Y

$$x_1'(e_2) = -p_{xe}(x_1,e_2) /p_{xx}(x_1,e_2)$$
$$-p_{ee} (x_1,e_2)e_2'(Y)Y -p_{ex}(x_1,e_2)x_1'(e_2)e_2'(Y)Y-p_e(x_1,e_2) =0$$

(7) $e_2'(Y) = - p_e(x_1,e_2)p_{xx}(x_1,e_2) /Y[p_{xx}(x_1,e_2)p_{ee}(x_1,e_2) - p_{xe}^2(x_1,e_2)] > 0$
(8) $x'(Y) = p_{xe}(x,e_2)p_e(x,e_2) /Y[p_{xx}(x_1,e_2)p_{ee}(x_1,e_2) - p_{xe}^2(x_1,e_2)] >0$

Since the game is symmetric, the same results hold for Game 2, in which individual 1 chooses e_1 and individual 2 chooses x_2.

Proposition 1: Helping effort (e_1,e_2) is positive if and only if $Y>0$ and is increasing in Y. i.e. $e_1'(Y) > 0$ and $e_2'(Y)>0$ if $Y>0$, and $e_1>0$ and $e_2>0$ if and only if $Y>0$.

Proposition 2: The level of crime increases as the group penalty is increased. i.e. $x_1'(Y) > 0$ and $x_2'(Y)>0$.

Proof for 1 and 2:

Individual's Problem Differentiating the first-order conditions of e_2 and x_1 with respect to Y, as given in (7) and (8):

$$e_2'(Y) = - p_e(x,e_2)p_{xx}(x,e_2) / Y[p_{xx}(x,e_2)p_{ee}(x,e_2) - p_{xe}^2(x,e_2)] = p_{xx} / AY^2$$
$$x'(Y) = p_{xe}(x,e_2)p_e(x,e_2) / Y[p_{xx}(x,e_2)p_{ee}(x,e_2) - p_{xe}^2(x,e_2)] = -p_{xe} / AY^2$$

From the assumptions made above, we know that:

$p_{xx} > 0$

$A=[p_{xx}(x,e_2)p_{ee}(x,e_2) - p_{xe}^2(x,e_2)] >0$

$p_{xe} < 0$

Therefore, we know that

$e_2'(Y) >0$; $x_1'(Y) >0$

Since the problem is symmetric, we also know that:

$e_1'(Y) >0$; $x_2'(Y) >0$

Social Problem The social loss function is given by:

(9) $L=R(x_1+x_2) + \beta[p(x_1,e_2)+ p(x_2,e_1)] (Z+Y)$

The policy-maker solves the following problem:

$$\text{Minimize } \{Y,Z\}\ Rx_1 + Rx_2 + \beta[p(x_1,e_2) + p(x_2, e_1)]\ (Z+Y)$$

First-order conditions for Z :

(10) $Rx_1'(Z)+Rx_2'(Z) + \beta(Z+Y)[p_x(x_1,e_2)x_1'(Z) + p_e(x_1,e_2)e_2'(Z) + p_x(x_2,e_1)x_2'(Z)+p_e(x_2,e_1)e'_1(Z)]+ \beta\ (p(x_1,e_2) + p(x_2, e_1))=0$

Using the results from above to substitute:

$$[R+ R\beta(Z+Y)/Z]\,(x_1'(Z) + x_2'(Z)) - \beta(Z+Y)/Y - (e_2'(Z) + e'_1(Z)) + \beta\,(p(x_1,e_2) + p(x_2, e_1))=0$$

Given that problem is symmetric, and substituting for terms, this reduces to:

$$(10')\quad -[2R^2(Z+ \beta(Z+Y)p_{ee}(x_1,e_2)Y+2R\beta(Z+Y)p_{ex}(x_1,e_2)Z] / Z^3Y^2[p_{xx}(x_1,e_2)p_{ee}(x_1,e_2) - p_{xe}^{\,2}(x_1,e_2)] + \beta(p(x_1,e_2) + p(x_2,e_1)) =0$$

As can be seen by evaluating the first-order condition for Z at Z=0, Z*>0.

First-order conditions for Y for an interior solution:

$$(11)\quad Rx_1'(Y)+Rx_2'(Y)+\beta(Z+Y)[p_x(x_1,e_2)x_1'(Y)+p_e(x_1,e_2)e_2'(Y) +p_x(x_2,e_1)x_2'(Y)+ p_e(x_2,e_1)e_1'(Y)]+ \beta(\, p(x_1,e_2) + p(x_2,e_1)\,)= 0$$

A change in Y has two competing effects on the social loss L*(Z*,Y*):

1. As Y increases, the level of help goes up and this causes the level of crime to go up, increasing social loss (See Result 1)
2. As Y increases, the probability of capture for a given level of crime goes down, and this decreases the expenditure on punishment and lowers social loss.

Proposition 3: Using group penalties will increase social loss when the probability of detection is separable in the number of crimes and effort devoted to evading detection.
i.e. When p(x,e) is separable in x and e, social loss is minimized by setting Y=0.

Proof of Proposition 3:

Show: For any given level of deterrence (i.e. for a given level of x) L*-L' > 0 where L' = minimum social loss when Y=0 and L* is the minimum level of social loss for Y*>0.

Suppose that the minimum level of social loss is given by L(Z*,Y*) with Z*>0 and Y*>0 and x = x*. Let p(x,e)=f(x)g(e) where f(x) and g(e) are such that p(x,e) satisfies all of the properties in Assumption 1 and p(x,0)=f(x).

Setting Y = 0 and Z = Z' such that x' = x*, it can be shown that $L'(Z_1')<L(Z_1^*,Z_2^*)$ for all (Z,Y) with Y>0. This contradicts the assumption that social loss is minimized for Y*>0. To see this, find L'(Z') and L(Z*,Y*) where Y'=0 and Z' is increased to maintain the same level of deterrence (i.e. to ensure that x' = x*).

Let $L' = 2Rx^* + 2\beta Z'(p(x^*))$
$L^* = 2Rx^* + 2\beta\, (Z^*+Y^*)p(x,e_2)$

Calculating Z' such that $x' = x^*$:

(a) Maximize $\{x\}$ $Rx - p(x,e_2)\, Z_1 - p(y,e_1)Z_2 - e_1$

First-order conditions:

$$R - p_x(x^*,e_2^*)\, Z_1 = R - f_x(x^*)g(e_2^*)\, Z_1 = 0$$

(b) Maximize $\{x\}$ $Rx - p(x)Z_1'$

First-order conditions:

$$R - p_x(x)\, Z_1' = R - f_x(x)\, Z_1' = 0$$

For $x' = x^*$, $Z' = g(e^*)Z^*$. Compare:

$$L' = 2Rx' + 2\beta Z'(p(x')) = 2Rx^* + 2\beta(Z^*g(e^*))\,(f(x^*))$$
$$L^* = 2Rx^* + 2\beta(Z^*+Y^*)(f(x^*)g(e^*))$$

The difference in social loss is given by:

$$L^* - L' = 2\beta Y^* f(x^*)g(e^*) > 0$$

Thus, social loss is minimized by setting Y=0.

Result: When p(x,e) is separable in x and e and the level of crime is held constant, the social loss is minimized by setting Y=0, i.e. $L^* - L' > 0$ for $Y>0$.

Example: Let $p(x,e)=p(x)/(e+1)$. Then $x' = x^*$ when $Z'=Z^*/(e^*+1)$ and $L^*(Z,Y) - L'(Z') = 2\beta Y^* p(x^*) / (e^*+1) > 0$

Appendix Three

Case 1 Group Penalties Have No Effect on Criminal Activity

Define: $R(x_1,x_2)$ = revenue function
x_1 = number of crimes committed by person 1, $0 \leq x_1 \leq \bar{x}$
x_2 = number of crimes committed by person 2, $0 \leq x_2 \leq \bar{x}$
e_1 = effort exerted by person 1 to help person 2, $0 \leq e_1 \leq \bar{e}$
e_2 = effort exerted by person 2 to help person 1, $0 \leq e_2 \leq \bar{e}$
$p(x_1)$ = probability that person 1 is caught committing crime
$p(x_2)$ = probability that person 2 is caught committing crime
Z = individual penalty level, given by the number of days in jail for person caught committing a crime
Y = group penalty level, given by number of days in jail for each of the remaining gang members if one of the members is caught committing a crime
β = social cost per day of keeping someone in jail, $0 < \beta < 1$

Assumption 3.1: $p(x)$ is a continuous, differentiable function which has the following properties: (i) $p(0)=0$ and $p(\bar{x})=1$; (ii) $p'(x)>0$, (iii) $p''(x)>0$.

Assumption 3:2: $R(x_1, x_2)$ is a continuous, differentiable function which has the following properties: (i) $R(0,0) = 0$, $R(\bar{x},\bar{x}) < \infty$; (ii) $R_1(x_1, x_2) > 0$, $R_2(x_1,x_2)>0$; (iii) $R_{11}(x_1,x_2)<0$, $R_{22}(x_1, x_2)<0$; (iv) $R_{12}(x_1, x_2)=R_{21}(x_1,x_2) < 0$.

Individual 1 chooses x_1 to solve:

$$\text{Maximize } \{x_1,e_1\} \; R(x_1, x_2) - p(x_1)Z - p(x_2)Y$$

and individual 2 chooses x_2 to solve:

$$\text{Maximize } \{x_2\} \; R(x_1, x_2) - p(x_2)Z - p(x_1)Y$$

First-order Condition for person 1:

$$(1) \quad R_1(x_1, x_2) - p'(x_1) Z = 0$$

We know from the first-order condition for person 1 that:

$$p'(x_1) = R_1(x_1, x_2) / Z > 0 \quad \text{for } x < \bar{x}$$
$$x_1'(Z) = R_1(x_1, x_2) / [R_1(x_1, x_2)\,Z - p''(x_1)\,Z^2] < 0$$
$$x_1'(Y) = 0$$

The equations are identical for person 2.

Proposition 4: The level of criminal activity is not affected by the level of the group penalty as long as the penalty is not high enough to drive both gang members out of the illegal market. i.e. For $x_1 > 0$ and $x_2 > 0$, $x_1'(Y) = x_2'(Y) = 0$.

Proof:

From the first-order conditions for each individual's optimization problem, it is clear that the choices of x_1 and x_2 do not depend upon the level of the group penalty Y.

$$R_1(x_1, x_2) - p'(x_1)\,Z = 0 \quad \rightarrow \quad x_1'(Y) = 0$$
$$R_2(x_1, x_2) - p'(x_2)\,Z = 0 \quad \rightarrow \quad x_2'(Y) = 0$$

Policy-maker's Optimization Problem The social loss function is given by:

$$L = 2\,R(x_1, x_2) + \beta[p(x_1) + p(x_2)](Y+Z)$$

Proposition 5a: It is socially efficient to set the group penalty equal to zero. i.e. $Y^* = 0$.

Proof:

The social problem is to minimize social loss, choosing Y and Z to solve:

$$\text{Minimize } \{Y, Z\}\ 2\,R(x_1, x_2) + \beta[p(x_1) + p(x_2)](Y+Z)$$

First-order condition for Z:

$$2R_1'(x_1, x_2)\,x_1'(Z) + 2\beta p(x_1) + 2\beta p'(x_1)x'(Z)(Y+Z) = 0$$

First-order condition for Y, employing the symmetry of the two person problem to simplify:

$$dL/dY = 2R_1(x_1,x_2)\, x_1'(Y) + 2\beta p(x_1) + 2\beta p'(x_1)x'(Y)(Y+Z)$$

Since $x_1'(Y) = 0$, this reduces to $dL/dY = 2\beta p(x_1) > 0$. Since this is a minimization problem, this implies that $Y^*=0$.

Proposition 5b: Where the gang members cooperate and select drug quantities to maximize joint profits, $Y^*>0$ and $Z^*>0$ when the loss function is a convex function of Y and Z, and either $Y^*>0$ and $Z^*=0$ or $Y^*=0$ and $Z^*>0$ when the loss function is a concave function of Y and Z (since in this model the group penalty and the individual penalty are interchangeable).

Using the same framework as above, suppose that gang members 1 and 2 cooperate and choose their criminal activity levels jointly instead of individually, choosing quantities to solve the following:

$$\text{Maximize } \{x_1,x_2\}\ 2R(x_1, x_2) - [p(x_1) + p(x_2)](Y+Z)$$

The first-order conditions for x_1 and x_2 are, respectively:

$$2R_1(x_1, x_2) - p'(x_1)(Y+Z) = 0$$
$$2R_2(x_1, x_2) - p'(x_2)(Y+Z) = 0$$

Solving for $x_1'(Y)$ and $x_2'(Y)$,

$$x_1'(Y) = p'(x_1) - 2R_{12}(x_1,x_2)x_2'(Y) / [2R_{11}(x_1,x_2) - p''(x_1)(Y+Z)]$$
$$x_2'(Y) = p'(x_2) - 2R_{21}(x_1,x_2)x_1'(Y) / [2R_{22}(x_1,x_2) - p''(x_1)(Y+Z)]$$

Using the symmetry of the problem, this becomes:

$$x_1'(Y) = p'(x_1) / [2R_{11}(x_1,x_2)+2R_{12}(x_1,x_2) - p''(x_1)(Y+Z)] < 0$$
$$x_2'(Y) = p'(x_2) / [2R_{22}(x_1,x_2)+2R_{12}(x_1,x_2) - p''(x_2)(Y+Z)] < 0$$

Similarly,

$$x_1'(Z) = p'(x_1) / [2R_{11}(x_1,x_2)+2R_{12}(x_1,x_2) - p''(x_1)(Y+Z)] < 0$$
$$x_2'(Z) = p'(x_2) / [2R_{22}(x_1,x_2)+2R_{12}(x_1,x_2) - p''(x_2)(Y+Z)] < 0$$

The social problem is to minimize social loss, choosing Y and Z to solve:

$$\text{Minimize } \{Y, Z\}\ 2\,R(x_1, x_2) + \beta[p(x_1) + p(x_2)](Y+Z)$$

First-order conditions for Z are given by:

$$\begin{aligned} dL/dZ &= 4R_1(x_1,x_2)x_1'(Z) + 2\beta p'(x_1)\, x_1'(Z)\, (Y+Z) + 2\beta p(x_1) \\ &= 2\beta p(x_1) + [4R_1(x_1,x_2) + 2\beta p'(x_1)(Y+Z)]\, p'(x_1) \,/ \\ &\qquad [2R_{11}(x_1,x_2)+2R_{12}(x_1,x_2) - p''(x_1)(Y+Z)] \end{aligned}$$

First-order conditions for Y are given by:

$$\begin{aligned} dL/dY &= 4R_1(x_1,x_2)x_1'(Y) + 2\beta p'(x_1)\, x_1'(Y)\, (Y+Z) + 2\beta p(x_1) \\ &= 2\beta p(x_1) + [4R_1(x_1,x_2) + 2\beta p'(x_1)(Y+Z)]\, p'(x_1) \,/ \\ &\qquad [2R_{11}(x_1,x_2)+2R_{12}(x_1,x_2) - p''(x_1)(Y+Z)] \end{aligned}$$

Second-order conditions for Z and Y are such that

$$d^2L/dY^2 = 4R_{11}(x_1,x_2)(x_1'(Y))^2 + 4R_1(x_1,x_2)x_1''(Y) + 2\beta p''(x_1)\,(x_1'(Y))^2\,(Y+Z) + 2\beta p'(x_1)\, x_1''(Y)\,(Y+Z) + 2\beta p'(x_1)\, x_1'(Y) + 2\beta p'(x_1)\, x_1'(Y)$$

and similarly for Z. If L is a convex function of Y and Z then loss will be minimized by setting Y=Z, and Y*>0. This condition holds if:

(i) $x_1''(Y)<0$ and
(ii) $-4R_{11}(x_1,x_2)(x_1'(Y))^2 - 4\beta p'(x_1)x_1'(Y) - 4R_1(x_1,x_2)x_1''(Y) - 4\beta p'(x_1)\ x_1''(Y)\,(Y+Z) < 2\beta p''(x_1)\,(x_1'(Y))^2\,(Y+Z)$
or
(i) $x_1''(Y)>0$ and
(ii) $-4R_{11}(x_1,x_2)(x_1'(Y))^2 - 4\beta p'(x_1)x_1'(Y) < 2\beta p''(x_1)\,(x_1'(Y))^2\,(Y+Z)\,)$ $+4R_1(x_1,x_2)x_1''(Y) - +4\beta p'(x_1)\, x_1''(Y)\,(Y+Z)$

If L is a concave function of Y and Z, then loss will be minimized by setting either Y or Z to zero.

Case 2 Group Penalties Have a Negative Effect on Criminal Activity

Define:

R	= revenue per crime, $0 < R < \infty$
x_1	= number of crimes committed by person 1, $0 \leq x_1 \leq \bar{x}$
x_2	= number of crimes committed by person 2, $0 \leq x_2 \leq \bar{x}$
e_1	= effort exerted by person 1 to help person 2, $0 \leq e_1 \leq \bar{e}$
e_2	= effort exerted by person 2 to help person 1, $0 \leq e_2 \leq \bar{e}$
$p(x_1,e_2)$	= probability that person 1 is caught committing crime
$p(x_2,e_1)$	= probability that person 2 is caught committing crime
$q(x_2,e_1)$	= probability that person 1 is penalized when person 2 is caught committing crime
$q(x_1,e_2)$	= probability that person 2 is penalized when person 1 is caught committing crime
Z	= individual penalty level, given by the number of days in jail for person caught committing a crime
Y	= group penalty level, given by number of days in jail for each of the remaining gang members if one of the members is caught committing a crime
β	= social cost per day of keeping someone in jail, $0 < \beta < 1$

Assumption 4.1: $p(x_i, e_j)$ is a continuous, differentiable function which has the following properties: (i) $p(0,e_j) = 0$, $0<p(\bar{x},e_i) \leq 1$; (ii) $p_x(x_i, e_j) > 0$, $p_e(x_i, e_j)>0$; (iii) $p_{xx}(x_i, e_j) > 0$, $p_{ee}(x_i, e_j) > 0$; (iv) $p_{xe}(x_i, e_j) = p_{ex}(x_i, e_j) > 0$.

Assumption 4.2: $q(x_i, e_j)$ is a continuous, differentiable function which has the following properties: (i) $q(0,e_j) = 0$, $0<q(\bar{x}, e_j) \leq 1$; (ii) $q_x(x_i, e_j) > 0$, $q_e(x_i, e_j)<0$; (iii) $q_{xx}(x_i, e_j) > 0$, $q_{ee}(x_i, e_j) > 0$; (iv) $q_{xe}(x_i, e_j) = q_{ex}(x_i, e_j) < 0$.

Criminal's Optimization Problem Individual 1 chooses x_1 and e_1 to solve:

$$\text{Maximize } \{x_1,e_1\} \; Rx_1 - p(x_1,e_2)Z - q(x_2,e_1)Y - e_1$$

and individual 2 chooses x_2 to solve:

$$\text{Maximize } \{x_2\} \; Rx_2 - p(x_2,e_1)Z - q(x_1,e_2)Y - e_2$$

There are two non-cooperative simultaneous moves games going on, the first involving choice of x_1 and e_2, the second involving choice of x_2 and e_1 where: $x_1 = f(e_2,Z)$, $x_2 = f(e_1,Z)$, $e_1 = g(x_2,Y)$, $e_2 = g(x_1,Y)$

Consider Game 1 (person 1 chooses x_1, person 2 chooses e_2)

First-order conditions for x_1 and e_2 respectively, for interior solutions:

(1) $R - p_x(x_1,e_2)Z = 0$
(2) $-q_e(x_1,e_2)Y-1 = 0$

Slope of reaction curve for person 1 in game 1 (choosing x given e_2):

$$- p_{xx}(x_1,e_2)Z- p_{xe}(x_1,e_2)e_2'(x_1)Z = 0$$

(3) $e_2'(x_1) = - p_{xx}(x_1,e_2) / p_{xe}(x_1,e_2) < 0$

Slope of reaction curve for person 2 in game 1 (choosing e_2 given x_1):

$$-q_{ee}(x_1,e_2)e_2'(x_1)Y-q_{ex}(x_1,e_2)Y=0$$

(4) $e_2'(x) = -q_{ex}(x_1,e_2) / q_{ee}(x_1,e_2) > 0$

Comparative Statics for Game 1:

Response of x to change in Z

$$-p_{xx}(x_1,e_2)\, x'(Z)Z - p_{xe}(x_1,e_2)e_2'(x)Z-p_x(x_1,e_2)=0$$

Solving for $e_2'(Z)$

$$-q_{ee}(x_1,e_2)e_2'(x_1)x_1(Z)Y - q_{ex}(x_1,e_2)x_1'(Z)Y = 0$$

$$e_2'(Z) = - q_{ex}(x_1,e_2)x_1'(Z) / q_{ee}(x_1,e_2)$$

(6) $x'(Z)=- p_x (x_1,e_2)\, q_{ee}(x_1,e_2) / Z[p_{xx}(x_1,e_2)q_{ee}(x_1,e_2) - p_{xe}(x_1,e_2)\, q_{xe}(x_1,e_2)]<0$

$e_2'(Z)= q_{ex}(x_1,e_2)\, p_x(x_1,e_2) /Z[p_{xx}(x_1,e_2)q_{ee}(x_1,e_2) - p_{xe}(x_1,e_2)q_{xe}(x_1,e_2)]<0$

Response of x_1 and e_2 to change in Y

$$x_1'(e_2) = -p_{xe}(x_1,e_2) /p_{xx}(x_1,e_2) < 0$$

$$-q_{ee}(x_1,e_2)e_2'(Y)Y -q_{ex}(x_1,e_2)x_1'(e_2)e_2'(Y)Y-q_e(x_1,e_2) =0$$

(7) $e_2'(Y) = - q_e(x_1,e_2)p_{xx}(x_1,e_2) /Y[p_{xx}(x_1,e_2)q_{ee}(x_1,e_2)-p_{xe}(x_1,e_2)\, q_{xe}(x_1,e_2)]>0$

(8) $x_1'(Y) = p_{xe}(x_1,e_2)q_e(x,e_2) /Y[p_{xx}(x_1,e_2)q_{ee}(x_1,e_2)-p_{xe}(x_1,e_2)\, q_{xe}(x_1,e_2)]<0$

Since the game is symmetric, the same results hold for Game 2, in which individual 1 chooses e_1 and individual 2 chooses x_2.

Proposition 6: The level of crime is a decreasing function of the group penalty. i.e. $x_1'(Y) < 0$ and $x_2'(Y) < 0$.

Proof :

From (8) above, we see that
$x_1'(Y) = p_{xe}(x_1,e_2)q_e(x_1,e_2) / Y[p_{xx}(x_1,e_2)q_{ee}(x_1,e_2)-p_{xe}(x_1,e_2)\, q_{xe}(x_1,e_2)]<0$
Similarly, given the symmetry of the problem,
$x_2'(Y) = p_{xe}(x_2,e_1)q_e(x_2,e_1) / Y[p_{xx}(x_2,e_1)q_{ee}(x_2,e_1)-p_{xe}(x_2,e_1)\, q_{xe}(x_2,e_1)]<0$

The Policy-maker's Optimization Problem The social loss function is given by:

$$L = R(x_1+x_2) + \beta[p(x_1,e_2)+p(x_2,e_1)]\, Z + \beta[q(x_1,e_2)+ q(x_2,e_1)]Y$$

The policy-maker's problem is given by:

$$\text{Min } \{Y,Z\}\ R(x_1+x_2)+\beta[p(x_1,e_2)+p(x_2,e_1)]Z+\beta[q(x_1,e_2)+ q(x_2,e_1)]Y$$

Proposition 7: It is socially efficient to have a positive group penalty when the beneficial effect of group penalties on the level of crime outweighs the cost of the increased frequency of punishment. i.e. $Y^*>0$ when
$-[2R+2\beta p_x(x_1,e_2)Z]x_1'(Y)>2\beta Z p_e(x_1,e_2)e_2'(Y)+2\beta q(x_1,e_2)$

Proof:

The policy-maker's problem is given by:

$$\text{Min } \{Y,Z\}\ R(x_1+x_2)+\beta[p(x_1,e_2)+p(x_2,e_1)]Z+\beta[q(x_1,e_2)+ q(x_2,e_1)]Y$$

First-order conditions for Y, using symmetry properties of the problem:

$$(10)\quad dL/dY = 2Rx_1'(Y) + 2\beta[p_x(x_1,e_2)x_1'(Y) +p_e(x_1,e_2)e_2'(Y)]Z + 2\beta[q_x(x_1,e_2)x_1'(Y) +q_e(x_1,e_2)e_2'(Y)]Y + 2\beta q(x_1,e_2)=0$$

which is equal to,
$[2R+2\beta p_x(x_1,e_2)Z+2\beta q_x(x_1,e_2)Y]x_1'(Y)+[2\beta p_e(x_1,e_2)Z+ 2\beta q_e(x_1,e_2)Y]e_2'(Y) + 2\beta q(x_1,e_2)=0$
or

$[2R+2\beta p_x(x_1,e_2)Z+2\beta q_x(x_1,e_2)Y]\ p_{xe}(x_1,e_2)q_e(x,e_2)\ /AY$
$-[2\beta p_e(x_1,e_2)Z+ 2\beta q_e(x_1,e_2)Y]\ q_e(x_1,e_2)p_{xx}(x_1,e_2)\ /AY+ 2\beta q(x_1,e_2)=0$
where $A = [p_{xx}(x_1,e_2)q_{ee}(x_1,e_2)-p_{xe}(x_1,e_2)\ q_{xe}(x_1,e_2)]>0$

$[2R+2\beta p_x(x_1,e_2)Z+2\beta q_x(x_1,e_2)Y]p_{xe}(x_1,e_2)q_e(x,e_2)$
$-[2\beta p_e(x_1,e_2)Z+ 2\beta q_e(x_1,e_2)Y]\ q_e(x_1,e_2)p_{xx}(x_1,e_2)+ 2\beta q(x_1,e_2)AY=0$

Evaluated at Y=0, this becomes:
$[2R+2\beta p_x(x_1,e_2)Z]p_{xe}(x_1,e_2)q_e(x,e_2)-[2\beta p_e(x_1,e_2)Z]\ q_e(x_1,e_2)p_{xx}(x_1,e_2)$

Result: $Y^*>0$ when

$$-[2R+2\beta p_x(x_1,e_2)Z]x_1'(Y)>[2\beta p_e(x_1,e_2)Z]e_2'(Y)+2\beta q(x_1,e_2)$$

or

$$-[2R+2\beta p_x(x_1,e_2)Z]p_{xe}(x_1,e_2)q_e(x,e_2)>-[2\beta p_e(x_1,e_2)Z]\ q_e(x_1,e_2)p_{xx}(x_1,e_2)$$

First-order Conditions for Z

$dL/dZ = 2Rx_1'(Z) + 2\beta[p_x(x_1,e_2)x_1'(Z) +p_e(x_1,e_2)e_2'(Z)]Z$
$\qquad + 2\beta[q_x(x_1,e_2)x_1'(Z) +q_e(x_1,e_2)e_2'(Z)]Y + 2\beta q(x_1,e_2)=0$
which is equal to:
$[2R+2\beta p_x(x_1,e_2)Z+2\beta q_x(x_1,e_2)Y]x_1'(Z)+[2\beta p_e(x_1,e_2)Z+ 2\beta q_e(x_1,e_2)Y]e_2'(Z)$
$\qquad + 2\beta q(x_1,e_2)=0$
or
$-[2R+2\beta p_x(x_1,e_2)Z+2\beta q_x(x_1,e_2)Y]p_x\ (x_1,e_2)\ q_{ee}(x_1,e_2)\ /\ AZ$
$\qquad + [2\beta p_e(x_1,e_2)Z+ 2\beta q_e(x_1,e_2)Y]\ q_{ex}(x_1,e_2)\ p_x(x_1,e_2)\ /AZ+ 2\beta q(x_1,e_2)=0$
where $A= p_{xx}(x_1,e_2)q_{ee}(x_1,e_2) - p_{xe}(x_1,e_2)\ q_{xe}(x_1,e_2)$

$-[2R+2\beta p_x(x_1,e_2)Z+2\beta q_x(x_1,e_2)Y]p_x\ (x_1,e_2)\ q_{ee}(x_1,e_2)$
$\qquad + [2\beta p_e(x_1,e_2)Z+ 2\beta q_e(x_1,e_2)Y]\ q_{ex}(x_1,e_2)\ p_x(x_1,e_2)\ + 2\beta q(x_1,e_2)AZ=0$
Evaluated at Z=0, this becomes:
$-[2\beta q_x(x_1,e_2)Y]p_x\ (x_1,e_2)\ q_{ee}(x_1,e_2) + [2\beta q_e(x_1,e_2)Y]\ q_{ex}(x_1,e_2)\ p_x(x_1,e_2)\ < 0$

This implies that $Z^*>0$.

Appendix Four

Application to Specific Statutes

Complicity

The penalty structure for person i, who is considering whether to devote effort to helping person j commit crimes, is given by $Y = f(e_i)Z$ where:

$$f(e_i) = \begin{cases} 1 & \text{for } e_i > \bar{e} \\ 0 & \text{for } e_i \leq \bar{e} \end{cases}$$

Proposition 8: Under the assumptions of the model, a complicity penalty structure has no effect on the level of crime or social loss.

Proof:

The penalty for complicity is given by $Y = f(e_i)Z$ where:

$$f(e_i) = \begin{cases} 1 & \text{for } e_i > \bar{e} \\ 0 & \text{for } e_i \leq \bar{e} \end{cases}$$

The Criminal's Problem: Person 1 selects effort e_1 and number of crimes x_1 to maximize:

$$\text{Maximize } \{x_1,e_1\} \; Rx_1 - p(x_1,e_2)Z - p(x_2,e_1)Y - e_1$$

If $0<e_1<\bar{e}$ then

$$E\Pi_1 = Rx_1 - p(x_1,e_2)Z - e_1$$

and, from the first-order condition for e_1 (where $dE\Pi_1/de_1<0$) it is clear that the optimal effort choice is $e_1=0$. If $e_1>\bar{e}$ then

$$E\Pi_1 = Rx_1 - p(x_1,e_2)Z - p(x_2,e_1)Z - e_1$$

Comparing the payoffs for $e_1 = 0$ and $e_1>0$, taking the actions of person 2 as given, it must be the case that:

$$Rx_1 - p(x_1,e_2)Z > Rx_1 - p(x_1,e_2)Z - p(x_2,e_1)Z - e_1$$

since $-p(x_2,e_1)Z - e_1<0$. Thus, an individual will always prefer to select $e_i=0$, taking the actions of others as given. The Nash Equilibrium in a multi-person game using this penalty scheme is given by $e_i=0$ for $i=1,2$.

When $e_i=0$ for $i=1,2$, then $Y=0$ and the criminal's decision problem is identical to that in which there are no group penalties (the "individualized penalty" case).

The Policy-maker's Problem: The policy-maker must choose $\bar{e}$ to minimize social loss, which is given by:

$$L=Rx_1+Rx_2 + \beta\,(p(x_1,e_2)+ p(x_2,e_1))\,(Z+Y)$$

Since for any level $\bar{e}$ the criminal will select $e_i=0$, and since $Y=0$ when $e_i=0$, social loss does not depend upon $\bar{e}$. Thus, the policy-maker can select any effort level $\bar{e}$ to minimize social loss.

Law Enforcement Error (e.g. guilt by association)

Suppose that effort is observed imperfectly, and that person 1 is sometimes punished as an accomplice even when $e_1=0$. Under complicity, the effective penalty structure can be approximated by the following, where $0<\beta<1$:

$$Y=\beta Z \quad \text{for } e_i \le \bar{e}$$

$$= Z \quad \text{for } e_i > \bar{e}$$

Proposition 9: Imposing a penalty for complicity will lead to an increase in crime and an increase in social loss where there is a positive probability β of error in identifying accomplices.

Proof:

If $\beta=0$ then the outcome parallels that in which $Y=0$ and $e=0$.

Where $\beta > 0$, the outcome parallels that in which there is a positive fixed group penalty. In this case, we know from Proposition 3 that both crime and social loss will be higher under such a penalty scheme than they would be with Y=0.

Note that if $\beta = f(e_i)$, where $f(e_i)$ is a standard probability function such that $0<f(e_i)<1$ for $e_i \leq \bar{e}$ and $f'(e_i)>0$, then the outcome would fall in between that of $\beta=0$ and a fixed penalty $\beta Y > 0$. In this case, there would be less incentive to help than under a fixed penalty, but more incentive to help than if there were no group penalty, and in equilibrium there would be a positive effort level which was positive but lower than under a fixed penalty scheme. Once again, it would be more efficient to set Y=0, using the same reasoning as that applied in Proposition 3.

Direct Benefit from Complicity

Let the optimal level of help for person i where there are no group penalties be give by e_i^*. Let the initial two person model be modified in the following way. Person 1's expected profit function is given by the following (with identical changes for person 2):

$$E\Pi_1 = Rx_1 + g(e_1)Rx_2 - p(x_1,e_2)Z - p(x_2,e_1)Y - e_1$$

$$E\Pi_1 = Rx_1 + g(e_1)Rx_2 - p(x_1,e_2)Z - p(x_2,e_1)f(e_1)Z - e_1$$

where the penalty structure under complicity is given by $Y = f(e_1)Z$ such that:

$$f(e_1) = 0 \quad \text{if } e_1 < \bar{e}$$
$$= 1 \quad \text{if } e_1 \geq \bar{e}$$

Assumption 5.1: $g(e_i)$ is a continuous, differentiable function which satisfies the following properties: (i) $g(0)=0$ and $g(e_i)>0$ fore $e_i>0$; (ii) $g'(e_i)>0$; (iii) $g''(e_i)<0$.

Proposition 10: Imposing a penalty for complicity will be efficient when the penalty fully deters gang members from helping each other. It may be efficient when it partially deters gang members from helping each other and the positive impact on crime level outweighs the higher cost of punishment.

Proof:

The Criminal's Problem Person 1's expected profit is given by:

$$E\Pi_1 = Rx_1 + g(e_1)Rx_2 - p(x_1,e_2)Z - p(x_2,e_1)Y - e_1$$

Person 1 chooses e_1 and x_1 to maximize his expected profit, taking x_2 and e_2 as given. Let e_1^* be the effort level which solves the individual's problem where there are no group penalties, i.e. e_1^* solves

$$E\Pi_1 = \max\{x_1,e_1\}\ Rx_1 + g(e_1)Rx_2 - p(x_1,e_2)Z - e_1$$

From the first-order condition for effort:

$$g'(e_1^*) = 1/Rx_2$$

If a penalty for complicity is imposed when $e^* \geq \bar{e}$ then the criminal's decision problem changes as follows:

(1) If $e_i^* < \bar{e}$ then the criminal faces the same effective decision problem. He chooses $e_i = e_i^*$, $Y=0$ and a penalty for complicity has no effect.

(2) If $e_i^* \geq \bar{e}$ and $p(x_2,e_1)Y + e_1 > g(e_1)Rx_2$ when evaluated at $e_i \geq \bar{e}$ then the criminal will choose $e_i < \bar{e}$ and a penalty for complicity reduces the level of helping effort without increasing the cost of punishment. Under these conditions a penalty for complicity decreases social loss.

(3) If $e_i^* \geq \bar{e}$ and $p(x_2,e_1)Y + e_1 < g(e_1)Rx_2$ for some $e_i \geq \bar{e}$ then the criminal will select e_i to maximize expected profits. His problem become:

$$E\Pi_1 = \max\{x_1,e_1\}\ Rx_1 + g(e_1)Rx_2 - p(x_1,e_2)Z - p(x_2,e_1)Y - e_1 \quad \text{if } e_1 \geq \bar{e}$$
$$= \max\{x_1,e_1\}\ Rx_1 + g(e_1)Rx_2 - p(x_1,e_2)Z - e_1 \quad \text{if } e_1 < \bar{e}$$

Suppose the following holds:

$$Rx_1 + g(\bar{e})Rx_2 - p(x_1,e_2)Z - \bar{e} > Rx_1 + g(e_1)Rx_2 - p(x_1,e_2)Z - p(x_2,e_1)Y - e_1$$

for all $e_1 > \bar{e}$. In this case, complicity has the same effect as in (1) and e_i is chosen to be $\bar{e}$. Suppose the following holds:

$$Rx_1 + g(\bar{e})Rx_2 - p(x_1,e_2)Z - \bar{e} < Rx_1 + g(e_1)Rx_2 - p(x_1,e_2)Z - p(x_2,e_1)Y - e_1$$

In this case, effort is selected to be $\bar{e} < e_i \leq e_i^*$ and effort will be lower under complicity. The benefit from lower crime must be compared to the increased cost of punishment in order to determine whether $Y^* > 0$.

Conspiracy

Taking the original model as a starting point, let the group penalty Y be given by an increasing function of helping effort such that the group penalty is given by $f(e_i)Y$.

Assumption 6.1: The function $f(e_i)$ is continuous and differentiable and has the following properties: (i) $f(e_i)>0$ for $e_i \geq 0$; (ii) $f'(e_i)>0$; (iii) $f''(e_i)>0$.

Proposition 11: Where the probability of detection is separable in effort and number of crimes, imposing a penalty for conspiracy (i.e. a penalty which is an increasing function of effort) increases social loss, and conspiracy penalties should be set equal to zero.

Proof:

From Result 1 we know that under the standard assumptions of Model 2, if $Y=0$ then $e_1=e_2=0$. If $Y>0$ then $e_1 = e_2>0$ and $x'(Y)$ and $e'(Y)$ may be either increasing or decreasing in Y. In either case, we can apply the same reasoning as contained in Proposition 3 to show that $Y^*=0$. See the full details of the problem below.

Person 1's decision problem becomes:

$$\text{Maximize } \{x_1, e_1\} \; Rx_1 - p(x_1,e_2)Z - p(x_2,e_1)f(e_1)Y - e_1$$

Likewise, person 2's decision problem becomes:

$$\text{Maximize } \{x_2, e_2\} \; Rx_2 - p(x_2,e_1)Z - p(x_1,e_2)f(e_2)Y - e_2$$

The first-order conditions for person 1 for quantity and effort are given by:

$$R - p_x(x_1,e_2)Z = 0$$
$$-p_e(x_2,e_1)f(e_1)\,Y - p(x_2,e_1)f'(e_1)Y - 1 = 0$$

For person 2:

$$R- p_x(x_2,e_1)Z = 0$$

$$-p_e(x,e_2)f(e_2)\ Y- p(x,e_2)f'(e_2)\ Y- 1 = 0$$

Differentiating with respect to Z:

$$-p_{xx}(x,e_2)x'(Z)Z-p_{xe}(x,e_2)e_2'(Z)Z-p_x(x,e_2)=0$$

$$x'(Z) =p_x(x,e_2) + p_{xe}(x,e_2)e_2'(Z)Z / -p_{xx}(x,e_2)Z$$

$$-p_{ee}(x,e_2)\ e_2'(Z)f(e_2)\ Y- p_{ex}(x,e_2)x'(Z)f(e_2)Y - p_e(x,e_2)f'(e_2)e_2'(Z)Y$$
$$-p_x(x,e_2)x_1'(Z)f'(e_2)Y- p_e(x,e_2)e_2'(Y)f'(e_2)\ Y-p(x_1,e_2)f''(e_2)e_2'(Z)Y=0$$

$$e_2'(Z)= [- p_{ex}(x,e_2)x'(Z)f(e_2) -p_x(x,e_2)x'(Z)f'(e_2)]$$
$$/ [p_{ee}(x,e_2)\ f(e_2) +2p_e(x,e_2)f'(e_2)+p(x,e_2)f''(e_2)]$$

$$x'(Z)= [p_xp_{ee}f(e_2) +2p_xp_ef'(e_2)+p_xpf''(e_2)]$$
$$/[-p_{xx}p_{ee}f(e_2)-2p_ep_{xx}f'(e_2)-p_{xx}pf''(e_2)+p_{xe}^2f(e_2)+p_x\ p_{xe}\ f'(e_2)]Z$$

$$e_2'(Z)= [- p_{ex}f(e_2) -p_xf'(e_2)]\ [p_xp_{ee}f(e_2) +2p_xp_ef'(e_2)+p_xpf''(e_2)]$$
$$/\ [p_{ee}f(e_2)\ +2p_ef'(e_2)+pf''(e_2)][-p_{xx}p_{ee}f(e_2)-2p_ep_{xx}f'(e_2)-p_{xx}pf''(e_2)+p_{xe}^2f(e_2)+p_x\ p_{xe}\ f'(e_2)]Z$$

Because of the competing effects of changes in the parameters, without further assumptions it is not possible to sign these derivatives, and effort and quantities may be increasing or decreasing in the individual penalty level.

Now differentiate with respect to Y:

$$e'(Y)= - p_{xx}(x,e_2)x'(Y) / p_{xe}(x,e_2)$$

$$-p_{ee}(x,e_2)f(e_2)e'(Y)\ Y-p_{ex}(x,e_2)f(e_2)\ x''(Y)Y-p_e(x,e_2)f'(e_2)\ e'(Y)Y$$
$$-p_e(x,e_2)f(e_2) - p_e(x,e_2)f'(e_2)\ e'(Y)Y- p_x(x,e_2)f'(e_2)\ x'(Y)Y$$
$$- p(x,e_2)f'(e_2) = 0$$

$$-p_{ee}f(e_2)e'(Y)\ Y-p_{ex}f(e_2)\ x'(Y)Y-2p_ef'(e_2)\ e'(Y)Y-p_ef(e_2)$$
$$- p_xf'(e_2)\ x'(Y)Y- pf'(e_2) = 0$$

$$e'(Y) = [-p_{ex}f(e_2)\ x'(Y)Y-p_ef(e_2) - p_xf'(e_2)\ x'(Y)Y- pf'(e_2)\ ]$$
$$/p_{ee}f(e_2)Y+2p_ef'(e_2)\ Y$$

Solving for e'(Y) and x'(Y):

$$x'(Y) = -p_{xe}p_ef(e_2) - p_{xe}pf'(e_2) /$$
$$[-p_{xx}p_{ee}f(e_2)-2p_{xx}p_ef'(e_2)+p_{ex}^2f(e_2)+ p_{xe}p_xf'(e_2)]Y$$

$$e'(Y) =\ p_{xx}\ p_ef(e_2) + p_{xx}pf'(e_2) /$$
$$[-p_{xx}p_{ee}f(e_2)-2p_{xx}p_ef'(e_2)+p_{ex}^2f(e_2)+ p_{xe}p_xf'(e_2)]Y$$

Once again, because of the competing effects of parameter changes on profits, these derivatives cannot be signed.

The Policy-maker's Problem The policy-maker's problem is to choose Z and Y to maximize social loss. In the basic model social loss is minimized by setting Y=0.

$$L= R(x_1+x_2) + \beta (p(x_1,e_2)+ p(x_2,e_1))Z+\beta p(x_1,e_2)f(e_2)Y +\beta p(x_2,e_1)f(e_1)Y$$

Given the symmetry of the problem, this simplifies to:

$$L= 2Rx_1+ 2\beta p(x_1,e_2)Z+ 2\beta p(x_1,e_2)f(e_2)Y$$

The first-order condition for Z is given by:

$$2Rx_1'(Z)+ 2\beta p_x(x_1,e_2)x'(Z)Z+ 2\beta p_e(x_1,e_2)e'(Z)Z+ 2\beta p(x_1,e_2)$$
$$+2\beta p_x(x_1,e_2)f(e_2)x_1'(Z)Y + 2\beta p_e(x_1,e_2)f(e_2)e'(Z)Y +2\beta p(x_1,e_2)f'(e_2)e'(Z)Y = 0$$

Simplifying:

$$(2R+ 2\beta p_x Z+2\beta p_x f(e_2)Y)\ x_1'(Z)$$
$$+ (2\beta p_e(x_1,e_2)\ Z+ 2\beta p_e f(e_2)Y+2\beta p(x_1,e_2)f'(e_2)Y)\ e'(Z)$$
$$+ 2\beta p(x_1,e_2) = 0$$

The first-order condition for Y is given by:

$$2R(1+\beta)x'(Y)+ 2\beta p_x f(e_2)x'(Y)Y$$
$$+ 2\beta p_e(1+f(e_2))\ e'(Y)Y+2\beta pf'(e_2)e'(Y)Y+ 2\beta pf(e_2) =0$$

When evaluated at Y=0, this first-order condition reduces to:

$$2R(1+\beta)x'(Y)+ 2\beta pf(e_2)$$

From the first-order condition, it is clear that if $x'(Y)>0$, then it is optimal to set $Y^*=0$.

Appendix Five

The Structure of Group-based Criminal Laws

Dimensions of the Criminal Rule

Criminal rules can be characterized in terms of their implications for: (1) investigation of criminal activities and use of evidence (i.e. instrumental process); (2) legal process; and (3) penalties available. Group-based criminal rules provide investigative and procedural advantages in addition to new theories of liability. Focusing first on instrumental advantages, investigators have been increasingly willing and able to adopt a large scale, proactive approach towards investigations of organized crime. Activities which might be too insignificant to address individually can become the profitable object of extended investigation when examined as a group. Extended undercover investigations have been used to uncover patterns of criminal activities and relationships between conspirators, and heavy use has been made of informants to provide information about related criminal activities and participants. Organization-based investigations do not produce evidence which maps easily into a reactive, individual based procedural system, however, and transforming information of this sort into prosecutable cases would be easier and more efficient if an organization-based procedural system was adopted.

Procedural advantages include the ability to evaluate individual conduct in the context of the criminal organization and its entire history of criminal activities. Allowing prosecutors to present individuals to the jury as members of a criminal organization that has been involved in a number of criminal activities will color the conclusions that jurors draw about the likelihood that this individual committed a crime. Under a conspiracy charge, hearsay by co-conspirators is admissible as evidence. Consolidated trials can further increase the success rate of prosecutions by allowing for prosecution of an entire pattern of related criminal activities and by allowing inferences regarding a specific defendant to be drawn from evidence about the existence of the organization and the activities of other members. Consolidation of related crimes and participants in a single mega-trial offers prosecutors greater flexibility in presenting evidence and drawing inferences from related activities pursued by a criminal organization. The proliferation of statutory crimes provides the prosecutor with more flexibility in deciding which charges to bring and raises the probability of conviction and the effectiveness of plea bargaining by increasing the number of charges and the range of penalties available.

Group-based criminal laws provide for compounded and expanded liability for crimes which take place in particular contexts. At the simplest level, group participation in a crime can lead to an enhancement of existing sentences for the crime based on inferences about the degree of intentionality and pre-planning involved. One method of extending liability beyond enhancement of penalties for substantive crimes has been to make participation in the criminal enterprise a source of criminal liability. Penalties can be expanded still further by holding each individual who agrees to participate in a criminal venture responsible for any act taken by any member to further the agreed upon criminal purpose. A newer form of compound liability imposes additional charges when substantive crimes are committed in the context of a criminal organization. Liability structures of this sort can be used to create incentives for group members to constrain each others' actions and to weaken the cohesiveness of the criminal group. If not carefully constructed, however, compound liability structures could have the perverse effect of increasing gang stability. The availability of a broader range of sentencing options confers more flexibility on prosecutors, and the higher penalties available through sentence enhancement and compounded liability can offset the group's increased criminal capacity.

It is important to keep in mind that the judicial system occupies an intermediate stage in the criminal justice process. Both the pre-conviction stages (e.g. apprehension of offenders) and the post-conviction stages (e.g. imprisonment and probation) are run by different institutional systems. Each institution will have its own approach towards organized criminal activity and its own set of limitations, and these differences will have consequences for other stages of the law enforcement process. The emergence of prison gangs in penal institutions, and the close connection between these gangs and some of the more well-established criminal street gangs, serves as a warning of the potential consequences of pursuing isolated legal strategies. There will also be differences between federal, state and local treatment of criminal organizations. The difficulty in drawing clear jurisdictional boundaries and manipulation of the system by sophisticated gangs requires consistency of approach and consideration of the compatibility of policy choices made at different stages of the enforcement process. An economic approach to enforcement emphasizes the net effect of different decisions made at different stages on the level of key variables such as the probability of detection and conviction. Changes at any of the stages involved in the criminal process will translate into changes in these key decision variables.

Requirements of Act and Intent

Criminal laws have traditionally been structured around requirements of knowledge and intentionality (mens rea) and act or result (actus reus). This structure corresponds to an individualized decision making paradigm and may not be suitable for a more complex organizational setting. Group-based criminal laws have retained this basic structure while allowing for more flexibility in methods of satisfying the necessary elements, requiring less stringent individualized findings of act and intent and allowing broader inferences from patterns of related criminal activities. While the Model Penal Code and many of the federal and state group-based criminal laws require as a necessary element of the crime a finding of purpose or intent to bring about the criminal result, alternative methods of proving intent have been allowed and liability has been extended to encompass reasonably foreseeable consequences of acts and conspiratorial agreements. The actus reus requirement is typically weaker than the mens rea requirement for group-based crimes, with no requirement of "but for" causation or even, in some cases, of materiality. Intent to further the criminal activities of a group and benefit received from concerted action are generally taken as touchstones of group responsibility.

More contemporary approaches towards group criminality have tried to substitute alternative requirements, such as knowing association with a criminal group, while retaining the same act and intent structure. Adopting an organizational approach would involve replacing this structure, with its emphasis on the state of mind and actions existing at the time of a specific event, with a set of requirements based on structural variables such as rank and stake in the organization.

Multiple Punishments or Different Crimes?

Adding a new layer of enterprise crimes to the system has generated concern that defendants will face multiple punishments for a single crime. There is also a fear that prosecutors will abuse the discretion offered by a proliferation of overlapping statutes, using the increased number and range of charges to increase the probability of conviction and to coerce defendants into accepting plea bargaining.[51] Excessive and arbitrary sentencing is problematic from both an economic and a constitutional standpoint. To achieve optimal deterrence the expected penalty attached to a criminal activity should match the expected harm (where harm is construed broadly to include support of the criminal enterprise). Increasing the penalties of certain types of crimes may induce substitution into other and potentially more harmful crimes and may prompt criminals to take inefficiently costly actions to avoid capture. Increasing the relative penalties for certain kinds of crimes where the crimes are not uniformly applied will exacerbate existing inequities and may confer competitive advantages on those groups subject to lesser scrutiny.

The constitutional debate centers around when and how enterprise crimes can be treated as separate offenses in order to avoid the Supreme Court prohibitions against excessive punishment and double punishment for the same activity.[52] The issue of double punishment has arisen in the context of prosecution under the Continuing Criminal Enterprise (CCE) statute and conspiracy, for example.[53] The debate reflects confusion and disagreement about the nature of enterprise crimes and their relationship to individual criminal activities and participants. The notion that supporting or participating in the criminal activities of a criminal organization is a substantive crime independent of the predicate crimes does not fit easily into the transaction-based framework. Adherents of this approach are more likely to view enterprise liability as imposing a double punishment on the same criminal transaction, whereas proponents of an organizational approach will find it easier to draw distinctions between criminalizing the mode of operation and criminalizing the activities that the organization produces. Similar issues arise in the context of constitutional restrictions on excessive punishment. Requiring that the severity of the punishment be proportional to the severity of the crime and that like crimes receive like treatment necessitates a method of determining the severity of enterprise crime. This includes a consideration of how context should be used in the evaluation of individual acts.

Punishing the Crime, Not the Individual

Criminal penalties can be used to reduce the incidence of harmful actions by increasing the relative cost and difficulty of performing them. Penalties should be targeted narrowly to ensure that legitimate activities are not inhibited, and they should be focused on variables over which decision makers have some control. Criminalizing status or membership per se does not satisfy these requirements. In addition to penalizing legitimate activities, it reduces the cost of criminal behavior by imposing penalties which are independent of actual criminal behavior and by increasing the pool of "criminals."

The American criminal law system prohibits punishment for mere status or group affiliation.[54] The high water mark of punishment for group membership in the United States occurred in the 1920s and 1930s in response to the widely perceived "Communist threat."[55] In 1927 the Supreme Court upheld the California Criminal Syndicalism Act outlawing "syndicalism," which was defined as associating for the purposes of accomplishing any desired end by illegal means.[56] During the McCarthy era the government continued to experiment with ways of criminalizing membership in the Communist Party. The ability to target group membership for criminal sanctions was limited in the Supreme Court decision of *Scales v. United States*, where the Court provided a limiting interpretation of membership statutes to confer no more than complicity and conspiracy. The Court held that a "blanket prohibition of association with a group having both legal and illegal aims" would pose a "real danger that legitimate political expression or association would be impaired,"[57] and therefore "mere membership in (an association) ...that embraces both illegal and legal aims" cannot be punished "unless the individual specifically intends to further the group's illegal aims."[58] In *Elfbrant v. Russell* the Court held that knowing membership "without any showing of 'specific intent' would run afoul of the Constitution."[59] Penalizing membership thus requires at a minimum proof of an individual's awareness of the organization's illegal purposes and his intent to further those illegal aims.[60] The relationship with the groups must be substantial enough to satisfy the due process requirement of personal guilt, and the rule must be limited in a way which avoids infringement on constitutionally protected freedoms of association and expression. Joining an organization engaged in criminal activity has been recognized as a form of expressive association which receives some protection under the First Amendment.[61] In the recent case of *Dawson v. Delaware* the Supreme Court extended this protection to cover gang membership.[62]

There has been some concern that anti-gang statutes such as the California Street Terrorism Enforcement and Prevention (STEP) Act and the Chicago anti-gang loitering ordinance come dangerously close to imposing guilt by association and to creating status crimes.[63] STEP makes it illegal for an individual to become a participant in and intentionally promote, further, or assist in a criminal street gang's unlawful activities when he knows that members of the gang are or have engaged in a pattern of criminal activity.[64] The Chicago loitering ordinance, whose constitutionality is currently being challenged in the state supreme court, authorized police officers to order groups of two or more "loiterers" to disperse or face arrest where the officers have a reasonable belief that one of the loiterers is a gang member. Although statutes such as the STEP Act do make group associations and prior history aggravating factors in a particular crime, they do so in combination with requirements of active engagement in criminal acts. While the recent sentence enhancement statute introduced in the 1994 Omnibus Crime Bill appears to focus even more directly on association as a source of liability, the addition of intent and primary purpose requirements in later versions of the bill substantially limit the reach of the provision.[65] While act, specific intent and primary purpose requirements ensure that status or membership per se is not explicitly criminalized, however, they do little to address the expanded role of discretionary character perceptions in criminal judgments.[66]

Designing statutes which make the criminal enterprise the cornerstone of prosecution is likely to involve problems of statutory definition and design. Finding an appropriate definition for a criminal organization is particularly difficult given the multiple forms and structures that organizations can adopt and the constitutional and practical limitations on scope and specificity of statutory definitions. Although it is important to address the special dangers of criminal organizations directly, it is difficult to target these dangers without encompassing legitimate and constitutionally protected associations and activities. The relative merits of organization-based statutes must be evaluated in a broader context which includes a weighing of the dangers of over inclusion and under inclusion. While it may sometimes appear as if constitutional and institutional restrictions are impediments to the economic efficiency of the system, in some respects they may be operating as methods of incorporating a broader set of factors into the analysis.[67] Most group-based statutes, including the "Racketeer Influenced and Corrupt Organizations" (RICO) statute, have had to rely on definitions which define the enterprise implicitly through the activities that it performs.

Putting the Criminal Enterprise Out of Business

Prison sentences and fines imposed on individual criminals have been the traditional methods of punishing crimes. Sentencing structures are gradated to reflect differences in the severity of crimes and to create incentives for shifting from greater to lesser crimes. A variety of enforcement methods have been employed, including enhanced sentencing for group related crimes, making new crimes out of participation in group activities, and injunctions for loitering and other activities associated with certain types of criminal groups. But prosecution and punishment of individual members has proven to be an ineffective way of attacking criminal organizations. Sophisticated organizations incorporate the risk of individual prosecutions into their "business planning" and have structures which can accommodate high membership turnover. Even loosely organized criminal groups tend to depend more upon certain shared resources, such as a physical territory, than on an unchanging membership, and when individual members are arrested they are quickly replaced with new recruits or previous members returning from jail. Having a long term impact on a criminal organization requires concerted measures designed to cripple its economic foundation.

Recognition of this fact prompted Congress to introduce new criminal forfeiture and money laundering statutes designed to cripple the economic base of criminal enterprises, particularly those involved in drug traffickers.[68] The Comprehensive Drug Abuse Prevention and Control Act of 1970[69] and RICO contained the first modern criminal forfeiture provisions.[70] In their current form, these criminal forfeiture provisions authorize the confiscation of a convicted offender's interest in and profits from any enterprise involved in the crime.[71] In contrast to civil forfeiture, criminal forfeiture attaches to the offender and can only be applied after conviction. Notice and tracing requirements further restrict the effective use of the provisions. If these limitations can be overcome, the combination of asset forfeiture and money laundering statutes provide an important basis for attacking the economic foundation of the enterprise.

Jurisdiction - Blurring the Local/State/Federal Divide

The variety in scale, level of sophistication and geographic dispersion of new criminal groups has created problems in defining the appropriate level of response to organized crime and initiatives have been taken at multiple levels of government. While attempts have been made to coordinate these responses, many of the statutes and rules introduced provide little in the way of rational guidance as to jurisdictional boundaries and allocation of responsibility. Loosely related umbrella groups of locally based organizations, such as the Los Angeles based Bloods and Crips, do not fit easily into existing jurisdictional boundaries.

In the past the higher level of intensity and sophistication of federal investigations and prosecutions led to concerted attempts by organized criminal groups to avoid involvement in federal crimes, especially those targeted as federal priorities. While most gang-related crimes are currently prosecuted in state courts, the Senate has recently introduced a bill which would make gang activity a federal crime. The proposed Federal Gang Violence Act doubles criminal penalties for gang members who commit a federal crime or a crime across state lines.[72] It expands the list of federal crimes to include activities more closely associated with gangs, such as drive-by shootings and firearms trafficking, and would make it a federal offense to recruit a juvenile to a street gang.[73] This is reflective of a continuing expansion of the federal role in prosecuting organized crime.[74] Many of the federal statutes aimed at criminal enterprises, such as the Racketeer Influenced and Corrupt Organization Act (RICO), make it a federal crime to commit a pattern of criminal activities which often include state-based predicate crimes. These statutes create overlapping jurisdiction without providing guidance as to how the different authorities should be reconciled. The rules governing jurisdiction correspond to a procedural framework which has been designed to accommodate unified, single-transaction crimes, and the natural dividing lines are obscured by crimes involving patterns of activities and multiple offenders who may be located in different places and engaged in different types of crimes.

Appendix Six

The Current System of Group-based Crimes

Complicity - A First Step Towards Affiliative Liability

Accomplice liability plays a central role in the current system of affiliative liability. Complicity doctrine has developed around the idea that individuals who share the primary offender's guilty intent and take deliberate facilitating acts are equally culpable and therefore deserving of the same treatment as primary offenders. Derivative liability is imposed for the commission of a substantive crime.[75] Of all the multiple offender crimes, complicity falls closest to the traditional paradigm of individual wrong-doing - the accomplice is presented as engaging indirectly in the same crime as the principle and is punished as if he performed the crime.[76] Imposing the same penalty on aider and primary offender can be justified on deterrence grounds by treating similarity of intended outcome as a legitimate alternative measure of liability. Section 2.06 of the Model Penal Code ("Code") provides a model crime of complicity under which an individual is "legally accountable" for the acts of the offender by causing an innocent person to engage in criminal conduct, by acting as an accomplice, or through legally imposed measures such as vicarious liability.[77] The individual is liable as an accomplice if his conduct is expressly declared by law to establish complicity or if "with the purpose of promoting or facilitating the commission of the offense," he solicits or aids or agrees or attempts to aid another person in planning or committing an offense or fails to make proper effort to prevent the offense where he has a legal duty to do so. Conviction can be obtained upon proof of commission of the offense and complicity even if the principal is not prosecuted or convicted.[78] While federal criminal law does not have a general crime of complicity similar to that contained in the Code, it employs the same paradigm in the form of 18 U.S.C. section 2(a), which holds a person liable as a principal if he "aids, abets, counsels, commands, induces or procures" the commission of an offense.[79] Federal accomplice liability applies automatically to all substantive federal crimes absent explicit statutory language to the contrary.[80] Exceptions to the accomplice rule include victims of the offense and individuals (such as employees of a culpable corporation) whose conduct is necessarily incident to its commission.[81] Liability is imposed for the crime and for consequences that "might reasonably be expected to result" from it, but is not imposed for conduct falling outside of the "criminal purpose"[82] or for the consequences of this conduct.[83]

The structure of the crime is consistent with the standard notion of individual punishment for a crime the individual intends to and takes active steps to accomplish, whether directly or indirectly through the aid of another. Federal prosecutions typically employ the standard developed by Learned Hand in *United States v. Peoni*, which requires that the aider and abettor "(i)n some sort associate himself with the venture, that he participate in it as something that he wishes to bring about, (and) that he seek by his action to make it succeed."[84] While the *Peoni* standard has been interpreted as requiring both association with the criminal plan and an affirmative act intended to promote its success, the act requirement has been liberally construed to encompass acts with even a minimal possibility of actual aid or encouragement so long as the individual acted with the required mens rea.[85] State and federal statutes have adopted slightly different mens rea requirements. The Code has required a relatively stringent showing of purposive attitude,[86] holding guilty knowledge without more insufficient for conviction but allowing purpose to be inferred from factors such as a "stake in the venture."[87] Some federal courts have applied the less restrictive Laurier standard to aiding and abetting, requiring purpose for lesser offenses but only requiring knowledge where major crimes are implicated.[88] The federal statutory scheme also permits accessorial liability to attach for criminally negligent homicide provided that the accessory shares the requisite culpable mental state for the crime (i.e. reckless indifference) and intentionally aids in its commission.[89] Courts have created special standards for certain types of offenses, such as sale of goods (where a "stake in the venture" standard was adopted for seller of legal goods destined for illegal uses), securities fraud and drug possession.[90] The New York Penal Code employs a more comprehensive approach by providing for a separate crime of "criminal facilitation" where a person, believing it probable that he is rendering aid to a person who intends to commit a crime, engages in conduct which aids the person.[91] These differences can be attributed in part to different views about the most effective ways of targeting facilitating acts and the relative costs of being over and under inclusive (including the possibility of a chilling effect on legitimate activities). All of these standards share the same focus on direct, intentional involvement in a specific crime (rather than in a criminal association) and vary only in the degree of intentionality required.[92]

Criminal Solicitation

According to section 5.02 of the Model Penal Code, a person is guilty of "criminal solicitation" if "with the purpose of promoting or facilitating its commission he commands, encourages or requests another person to engage in specific conduct which would constitute such crime or an attempt to commit such crime or which would establish his complicity in its commission or attempted commission."[93] Actual communication is not required as long as the individual engages in conduct "designed to effect such communication."[94] The rationale for imposing equal liability on both the perpetrator and the solicitor of a crime is similar to that of complicity. It reflects the notion that inducing someone else to perform a crime is functionally equivalent to performing it yourself - although the method differs, the intended outcome is the same. Liability for solicitation can be avoided by preventing commission of the crime under circumstances "manifesting a complete and voluntary renunciation" of the criminal purpose.[95] Recent proposals have sought to increase the penalties for solicitation to aid in the criminal activities of a street gang, and to make solicitation of a minor into a street gang a federal offense. This measure reflects the need to address the harmfulness of recruitment activities (which may expand the number of active criminals) and to reduce the benefits from employing individuals who face lesser sentences as a way of minimizing criminal liability (e.g. juveniles and first offenders).

Conspiracy: The Criminalization of Criminal Combinations

Criminal conspiracy is an agreement or combination by two or more persons to commit a crime. An individual can be charged with conspiracy if he agrees to engage or aid in the commission of a specified crime with the purpose of ensuring its successful completion and he takes some action to further this purpose. Conspiracy functions both an inchoate crime designed to reach preparatory conduct and as a group-based crime designed to penalize combined criminal action. Unlike attempt and solicitation, the charge of conspiracy is not merged into other substantive offenses, and unlike complicity, conspiracy allows imposition of liability both for the crimes that the conspiracy produces and for the conspiracy itself. These differences are attributable to the additional role that it plays in addressing the "special dangers" of group crime.[96]

Federal and state conspiracy statutes have been modeled after the Model Penal Code conspiracy provision, under which a person is guilty of conspiracy to commit a crime if "with the purpose of promoting or facilitating its commission he...agrees with such other person or persons that they or one or more of them will engage in conduct which constitutes such crime or an attempt or solicitations to commit such crime."[97] The Code provides that no person may be convicted of conspiracy to commit a crime other than a felony of first or second degree unless "an overt act in pursuance of such conspiracy is alleged and proved to have been done by him or by a person with whom he conspired." Courts in some jurisdictions have held that the agreement itself can be used to satisfy the act requirement. If convicted for conspiracy, members of the same conspiracy and of conspiracies which are so closely related that they constitute "different aspects of a scheme of organized criminal conduct" can be prosecuted jointly, although the evidence brought against each offender cannot be enlarged as a result of this joinder.[98] An individual can abandon the conspiracy by thwarting its success under "circumstances manifesting a complete and voluntary renunciation of his criminal purpose."[99]

Before 1970, compound liability (i.e. multiple forms of liability attached to a single act) was purely a matter of common law and courts generally preferred the traditional model of one act-one crime.[100] A more flexible approach to "duplicative" liability was adopted by the Supreme Court in *Clune v. United States*, where the Court held that conspiracy could be punished as a separate offense.[101] Half a decade later the court revisited the issue *in Pinkerton v. United States*, reiterating the punishability of conspiracy as an independent offense and introducing a "criminal agency" theory that made conspirators liable for substantive crimes that other conspirators committed in furtherance of the conspiracy.[102] This has been developed into the judicially-created "Pinkerton rule," which makes each member of a conspiracy liable for the crimes committed by any member in furtherance of the criminal purpose of the conspiracy. Although rejected by the Model Penal Code, Pinkerton liability has been accepted into federal criminal law and a number of states have followed suit.[103] Imposing the same liability on all members of a conspiracy regardless of the importance of their role and the extent of their knowledge has led to troubling results, however, as illustrated in *United States v. Alvarez*.[104] Cases like *Alvarez* suggest that liability should be made a function of the level of participation rather than being determined on a threshold basis with full liability once the threshold is crossed. In 1981 the Court upheld compound liability for multiple conspiracy charges.[105]

Modern conspiracy doctrine is based on the potential for concerted action, requiring neither a consummated criminal agreement nor the prosecution and conviction of other conspirators.[106] Conspiracy is treated as a crime of the same grade and degree as the most serious offense which is the object of the conspiracy.[107] This limited departure from the transaction-based approach is sometimes justified on a theory of mediate causation for the crimes of group members.[108] It is also justified on deterrence grounds as a means of discouraging combined crimes by forcing participants to assume the risk of being held responsible for each others' criminal actions. While it may make sense to target concerted criminal action directly, however, provisions that do so should be designed in light of the structure of the organization and the likely impact of the penalty structure on the incentives of participants. If groups pose special dangers, then a crime such as conspiracy that focuses explicitly on the group should respond to these dangers and penalties should be graduated based on the nature of the participation.

Applying Conspiracy to Gangs With its focus on concerted criminal activities, conspiracy can be used to address the operations of criminal street gangs. The conspiracy charge is particularly suitable for drug trafficking organizations, since 21 U.S.C. section 1846 eliminates any overt act requirement in federal drug conspiracy prosecutions and a number of states have weakened the requirements for finding a drug trafficking conspiracy under state law. Washington conspiracy law, for example, has been applied to street gangs by inferring a tacit, continuos agreement between gang members to secure a geographical area for drug trafficking and interpreting attacks on rival gang members as substantial steps taken in pursuit of the agreement to secure territory.[109] An under-utilization of conspiracy provisions has been attributed in part to the generality of conspiracy statutes which, it is argued, makes them difficult to apply to specific contexts, and in part to the availability of new statutes which confer greater procedural and evidentiary advantages. The modern trend towards combating criminal enterprises has been to develop more explicit statutory conditions for attacking specific types of criminal organizations and specific patterns of criminal activities.

Corporate Criminal Liability: Falling Short of Enterprise Criminality

Corporate criminal liability is used to hold corporations and certain specified unincorporated organizations responsible for any act of an employee done within the scope of employment in the interest of the corporation. According to the Code, a corporation or a statutorily specified unincorporated association may be convicted of the commission of an offense if there is a clear legislative purpose to impose liability on the corporation and the conduct was performed by an agent of the corporation acting on its behalf and within the scope of employment.[110] Liability can also be imposed if the commission of the offense was authorized, requested, commanded, performed or recklessly tolerated by the board of directors or by a high managerial agent acting on behalf of the corporation within his scope of office or employment.[111] Attaching liability to managers for crimes committed by subordinates if the managers are reckless in supervising has been proposed and rejected. The corporation is assumed liable unless otherwise specified, although a due diligence defense is available, and the corporation is held liable for the same offense as a natural person would be.[112]

This provision does not apply to criminal organizations, does not employ the doctrine of respondeat superior, and does not allow liability based on reckless supervision. These limitations have prevented prosecutors from applying the provision to address enterprise criminality despite the many similarities between legitimate and illegal organizations. One option would be to expand corporate criminality in scope and coverage to encompass enterprise criminality. Alternatively, one could rely on existing group-based criminal laws such as conspiracy reinterpreted to apply more specifically to an organizational setting. These provisions could be adapted to an organizational framework by interpreting key terms within the context of criminal organizations and modifying penalty structures in light of existing incentive structures.

RICO: Departure from the Transaction-based Model

Congress adopted the "Racketeer Influenced and Corrupt Organizations" (RICO) and the "Continuing Criminal Enterprise" (CCE) statutes in 1970 as part of a comprehensive attempt to combat organized crime by making organizations the focus of the law. [113]At least thirty-three states have followed suit, adopting statutes comparable to RICO and CCE. RICO targets crimes committed by, or in the context of, an "enterprise," where "enterprise" is construed broadly to include any form of organized activity. According to the framework provided by the Eighth Circuit, an association must exhibit "commonalty of purpose," "continuity of both structure and personality" and "an 'ascertainable structure' distinct from that inherent in the conduct of a pattern of racketeering activity" in order to qualify as an enterprise under RICO, although other circuits have been more lax in this requirement.[114] It imposes additional liability where predicate crimes are related to each other in a particular kind of causal nexus.[115]

The statute creates three substantive crimes and the crime of RICO conspiracy.[116] The substantive crimes require that a "person" use the collection of unlawful debt or a "pattern of racketeering activity" in order to: (i) acquire an interest in, establish, or operate an enterprise; (ii) acquire or maintain an interest in or control of an enterprise; and/or (iii) conduct or participate in conducting an enterprise.[117] In a typical RICO charge the prosecutor must establish that the enterprise existed, that the defendants engaged in the charged acts and that they used the resulting pattern of racketeering activity to affect the enterprise in one of the prohibited ways. A pattern of racketeering activity is established if the individual commits at least two of the "predicate offenses" specified by state and federal statutes within ten years of each other, excluding time spent in prison.[118] The Supreme Court has held that racketeering activity must exhibit "continuity plus relationship,"[119] where "relationship" requires that the activity have "the same or similar purposes, results, participants, victims, or methods of commission" or be "otherwise related and not isolated," and "continuity" requires repetitious activity.[120]

Although Congress originally viewed RICO principally as a tool for attacking the infiltration of legitimate business by organized crime, in practice it has been applied primarily to the operations of illegitimate criminal enterprises.[121] Difficulties in arriving at a legally and socially acceptable definition of organized crime and problems with criminalizing certain actions when performed by members of specific, named organizations led to a definition of organized crime in terms of particular behavior rather than particular groups.[122] Defining a criminal organization implicitly "by what it does rather than by what it (is)" allowed for an expansive interpretation of the statute.[123]

While convictions must be based on particular predicate crimes, the focus of a RICO prosecution is typically aimed at the individual's associations with an ongoing criminal organization.[124] RICO provides that if an offender commits two of the listed crimes in furtherance of a business enterprise, then the penalties for these two crimes are aggravated and participants can be brought together in a single trial. The crimes need not be related to the same transaction as long as they were committed in the operation of a criminal organization that all had agreed to join.[125] The jury can be presented with what are often loosely related charges in the context of a broader pattern of criminal activity conducted by multiple offenders and jurors are allowed to draw inferences about individual conduct from the organizational context. By viewing individual actions in the context of a broader pattern of events, the jury is invited to judge individuals as group members and to hold individuals responsible for the actions of the group. When the appropriate relationship between the predicate offenses is established, liability can be imposed both for the substantive crimes and the crime of conspiracy and for the conspiracy to commit substantive RICO offenses. Treating the operation of a criminal enterprise through criminal acts as a single unified crime provides a number of procedural advantages in a legal system which is designed to process single transactions. Section 1962(c) can be used to join loosely related acts and actors in a single trial, and the prosecution is allowed to introduce evidence regarding the existence, purposes and structure of the criminal organization and the defendant's membership in it. RICO can significantly reduce jurisdictional and venue problems and also extends the time available for prosecuting criminal acts since the statute of limitations for a RICO offense runs from completion of RICO.

While RICO has become the primary federal tool in prosecuting criminal organizations, it has a number of weaknesses which need to be addressed. First, since the statute has received a more expansive interpretation than its designers planned for, it lacks the structure and guidelines necessary to ensure consistent and effective application. It also provides for expanded federal jurisdiction without providing rational principles for coordinating federal and state authority. Second, the statute attacks organizations indirectly by focusing on particular patterns of acts while failing to address the special nature and structure of criminal organizations. The statute recognizes the importance of the ongoing criminal organization as an operational unit by targeting the network of relationships between multiple crimes and offenders for additional liability and procedural innovations. It does not include a sufficient consideration of organizational variables such as rank or degree of effective control of the organization, however, and penalties are not designed in light of the organization's incentive structure. Third, the statute is broad in coverage and employs a number of terms and requirements which are vague and difficult to apply, making prosecutors wary of using RICO provisions in areas where they would be useful and creating the potential for discriminatory law enforcement.[126] Questions arise as to what the new set of crimes created by RICO add to existing crimes such as conspiracy and whether the additions it makes could be introduced more directly.[127] There is also a concern that RICO is setting the stage for criminalization of status and group membership by effectively criminalizing participation in a criminal organization. Indeed, one of the predecessor bills, S.2187 introduced by Senator McClellan, would have outlawed membership in the Mafia and other named criminal syndicates.[128] Finally, while a departure from the transactions-based model of criminal law may be advisable, a corresponding departure from the existing procedural framework may be required. By making illicit associations an integral part of a crime, statutes such as RICO might allow prosecutors to override the procedural and evidentiary protections of a legal system that is not designed to accommodate these statutes.[129]

According to one scholar, the use of RICO as an "expanded conspiracy statute" to prosecute members of a criminal organization "represents an expansion of trends visible in federal conspiracy law that move it farther away from a traditional concentration on conduct in specific transactions and towards the presentation of a broader pattern of conduct and association in criminal proceedings."[130] He argues that the traditional approach to criminal law has been closely tied to a transaction-based model of crime that focuses on specific criminal behavior rather than on the criminal. This model targets criminal behavior which "represents a free choice at a particular moment in time to commit an immoral act," with little if any attention paid to a defendant's past conduct or current group affiliations.[131] RICO prosecutions depart from this model by directing attention to a pattern of related crimes and offenders and assessing criminality in the context of this overall pattern. Indeed, "the defining characteristic of the 'pattern of racketeering' is the relationship of certain conduct to other conduct and to the 'enterprise', which itself is an abstract construct of certain interpersonal relationships."[132] The statute reflected a shift in focus from individual prosecutions to organizational foundations. "Under RICO," suggests another scholar, "the criminal enterprise replaces the individual as the cornerstone of each trial. Though individuals are still prosecuted, their illicit use of an enterprise potentially triggers the application of enhanced sanctions, civil remedies, and procedures aimed at the foundation of group crime."[133] The departure is most significant in RICO cases of illicit association, where a defendant can be prosecuted essentially for becoming involved in a network of criminal activities and associations.[134] Like RICO, conspiracy law allows prosecutors to bring a pattern of related events within a single proceeding. But by focusing on participation in a related network of activities rather than on the agreement to pursue a set of related, or "unified," activities, and by allowing a greater role for inferences among multiple acts and actors, RICO makes a more substantial departure from the transaction-based framework than does conspiracy. It stops short of a purely organizational approach, however, constrained in part by its effort to fit enterprise criminality into the existing legal framework of unified criminal transactions.[135]

Applying Federal and State Anti-racketeering Laws to Gangs An analysis of patterns of use of RICO suggest that its principal use has been for direct attack on the criminal activities of groups or individuals thought to constitute particularly severe threats.[136] The combination of procedural and evidentiary advantages, enhanced sentencing, and forfeiture provision offered by the statute make it a useful tool for combating the activities of criminal street gangs. But while several jurisdictions have begun to use the RICO statute to prosecute the activities of street gangs, this use has generated substantial controversy about whether street gangs are criminal enterprises within the meaning of the statute.[137]

The court in *United States v. Elliot* supported the use of RICO against loosely knit associations of criminals, suggesting that RICO is applicable "when groups of people, through division of labor, specialization, diversification, complexity of organization, and the accumulation of capital, turn crime into an ongoing business."[138] The Supreme Court refused to review this decision and subsequently endorsed the "illegitimate enterprise" prosecution in *United States v. Turkette*,[139] a case involving a loosely organized gang involved in a number of different arson-for-profit schemes orchestrated by Turkette and carried out by a frequently changing personnel. While application of RICO requires proof of an ongoing organizational form, Turkette suggests that the evidentiary requirements are weak and that loose associations with one or two enduring members are sufficient. According to one commentator, "(a)fter Turkette, RICO makes it a crime...to be a gangster, whether in the Mafia or in a much more loosely affiliated criminal combine."[140] Congress implicitly endorsed the use of use of RICO against criminal enterprises in the Comprehensive Crime Control Act of 1984, which expanded RICO's forfeiture provisions to include both interests in and proceeds or profits from illegitimate enterprises and provided for forfeiture of assets upon commission of the RICO violation.[141]

The 1986 Presidential Commission Report provides a framework for defining criminal organizations. Criminal organizations are defined as groups which satisfy the following structural and behavioral characteristics: continuity of operation; a hierarchical management structure; restricted membership based upon a shared trait; financial reliance on continuing criminal activity; systematic violence used as a means of control and protection; and motivation to enhance its power and profitability.[142] Many of the more sophisticated street gangs have developed an organizational structure and engage in an ongoing pattern of activities which clearly satisfy these requirements. In *United States v. Coonan*, the Second Circuit found RICO to be constitutional as applied to the activities of gangs and accepted evidence of gang activities and position in illegal markets as proof that it was a criminal "enterprise." *Coonan* involved the prosecution of the Westies, a gang which emerged in the Hell's Kitchen area of Manhattan in the early 1960s and engaged in loan sharking, narcotics trafficking and sales, and extortion, exercising control over this area through violent means.[143] The conviction of members of the Chicago based El Rukns gang under RICO was similarly upheld in United States v. Andrews on the grounds that the gang had a structure and pattern of activities similar to that of the mafia groups that RICO was originally designed to handle.[144]

Continuing Criminal Enterprise: Attacking the Organization

The Continuing Criminal Enterprise (CCE) Statute[145] provides a method by which the leadership and key players, or "kingpins," of a sufficiently large drug-trafficking criminal organization can be severely punished and the enterprise dismantled through asset forfeiture. The statute includes a mandatory minimum sentencing provision of 10 years for first time offenders, 20 years for second offenders and life sentences for principal leaders or organizers of a particularly large drug ring, fines and forfeiture of property obtained from or used in a CCE.[146] It has been applied both to kingpins and, more recently, to third party aiders and abettors of kingpins.[147] Like RICO, CCE is a compound offense committed by perpetrating predicate crimes, but unlike RICO these predicate crimes are limited to drug crimes and CCE creates only one offense, which the Supreme Court has construed as resembling conspiracy more than a substantive offense.

To secure a conviction under the CCE statute, the prosecutor must establish that: (1) the suspect has committed a felony in violation of the federal narcotics laws;[148] (2) which was part of a continuing series of violations;[149] (3) in concert with five or more people;[150] (4) for whom the defendant was an organizer or supervisor; and (5) from which he derived substantial income or resources.[151] The last three requirements are used to target the leadership of drug-trafficking criminal enterprises which are of a sufficient scope and magnitude by focusing on the size and organizational structure of the criminal activities and the degree of control exercised by the participant(s). These elements can be proven through direct and circumstantial evidence, and the requirements have been interpreted liberally within the context of CCEs in order to restrict the ability of shrewd leaders to insulate themselves through measures such as delegation of tasks or outside contracting. The third requirement has been construed to mean an "agreement in plan or design" involving five or more people. Personal interaction between all five is not required and they may be involved in different but related criminal transactions. "Managerial capacity" can be inferred from structure (easiest to do where the organization is hierarchical), or can be established by demonstrating controlling authority over subordinates. It can also be determined according to the "central role" standard, which looks to conduct which is sufficiently central to the operations of the organization.[152] The final requirement is directed solely at the magnitude of the operation, although courts have refused to establish an income floor and have been liberal in allowing inferences of substantial income from position in the drug dealing hierarchy, number of drug sales made or supervised, and unjustified conspicuous consumer purchases.[153]

The requirements for applying CCE are designed to target the kingpins of gang-controlled narcotics distribution network in an effort to shut down the operations of the enterprise while preserving gradated and proportional penalties for those involved. Attention is paid to the structure of the criminal enterprise, and definitions under the CCE are construed in the context of the organization. Criteria for prosecution and methods of proof are designed to accommodate limited differences in the nature and structure of organizations (e.g. by allowing for different methods of establishing managerial capacity and substantial income). CCE provides an effective vehicle for attacking organizations by including provisions for the removal of both the leadership and the asset base of the organization and by defining statutory requirements within the organizational context.[154] It fails to take the further steps of actively incorporating the criminal organizational structure into the sentencing structure and utilizing organizational information to intervene strategically in the functioning of the organization.

Applying Accomplice Liability to CCE -- Broadening the Net Attempts have been made to broaden the radius of CCE to encompass the network of relationships between drug organizations and independent third parties by applying aider and abettor liability to the operations of an illegal narcotics network.[155] There has been a divided judicial response to CCE aider and abettor liability. The Seventh Circuit has upheld the validity of applying aider and abettor liability to the CCE for third parties who are not employees of the organization, but has replaced the traditional threshold sentencing approach with a "degree of culpability" test which makes the applicability of aider and abettor liability a function of the defendant's degree of culpability.[156] Where third parties are providing substantial support to an organization, it is argued, they are making themselves as culpable as the kingpins, whereas the exclusion of employees is necessary (for deterrence and fairness reasons) to preserve the gradation of punishments for members of different ranks within the same organization.[157] The Second Circuit has adopted the opposite position, focusing on the limited class of targeted offenders identified by the statute to argue that CCE was intended to apply only to the leadership of the drug enterprises.[158] Adopting the Seventh Circuit approach gangs, such as the

Los Angeles based Bloods and Crips, which have forged connections with local gangs and established distribution networks in multiple cities, could be held liable as aiders and abettors of continuing criminal enterprises.

The controversy which application of aider and abettor liability to the CCE has generated highlights a number of issues concerning the use of enterprise criminality statutes. Areas of concern include the potential conflict of new penalty systems with the sentencing structure of the drug laws, which creates the prospect of irrationalities in sentencing structure, differential treatment of equally culpable offenders, and interference with the existing system of gradated punishment for drug offenses, and the role of context in interpreting statutory requirements.[159] There are also methodological questions concerning how group criminality provisions should be introduced. One method has been to attach group criminality provisions such as accomplice liability automatically to the substantive crime. A second approach has been to implement complex criminal statutes (such as RICO and CCE) which rest on a triggering pattern of predicate crimes. There is also a choice between use of threshold tests and mandatory sentencing (as employed in Pino-Perez) as compared to broader application of the crime accompanied by sentencing discretion (as employed in *Ambrose*).[160]

Continuing Financial Crimes Enterprises (CFCE)

Congress added a white-collar version of CCE to its arsenal in late 1990 with the adoption of 18 U.S. C. Sec 225, which makes it a crime to organize, manage, or supervise a "continuing financial crimes enterprise" (CFCE) from which one receives five million dollars or more in gross receipts in any two year period. A "continuing financial crimes enterprise" is defined as "a series of violations" of federal bank bribery, fraud, and false statements statutes which affect a financial institution and are committed by four or more persons "acting in concert." CFCE adopts the same liability structure as CCE.

Criminal Forfeiture: Attacking the Economic Foundation

The Comprehensive Drug Abuse Prevention and Control Act of 1970[161] and RICO contained the first modern criminal forfeiture provisions.[162] The criminal forfeiture provisions contained in RICO and CCE now authorize the confiscation of a convicted offender's interest in and profits from any enterprise involved in the crime.[163] In contrast to civil forfeiture, criminal forfeiture attaches to the offender and can only be applied after conviction.

The extent of this "enterprise forfeiture" is determined by the jury in the same proceedings for determining the guilt or innocence of the individual involved, and the nexus of the property forfeited to the criminal enterprise must be established prior to forfeiture.[164] There has been concern that use of enterprise forfeiture will yield unconstitutionally excessive punishment and unequal punishment of like crimes. Alternative such as a profit fine for illegal earnings have been suggested as a preferable way of punishing criminal gain.[165] The dispute over appropriate methods and scope of forfeiture reflects a confusion about the nature and the target of enterprise crimes. Where the primary objectives are to put the criminal organization out of business and to deter new organizations, enterprise liability seems well suited to the task, and individuals who contribute assets or services to the organization should be put on notice that they run the risk of losing their investments.

Unfortunately the nature of the criminal forfeiture procedure has prevented effective use of this measure. Requiring notice prior to seizure and failing to make pre-notice protective measures easily available allows sophisticated organizations to avoid asset forfeiture. Poorly specified requirements of "nexus to the criminal enterprise" and tracing requirements have made it difficult to identify seizable assets. An organizational approach would design the procedures for criminal forfeiture in light of the objectives of the statute (i.e. shutting down the criminal enterprise), the target of the statute (i.e. the criminal enterprise) and the anticipated reactions of criminal organizations (e.g. evasive responses, hiding and shifting assets). The procedure employed must anticipate and preempt evasive responses from sophisticated criminal players.[166]

"Anti-gang Statutes": A More Direct Attack

State and federal governments have introduced a number of "anti-gang" statutes designed to combat gang-related criminal activities. Although sharing the same objective, these statutes vary in their target(s) and the nature of their penalty structures. Federal statutes have focused on the leadership of criminal organizations that have achieved a certain size and complexity, although more recent proposals have sought to extend the coverage of federal criminal law to include a broader range of gang participants and activities. State statutes have been targeted more broadly at gang participants and at the resources used and activities engaged in by gangs (such as loitering and intimidating others in public spaces). A variety of enforcement methods have been employed, including enhanced sentencing for gang related crimes, making new crimes out of participation in gang activities, and injunctions for loitering and other activities held to constitute a threat to public safety.

Given the legal tools already available for addressing criminal organizations, new statutes aimed exclusively at street gangs should focus on the special characteristics of these groups. Defining characteristics include the protection and use of a demarcated territory, use of membership restrictions and identifying signs such as clothing and hand signals to maintain a visible group identity, some sort of control structure and shared guidelines, and an ongoing association for criminal purposes. Coverage should include gang participants, leadership and gang-related activities, but should be limited to the criminal operations of the gang. Enforcement methods should be designed with an eye to the organizational structure of the gang and should include gradated sentences based on level of involvement and asset forfeiture methods designed to put the organization out of business. Translating these prescriptions into a statutory framework which targets the desired behavior without encompassing legitimate activities and protected associations has proven difficult. Many of the statutory experiments with comprehensive anti-gang statutes have run into problems of over breadth and vagueness. Some of them have also come too close to transforming gang membership into a status crime, imposing guilt by association and criminalizing gang membership.

Examples of "Anti-gang" Statutes In 1994 Congress introduced the Omnibus Crime Bill, which contains a criminal street gang provision that lengthens the sentence of any street gang member who is convicted of committing listed felonies and who has a prior record for committing one of the listed felonies within five years of the current conviction.[167] The section effectively criminalizes association with the specific intent to engage in criminal activities. Its application is limited by an intent requirement (participation with knowledge that the gang engages in felonious activities) and a primary purpose requirement (one of the primary purposes of the gang must be to commit felonies). The latter condition weakens the strength of the section, perhaps unnecessarily, in the attempt to avoid constitutional problems.[168]

Within the last decade a number of states have adopted gang statutes that criminalize activities which promote or facilitate the operations of a "criminal street gang." These statutes make it a crime to commit, to aid and abet in the commission of and/or to conspire to commit crimes that are intended to further the criminal activities of a "criminal street gang" as defined by statute. While statutes differ in their definitions, a "street gangs" can be defined in general terms as "an association of individuals who exhibit characteristics including: a gang name and recognizable symbols, a geographic territory, a regular meeting pattern, and an organized continuos course of criminality."[169] California's anti-gang statute, for example, which has been used as a model by a number of other states, defines a "criminal street gang" as "any ongoing organization, association, or group of three or more persons, whether formal or informal, having as one of its primary activities the commission of one or more of the criminal acts...which has a common name or common identifying sign or symbol, whose members individually or collectively engage in or have engaged in a pattern of criminal gang activity."[170]

California took the lead in the battle against gang violence by enacting the Street Terrorism Enforcement and Prevention (STEP) Act.[171] STEP makes it illegal for an individual to become a participant in and intentionally promote, further, or assist in a criminal street gang's unlawful activities when he knows that members of the gang are or have engaged in a pattern of criminal activity.[172] The statute focuses on "patterns of criminal gang activity and upon the organized nature of street gangs, which together, are the chief source of terror created by street gangs," at least according to the State Legislature.[173] In order to prosecute an individual under STEP, the prosecution must show that a criminal street gang exists and has engaged in a pattern of criminal activity, that the defendant was a knowing participant, and that he knew of this pattern of criminal activity and had the intent of assisting criminal conduct.[174] Showing a "pattern of criminal gang activity" requires proof of "the commission, attempted commission, or solicitation of two or more of the (enumerated)...offenses, provided at least one of those offenses occurred after the effective date of this chapter and the last of these offenses occurred within three years after the prior offense, and the offenses are committed on separate occasions, or by two or more persons."[175] It can be established "by two or more incidents each with a single perpetrator, or by a single incident with multiple participants committing one or more of the specified offenses."[176]

By focusing on knowing association with and facilitation of criminal street gangs, the statute has the potential to sweep quite broadly. Indeed, there has been concern that STEP sweeps too broadly, infringing upon the constitutional right to free association by criminalizing association with a criminal street gang and depriving gang members of due process by imposing guilt through association.[177] Moreover, it is argued that even if combating gang-related crime is treated as a compelling state interest sufficient to justify these infringements, the court has available other less drastic measures, such as conspiracy charges or additional policing measures.[178] While the constitutionality of STEP has been upheld in several

California courts of appeal, where it has been argued that the Act punishes only groups that have the commission of crimes as their primary activities,[179] the effect of the statute on the associational rights of gang members and the potential for arbitrary and discriminatory enforcement have not been adequately addressed.[180]

Similar statutes have been adopted in about fourteen other states, including Colorado, Florida, Georgia, Illinois, Kansas, Minnesota and Missouri.[181] Florida has recently introduced a Criminal Street Gang Prevention Act, which adds sentence enhancements for gang members.[182] Colorado has enacted a controversial "street terrorism bill" that would make membership in a criminal street gang a felony-level enhancement.[183] Concern has been voiced that the Colorado bill would promote de facto guilt by association. Evidence of gang membership includes identification by parents or reliable informants, adoption of the gang style of dress, use of hand signs, association with known gang members, or having been stopped in the company of known members more than three times.

Some states have chosen to rely on existing sentence enhancement laws in the battle against street gangs. In a recent decision the Washington State Supreme Court decided that criminal sentencing may be based in part on gang motivation, holding that gang-motivated crime is an aggravating factor that justifies extending the presumptive sentencing range set forth by the state's Sentencing Reform Act.[184] Evidence supporting the aggravated sentence in this case included the defendant's membership in the Black Gangster Disciples, the positive impact of violent acts against rival gangs on status in the gang hierarchy, and the defendant's participation in earlier gang confrontations during which he used gang signs and boasted of his membership.[185] The evidence relied upon could have been (but was not) used to charge the defendant with leading organized crime and conspiracy.[186]

Local governments have taken imitative measures, although the legality of these measures has been questioned because of the focus on restricting criminals rather than criminal activities. The San Fernando City Council, for example, passed a local ordinance modeled after STEP which bans gang members from a public park in which gang violence frequently occurs. The ordinance bans those gang members classified as active under STEP "based on their criminal records, associates, street names, tattoos and other signs of gang involvement" who have been "served with papers notifying them of the classification" from using the park.[187]This approach is troubling because it seeks to restrict the movement of criminals rather than the performance of criminal activities. When evaluating anti-gang statutes, issues to consider include whether the statutes are adding anything new to existing group-based statutes, what it is they are targeting, and whether they are targeting it in the right way.

Criminal Syndicate Statutes

Two states, Arizona and Nevada, have statutes that outlaw "criminal syndicates." Ohio had such a statute until 1980, and North Dakota has a functionally identical statute that prohibits "leading organized crime." Arizona's statue makes it a crime to "participate in" or "assist" a criminal syndicate, defined as a "combination of persons or enterprises engaging, or having the purpose of engaging, on a continuing basis" in one or more felonies under Arizona law. Participation in a syndicate can include organizing, managing, or financing the syndicate, inducing others to engage in violence or intimidation to promote it, giving advice on conducting or financing its affairs, inducing a public servant to violate an official duty to promote its goals, or using a minor to commit an offense under the statute. One "assists" a criminal syndicate by committing any felony "with the intent to promote or further" its criminal objectives.[188] Nevada defines a "criminal syndicate" as a group of persons who engage in, or intend to engage in "racketeering activity," defined in the same way as under federal statute, such that the group will "continue its operation even if individual members enter or leave the organization."[189] These syndicate statutes do not stand alone, but rather are related to RICO and gang provisions. While there is some degree of overlap between the two approaches, they differ in that syndicate crimes focus on the formation of a criminal enterprise through organized criminal activity, whereas RICO focuses on the ways in which crimes are used to exploit an enterprise.[190]

Leading Organized Crime Statutes

New Jersey and Washington have statutes that prohibit "leading organized crime."[191] According to the Washington statute, one leads organized crime by organizing, managing, or financing "three or more persons with the intent to engage in a pattern of criminal profiteering activity;" or by inducing violence or intimidation to promote a pattern of criminal profiteering activity, where the required pattern involves committing at least three related acts of criminal profiteering in five years.[192] Rather than imposing aiding and abetting liability, this statute carves an additional offense out of the conduct involved in committing a substantive violation of Washington's RICO statute, making leading organized crime a RICO predicate. The New Jersey statute is designed to target the controlling members of a group engaged in racketeering activity.[193] One scholar suggests that the offense is akin to CCE, a "super-conspiracy" aimed at criminal executives.[194]

Loitering Laws

Some local governments have looked to loitering laws as a means of controlling the street-based activities of criminal groups involved in drugs, prostitution and violent crime. Examples include a drug loitering ordinance enacted in Seattle, Washington, which prohibits loitering in public places with the intent to sell drugs, and a similar loitering ordinance enacted in Tampa, Florida, which is aimed at prostitution. The Seattle ordinance, which authorized police officers to make arrests for signaling to passersby, possessing drug paraphernalia or being a known drug dealer, was upheld.[195] The Tampa ordinance was struck down by the Florida Supreme Court as unconstitutionally overbroad and vague.

Loitering laws can be used to target an important group resources utilized by the criminal gang - the territory over which they have established control. Control over an identifiable territory provides the gang with a market base, an identity and a locus for group activity. Criminal street gangs establish control over selected areas by loitering in those areas and intimidating others from entering. In the absence of loitering laws, the gangs are able to police their territory without fear of arrest. An anti-gang loitering ordinance was introduced in Chicago in 1992 as part of a concerted strategy to control a spiraling crime rate allegedly resulting from gang violence.[196] This loitering ordinance authorized police officers to order groups of two or more "loiterers" to disperse or face arrest where the officers have a reasonable belief that one of the loiterers is a gang member, where "loiter" is defined as "to remain in any one place with no apparent purpose." The ordinance was passed by the City Council on the basis of legislative findings linking criminal street gangs with the increased violent and drug related crimes in Chicago and linking loitering activities with the establishment of control over identifiable areas and intimidation of entrants into the area without direct violation of any offenses covered by existing law.[197] This ordinance was declared unconstitutional in an Illinois appellate court in 1995 and is under review by the Illinois Supreme Court.[198] The Illinois appeals court held that, among other things, the gang loitering ordinance infringed on freedoms of association and expression and criminalized the status of being a gang member.

Loitering laws of this sort have given rise to concerns about the scope for discriminatory and arbitrary enforcement against undesirable groups (vagueness) and the over-inclusive nature of the statutes (overbreadth). Although many of the newly enacted loitering ordinances have tried to design their ordinances to proscribe only a narrow range of activities, the use of these types of rules continues to pose concerns about the consequences for freedom of association and freedom from arbitrary state action. Moreover, as noted by commentators such as Malcom Klien, these types of ordinances may serve to increase the cohesion of the groups they are aimed at suppressing, providing them with additional means of maintaining group identity. The Supreme Court has strongly indicated that laws that proscribe mere loitering are unconstitutional, but has not ruled out loitering laws that are narrowly tailored and more restricted in coverage.[199]

Nuisance Laws

California prosecutors were the first to employ civil injunctions barring gang activities. A Los Angeles City Attorney became the first to initiate a nuisance abatement action against a street gang in the civil suit of *People v. Playboy Gangster Crips*. The suit asked the court to issue an injunction against more than two hundred gang members which prohibited both legal and illicit conduct including wearing gang colors, associating with other gang members, remaining in public more than five minutes and leaving their residences after nightfall. Prosecutors argued that collective liability of this sort was necessary to combat sophisticated street gangs.[200] Superior Court Judge Major issued an even more sweeping preliminary injunction against a 350 member Los Angeles gang in *People v. Blythe Street Gang*, explaining his imposition of collective liability based on observations that the Blythe Street Gang "shares common purposes to recruit new members, to control the ... area as their "turf" and to engage in activities designed to further their rein of terror." This approach targets a pattern of activities relied upon by street gangs as a means of interfering with the continued existence of the group.

Attention has recently been focused on San Jose's use of a 19th century anti-nuisance law to combat youth gangs by banning gang activities such as vandalism, applying graffiti, using drugs, using gang hand signs and beepers in public, and appearing with known gang members. In an appellate court ruling the city has been allowed to use injunctions to address gang-related criminal activity but not non-criminal activity as a public nuisance.[201] The San Jose injunction is currently under consideration by the California Supreme Court and city officials await this first higher court ruling on this strategy.[202] More specific injunctions have been applied in other Californian cities as part of a larger program being called "Strategy

Against Gang Environments."

Curfews and Parent Liability

Curfew laws have been upheld in a number of cities, including Dallas and New Orleans, and according to a Justice Department Report curfews are now in effect in nearly three-quarters of the nation's largest cities.[203] Curfew violators and truants in Ventura County, California now face tough new penalties which include fines and loss of driving privileges for children and fines of up to $2,500 for parents.[204] Washington, D.C.'s curfew law, which set hours of 11 p.m. to 6 a.m. on weekdays and midnight to 6 a.m. on weekends for children up to the age of 17, was ruled to be an unconstitutional violation of the rights of minors and parents.

Other measures have included warrantless searches of probationers. For the last four years Ventura County authorities have performed unannounced dawn searches of the homes of probationers as part of a crackdown on gang members.[205] San Antonio police are embarking on a "Knock and Talk" Program which allows police to enter homes (with parents' permission) and confiscate illegal firearms without making arrests.[206] In 1988 the California Supreme Court upheld the constitutionality of a provision which hold parents or guardians who engage in conduct or omissions which cause, encourage or contribute to the delinquency of a minor guilty of a misdemeanor.[207]

Notes

[1] See Truan, D. (1995), 'The Jets and Sharks Are Dead: State Statutory Responses to Criminal Street Gangs', *Washington University Law Quarterly*, vol. 73, p. 683. Armstrong,S. (1987), 'In L.A. Line Blurs Between Street Gangs and Organized Crime', *Christian Science Monitor*, June 12, p.8.

[2] See Vigil, J.D. (1988), *Barrio Gangs: Street Life and Identity in Southern California*, ,University of Texas, Austin. In his book on barrio gangs, Vigil looks at the emergence of street gangs as substitute for family and community network.

[3] See Genelin, M. (1993), 'Gang Prosecutions; The Hardest Game in Town', in A. Goldstein and R. Huff (eds), *The Gang Intervention Handbook*, p. 417.

[4] The federal Racketeer Influenced and Corrupt Organizations Act (RICO) and similar state substitutes have been increasingly utilized to prosecute criminal street gangs, for example, as has the federal Continuing Criminal Enterprise (CCE) statute.

[5] California took the lead in this battle with enactment of the Street Terrorism Enforcement and Protection Act (STEP Act) in 1988. See Cal.Penal Code §§ 186.20-28 Twelve other states followed suit with some form of anti-gang statute. Florida (Fla.Stat.An. §874.03) South Dakota (S.D.Codified Laws Ann. § 22-10-14) and Illinois (Ill.Ann.Stat. ch. 730) went even further than California by criminalizing mere association with criminal gangs.

[6] The Southern District of Florida was shaken by a trial of two criminal defense lawyers who had often been seen in Miami courts defending others. The lawyers were charged as conspiracy members in the Cali Cartel because of the actions they took in defending cartel members.

[7] Positioning on this spectrum will be influenced by theories about the appropriate role of criminal penalties and the influence of organization on individual decision-makers. An organizational approach will be adopted if deterrence is regarded as the primary goal.

[8] Gang members who spend time in jail face even fewer legitimate opportunities upon release, making membership more attractive, and detention of gang members leaves openings to be filled by new recruits.

[9] The likelihood of ending up in prison, for example, where gangs are active and gang affiliation is extremely important, enhances the incentive of a gang member to behave according to the dictates of his gang. Pressure from external threats and the offer of protection against these threats increase the ability of a gang to operate as a cohesive group.

[10] It was this concern that fueled the passage of the first federal racketeering statute.

[11] At one point the El Rukns even sought legal recognition as an independent nation and maintained secret political ties with a foreign government.

[12] Becker, G. (1968), 'Crime and Punishment: An Economic Analysis', *Journal of Political Economy*, vol. 76, pp. 169-217.

[13] See e.g. Sah, R. K. (1991), 'Social Osmosis and Patterns of Crime', *Journal of Political Economy*, vol. 199, no. 6, pp. 1272-1295, 1272.
[14] Alternative starting points include looking at the effect of gang membership on crime production costs and the effect of gang membership on revenue.
[15] Investing in group resources will give rise to free rider and moral hazard problems. Information sharing increases the risk of a given transaction by increasing the number of potential informants. By increasing the number of participants in a criminal endeavor, specialization of labor may lead to an increase in risk (particularly where higher numbers lead to higher probability of detection), inability to diversify risk due to larger stakes, and problems of revenue sharing.
[16] Alchian, A. and Demsetz, H. (1972), 'Production, Information Costs, and Economic Organization,' *American Economic Review*, vol. 62, pp. 777-795; Holmstrom, B. (1982), 'Moral Hazard in Teams', *Bell Journal of Economics*, vol. 13, pp. 324-340.
[17] See Grossman, S. and Hart, O. (1983), 'An Analysis of the Principal-Agent Problem', Econometrica, vol. 51, pp. 7-45; Itoh, H. (1991), 'Incentives to Help in Multi-Agent Situations', Econometrica, vol. 59, no. 3, pp. 611-635. Using the standard principal-agent model in this context raises questions about the appropriateness of applying this framework, originally designed to solve problems of risk allocation and incentives to produce between an owner and an agent, to a situation of joint management and production by a group of individuals who are both principals and agents.
[18] The current policy of "getting tough on drugs," which has translated into larger sentences for larger groups of people, has put a severe strain on the existing prison system. The increase in prison population has resulted in overcrowding, large expenditures on building new prisons, and early release of other types of criminals. All of these measures are costly, and as the prison population swells the cost of punishment is likely to increase.
[19] This has an interesting parallel in criminal law, where the cost of imposing the death penalty as opposed to the maximum life sentence jumps dramatically.
[20] This expenditure reducing effect is in part an artifact of the unchanging detection technology, and in an expanded model the detection technology should be incorporated into the policy-maker's decision problem as an endogenous variable.
[21] Brenner, Susan W. (1991), 'Of Complicity and Enterprise Criminality: Applying Pinkerton Liability to RICO Actions', *Missouri Law Review*, vol. 56, p. 931 at 931.
[22] Model Penal Code § 5.02 (1).
[23] Model Penal Code § 5.02 (2).
[24] See eg. *Callanan v US*, 364 U.S. 587, 593 (1961).
[25] RICO was enacted as Title IX of the Organized Crime Control Act, codified as 18 U.S.C. §§ 1961-1968. CCE was enacted as part of the Comprehensive Drug Abuse Prevention and Control Act of 1970, Pub.L. No. 91-513, 84 Stat. 1236 (1970), codified as 21 U.S.C. § 848 (1988).
[26] The Supreme Court has construed CCE as a "super-conspiracy" offense that subsumes the predicate conspiracy defined by 21 U.S.C. § 846 (1988).

[27] See 18 U.S.C. § 1962 (1988).
[28] See 18 U.S.C. § 1962(a)-(c).
[29] 21 U.S.C. § 848. To secure a conviction under the CCE statute, the prosecutor must establish that: (1) the suspect has committed a felony in violation of the federal narcotics laws; (2) which was part of a continuing series of violations; (3) in concert with five or more people; (4) for whom the defendant was an organizer or supervisor; and (5) from which he derived substantial income or resources. The last three requirements are used to target the leadership of drug-trafficking criminal enterprises which are of a sufficient scope and magnitude by focusing on the size and organizational structure of the criminal activities and the degree of control exercised by the participant(s).
[30] 21 U.S.C. § 853(a) (1988) provides that those convicted under § 848 "shall forfeit to the United States...any property constituting, or derived from, any proceeds the person obtained, directly or indirectly, as the result of such violation," any property used to facilitate the operations of the CCE, and any property or contractual rights representing an interest in or affording control over the CCE. The defendant's assets can sometimes be frozen even before trial.
[31] Skalitzky, W. (1996), 'Aider and Abettor Liability, the Continuing Criminal Enterprise, and Street Gangs: A New Twist in an Old War on Drugs', *Journal of Criminal Law and Crimonology*, vol. 81, p. 348, 368 (application of aider and abettor liability to CCE convictions).
[32] Once the basic penalty structure has been selected, there is a further choice as to what type of penalty to use. The options include jail, fines and asset forfeiture. There is also a choice as to method for imposing group based liability - it can be introduced as sentence enhancement for individual crimes, compound liability, or new substantive crimes for involvement in an organization. There is a further range of choice as to which organizational variables to include and how to include them (e.g. as gradated sentencing or separate crimes for leadership roles). Some statutes (such as CCE) are targeted at leaders and key players of the organization. Some statutes (such as RICO) have a threshold requirement based on size, magnitude of earnings and pattern of activities engaged in. The crime of conspiracy allows for a broader application of group based liability to all involved parties, particularly if the Pinkerton Rule is applied.
[33] Sah, R. K. (1991), 'Social Osmosis and Patterns of Crime', *Journal of Political Economy*, vol. 199, no. 6, pp. 1272-1295, 1272. See Bureau of Justice Statistics (1988) for U.S. data . For a review of empirical studies see Pyle, D.J. (1983), *The Economics of Crime and Law Enforcement*, St. Martin's, New York.
[34] See e.g. Becker, G.S. (1968), 'Crime and Punishment: An Economic Approach', *Journal of Political Economy*, vol 76, pp. 169-217; Ehrlich, I. (1973), 'Participation in Illegitimate Activities: A Theoretical and Empirical Investigation', *Journal of Political Economy*, vol. 181, pp. 521-65 and Pyle, D.J. (1983), *The Economics of Crime and Law Enforcement*. St. Martin's, New York, pp. 1272-95.
[35] See Sah, R. K. (1991), 'Social Osmosis and Patterns of Crime', *Journal of Political Economy*, vol. 99, no. 6, pp. 1272-1295.

[36] Sah models the propensity of an individual to commit a crime as a function and uses this function to construct an economy wide crime participation rate which is then used to determine the information available to the individual in determining his own probability of being caught, and hence his own participation decision. This model is used to demonstrate that an individual's current propensity for crime is higher if past crime participation rates were higher, if fewer resources were spent on criminal apprehension, or if the current relative payoff from crime is larger.

[37] See Bureau of Justice Statistics for 1983.

[38] According to Drug Enforcement Agency statistics.

[39] See Davison, P. (1993), 'Rivals Muscle in on Excobar Drug Empire', *The Independent*, March 23, p. 13 (the Cali Cartel emerges as the new financial leader of the Colombian cocaine trade); Wilson, G. (1994), 'The Changing Game: The United States Evolving Supply-Side Approach to Narcotics Trafficking', *Vanderbilt Journal of Transnational Law*, vol. 28, p. 1163.

[40] See Farah , D. and Coll, S. (1993), 'Cocaine Dollars Flow Via Unique Network', *Washington Post*, September. 19, p. A1.

[41] See Wilson, G. (1994), 'The Changing Game: The United States Evolving Supply-Side Approach to Narcotics Trafficking', *Vanderbilt Journal of Transnational Law*, vol. 26, p. 1163, 1194.

[42] Kacarab, P. J. (1991), 'An In-depth Analysis of the New Money Laundering Statutes', *AKRON Tax Journal*, vol. 8, p. 1, 3.

[43] See Wilson, G. (1994), 'The Changing Game: The United States Evolving Supply-Side Approach to Narcotics Trafficking.' *Vanderbilt Journal of Transnational Law*, vol. 26, p. 1163, 1194. The United States has engaged in three large scale operations to slow the drug trade - Operation Blast Furnace (involving a U.S. attempt to use the military to attack the drug trade by destroying cocaine laboratories in Latin America), the Andean Strategy, and Operation Green Ice (an anti-money laundering sting operation aimed primarily at the Cali cartel). Operation Green Ice was a large scale three year investigation aimed primarily at the financial operations of the Cali Cartel. DEA operators established leather good stores across the U.S. and posed as money laundering facilitators in the attempt to create legitimate paper trails for illicit funds. See Staff writer. (1992), 'Follow the Money; Operation Green Ice Breaks Up the Cali Cartel's Financial Network', *Time Magazine*, October 22, p. 26; Staff writer. (1992), 'Seven-Nation Green Ice Effort Deals Blow to Cartels', *Money Laundering Alert*, October, p. 6.

[44] Criminal forfeiture is the post-conviction divestiture of the defendant's property and any financial interests associated with his criminal activities or the criminal organization. See Wilson, G. (1994), 'The Changing Game: The United States Evolving Supply-Side Approach to Narcotics Trafficking', *Vanderbilt Journal of Transnational Law*, vol. 26, p. 1163, 1194.

[45] Complex laundering schemes involving multiple transfers of property make forfeiture difficult, particularly where the assets must be shown to have a nexus with the criminal enterprise (as under CCE). See *United States v. Daccarett*, 6 F.3d 37, 44-50 (2d Cir. 1993) (Three associates of the Cali Cartel had been arrested

after opening hundreds of bank accounts, depositing large sums of money and conducting countless EFTs, and $12 million dollars were seized, court's decision that warrantless seizure of electronic fund transfers (EFTs) not unconstitutional appears to provide necessary legal weapons to seize EFTs and disrupt the Cali financial empire); *United States v. Meinster*, 488 F. Supp. 1342 (S.D. Fla. 1980) (Proof at trial that 'Black Tuna' marijuana smuggling ring, composed of at least 60 people, had handled over one million pounds of marijuana, earning gross receipts estimated to be at least $300 million, but investigation never sufficiently penetrated the organization's financial set up and did not find location of the profits. According to the prosecutor, most of the money was transferred out of the country by wire, possibly to the Cayman Islands, which offers complete secrecy regarding bank accounts. The FBI discovered bribe arrangements with jurors, intimidation of jurors and financial arrangements with local organized crime groups to cause a mistrial.). See Pianin, I. A. (1982), 'Criminal Forfeiture: Attacking the Economic Dimension of Organized Narcotics Trafficking', *American University Law Review*, vol. 32, p. 227.

[46] 18 U.S.C. § 1956 (1988). The Money Laundering Control Act authorizes the seizure and forfeiture of cash and related property where the owner causes a financial institution to fail to file a required Bank Secrecy Act report. It also substantially increases the fines and prison penalties for violating the Bank Secrecy Act, extends to negligent reporting, and provides exceptions to financial privacy.

[47] See Zagaris, B. (1989), 'Money Laundering: An International Currency Problem' in S. MacDonald and B. Zagaris (eds), *International Handbook on Drug Control*, Greenwood Press, London, Chapter Two.

[48] Schemo, D. J. (1996), 'Turning Colombia's Drug Plots Over to Peasant Plowshares', *The New York Times*, Wednesday December 18, p. A15.

[49] The criminal law approach towards group based crimes is the product of an amalgamation of different objectives and procedural constraints. More so than in other areas of law, the criminal law implicates a wide range of political, social and economic concerns and a wide variety of people (including both criminals and victims). Statutory crimes are designed with an eye to avoiding infringement upon constitutionally protected activities such as freedom of association and expression and satisfaction of constitutional restrictions on the criminalization of membership and proportionality in punishment. They are also designed in response to public concerns about particular types of crimes, such as street violence and drug trafficking, and political concerns about the special dangers of organized crime. The legal structure imposes its own set of constraints, including act and intent requirements and an emphasis on individual liability for specific conduct. Finally, there are institutional constraints, such as enforcement capacity and scope for abuse of prosecutorial discretion, and procedural constraints, such as issues of venue, jurisdiction and restrictions on use of consolidated trials, which have implications for the effectiveness of criminal statutes. The legal framework affects criminal organizations by altering the relative and absolute costs of different actions and methods of organization.

[50] By explicitly recognizing the importance of the organizational structure and allowing direct use of organizational variables, this approach would facilitate consistent treatment of the multiple aspects of a group-based provision, including evidentiary restrictions, trial consolidation and sentencing structure. Ideally, it would also facilitate development of a unified system by focusing attention on the functional affects of criminal provisions and ensuring that the provisions are aimed more directly at their intended objectives.

[51] See *Ex parte Lange*, 85 U.S. 163, 305 (1873).

[52] Double punishment for the same crime would violate the Supreme Court rule that "no man can be twice lawfully punished for the same offense." See *Ex parte Lange*, 85 U.S. 163, 168 (1873).

[53] See Schuler, K. G. (1993), 'Continuing Criminal Enterprise, Conspiracy, & Multiple Punishment Doctrine', *Michigan Law Review*, vol. 91, p. 222.

[54] California's attempt to create a status crime of being a narcotics addict was held unconstitutional in *Robinson v. California*, 370 U.S. 660 (1962).

[55] Closely related to criminalizing group membership are provisions making support of certain groups illegal. A recent Clinton initiative makes it illegal to provide financial support to certain named terrorist and criminal organizations.

[56] *Whitney v. California*, 274 U.S. 357, 371(1927).

[57] *Scales v. United States*, 367 U.S. 203, 224-25 (1961) (Court upheld Smith Act against facial challenge by reading a requirement of individualized intent into statute).

[58] *United States v. Lemon*, 723 F.2d 922, 939 (D.C. Cir. 1983).

[59] *Elfbrant v. Russell*, 384 U.S. 11, 16 (1966) (Court held unconstitutional Arizona statute requiring teachers to disavow membership any organization advocating violent overthrow).

[60] *Healy v. James*, 408 U.S. 169, 186 (1972).

[61] See *Healy v. James*, 408 U.S. 169, 194 (1970) (refusal to allow college students to establish local chapter of political organization known for violence without sowing that these students contemplated violent action violates First Amendment). While freedom of intimate association may extend beyond the family unit, the Supreme Court has placed weight on family-like values and personal connections, and has found the organizations it has considered too impersonal to receive protection. See e.g. *New York State Club Ass'n v. New York City*, 487 U.S. 1, 12 (1988).

[62] *Dawson v. Delaware*, 112 S.Ct. 1093 (1992) (Court held that admission of evidence of defendant's gang membership in murder conviction was reversible error since associational beliefs had no bearing on the issue).

[63] See Cal. Penal Code Section 186.20-.27 (Deering Supp. 1992) and See Section 8-4-015 of the Chicago Municipal Code.

[64] Section 186.22(a) of STEP provides that "[a]ny person who actively participates in any criminal street gang with knowledge that its members engage in or have engaged in a pattern of criminal gang activity, and who willfully promotes, furthers, or assists in any felonious criminal conduct by members of that gang, shall

be punished by imprisonment in the county jail for a period not to exceed one year, or by imprisonment in the state prison for one, two, or three years."

[65] Omnibus Crime Bill, 18 U.S.C. § 521 (West Supp. 1995).

[66] Lynch notes that studies of juror behavior indicate that juror's reactions to the characteristics of the defendant play a major role in explaining verdict disagreement between judges and juries and emphasizes the potential impact of context on conviction and sentencing. See Lynch, G.E. (1987), 'RICO: The Crime of Being a Criminal Parts III,IV', *Columbia Law Review*, vol. 87, p. 920, 958-67.

[67] The Constitution can be seen as a system of general equilibrium rules designed to regulate the interactions between self-interested individuals with interdependent interests. Narrow rules may have broad derivative effects which need to be included in the evaluation. In this sense the constitutional requirements are playing a role which is entirely consistent with economic analysis.

[68] See S. Rep. No. 225, 98th Cong., 1st Sess. 191 (if law enforcement efforts to combat racketeering and drug trafficking are to be successful, they must include an attack on the economic aspects of these crimes. Forfeiture is the mechanism through which such an attack may be made.)

[69] Pub. L. No. 91-513, 84 Stat. 1236 (also known as the Drug Control Act and the Controlled Substances Act).

[70] See Reed, R. (1985), 'Criminal Forfeiture Under the Comprehensive Forfeiture Act of 1984: Raising the Stakes', American Criminal Law Review, vol. 22, p. 747, and also Webb, D.K. and Turow, S.F. (1983), 'RICO Forfeiture in Practice, A Prosecutorial Perspective', *University of Cin. Law Review*, vol. 52, p. 404.

[71] Both provisions have been expanded. The Comprehensive Crime Control Act of 1984 expanded RICO's forfeiture provisions to include both interests in and proceeds or profits from illegitimate enterprises and provided for forfeiture of assets upon commission of the RICO violation. Pub. L. No. 98-473, 98 Stat. 1837 (1984). While application of the criminal forfeiture provision introduced under the Drug Control Act was originally restricted to convictions under the CCE statute, the statute was subsequently amended to impose forfeiture upon all defendants convicted of drug felonies. Comprehensive Forfeiture Act of 1984, Pub. L. No. 98-473, §§ 301-309, 98 Stat. 1837, 2040-57. The provision is now applied under 21 U.S.C. § 853. For further discussion see Smith, S.D. (1988), 'The Scope of Real Property Forfeiture for Drug-Related Crime Under the Comprehensive Forfeiture Act', *Univ. of Penn. Law Review*, vol. 137, p. 303 (considers the use of § 853 in the forfeiture of real property, argues that entire parcels should be forfeited even if only a porition was used directly in offense).

[72] Black,C. (1996), 'Senate proposal targets street gangs', *Boston Globe*, April 25, p. 14.

[73] Id.

[74] See Bradley, R. (1984), 'Racketeering and the Federalization of Crime', *American Criminal Law Review*, vol. 22, p. 213.

[75] Brenner, S. (1991), 'Of Complicity and Enterprise Criminality: Applying Pinkerton Liability to RICO Actions." *Missouri Law Review*, vol. 56, p. 931.

[76] The American approach to punishment of accomplices is to make them subject to the identical punishment as principals. This can be contrasted to the German approach, which imposes different punishments for perpetrator, instigator and aider.

[77] Model Penal Code § 2.06 commentary at 300, 305.

[78] Model Penal Code § 2.06 (7). There must be a guilty principal before there can be an aider and abettor, since what is at issue is the responsibility of the secondary actor for the principal actor's violation of the law. See *U.S. v. Jones*, 425 F.2d 1048, 1056 (9th Cir, 1970).

[79] 18 U.S.C. § 2 (1988). Enacted in 1909, the original version of this statute was the first federal statute authorizing prosecution for aiding and abetting another in the commission of a crime. See Brenner, S. (1991), 'Of Complicity and Enterprise Criminality: Applying Pinkerton Liability to RICO Actions', *Missouri Law Review*, vol. 56, p. 931.

[80] *United States v. Rector*, 538 F.2d 223, 225 (8th Cir. 1976).

[81] Model Penal Code § 2.06 (6).

[82] Model Penal Code § 2.06 commentary at 311.

[83] See e.g. *Regina v. Anderson and Morris* ,2 W.L.R. 1195 (1966) (where two persons embark on joint enterprise, each is liable for the acts done in pursuance of that joint enterprise including liability for unusual consequences but if one of the actors goes beyond what has been tacitly agreed as part of the common enterprise, his co-actor is not liable for the consequences). See Model Penal Code § 2.06 comments at 310 (the liability of an accomplice ought not to be extended beyond the purposes that he shares, probabilities have an important evidential bearing on these issues but are not independently sufficient).

[84] *United States v Peoni*, 100 F.2d 401, 402 (2nd Cir. 1938). The *Peoni* standard is also used in a number of states. See e.g. *State v. Harper*, 365 S.E. 2d 69 (W.Va. 1987); *Miller v. United States*, 479 A.2d 862 (D.C. 1984); *Jahnke v. State*, 692 P.2d 911 (Wyo. 1984).

[85] See e.g. *State ex rel. Attorney General v. Tally, Judge*, 102 Ala. 25, 69 (1894) (Judge Tally sent telegram requesting that warning telegram not be delivered, victim not warned and ultimately killed, act need not be "but for" cause as long as it facilitated a result).

[86] Where causing a particular result is an element of the offense, the accomplice must act with the kind of culpability required for liability but the Model Penal Code is silent as to whether the mens rea requirement of purpose applies to attendant-circumstance elements. See Model Penal Code § 2.06 comment at 311, argues that "(t)here is deliberate ambiguity as to whether the purpose requirement extends to circumstance elements of the contemplated offense or whether, as in the case of attempts, the policy of the substantive offense on this point should control. The result, therefore, is that the actor must have a purpose with respect to the proscribed conduct, with his attitude towards the circumstances to be left to resolution by the courts...."

[87] *Nye & Nissen v. U.S.*, 336 U.S. 613, 619 (1949). See *Hicks v US*, 150 U.S. 442

(1893) (acts or words of encouragement must have been used with the intention of encouraging and abetting principal in committing crime); *State v Gladstone*, 78 Wash. 2d 306 (1980) (conviction of person who aided seller in unlawful purchase of marijuana overturned b/c not proof of purposive attitude - no communication with seller and no benefit, and therefore insufficient nexus between accused and offender). See also *US v. Peoni*, 100 F.2d 401, 402 (1938) (stake in the venture as suggesting purposive attitude); *Backun v. U.S.*, 112 F.2d 635, 637 (4th Cir. 1940) (require knowledge that there is a purpose to commit a crime and that one's own behavior renders aid).

88 See *U.S. v. Fountain*, 768 F.2d 790 (7th Cir. 1985) (Gometz held liable for aiding and abetting another inmate to murder guard by providing knife, Posner held it sufficient to show that Gometz knew when he helped Silverstein obtain the knife that Silverstein would use it to attack the guard); U.S. v. Barnett, 667 F.2d 835 (9th Cir. 1982) (Hensley manufactured PCP using formula and supplier information purchased from Barnett).

89 See e.g. *People v. Abbot*, 84 App.Div.2d 11 (1981) (Moon and Abbott jointly indicted for negligent homicide resulting from Abbot's collision with victim during drag race because Moon intentionally aided Abbott to engage in criminally negligent conduct resulting in deaths); *Story v U.S.*, 16 F.2d 342, 344 (D.C. Cir. 1926) (owner of car permitted drunk to take wheel and was held liable for aiding and abetting him in his criminal negligence when he drove car into head-on collision).

90 See Lynch, S.C. (1991), 'Drug Kingpins and their Helpers: Accomplice Liablity Under 21 USC Section 848', *University of Chicago Law Review*, vol. 58, p. 391, 410 (1991). See also *United States v. Pino-Perez*, 870 F.2d 1230, 1239 (7th Cir. 1989)(the scope of accomplice liability under 18 U.S.C. 2(a) "depends on the structure and functions of the substantive statute").

91 New York Penal Code § 115.

92 The conditions for abandonment are also consistent with the notion of punishment only for direct purposive criminal activity. In general, an aider and abettor can terminate his complicity prior to the commission of the offense by preventing the commission of the crime or making proper effort to do so. See Model Penal Code § 2.06. Some states have imposed additional requirements which make abandonment more difficult. The New York Penal Code, for example, requires in addition to acts of withdrawal and substantial efforts to prevent the crime that the offender has acted under circumstances manifesting a "voluntary and complete renunciation" of his criminal purpose rather than postponement of plans or an increased expectation of punishment. New York Penal Code § 40.10(1). While this may increase initial deterrence, it does so at the expense of discouraging withdrawal at later stages of the crime.

93 Model Penal Code § 5.02 (1).

94 Id. § 5.02 (2).

95 Id. § 5.02 (3).

96 See eg. *Callanan v US*, 364 U.S. 587, 593 (1961).

[97] Model Penal Code § 5.06 (1). State and federal provisions resemble the Code provision. See, e.g., Wash. Rev. Code § 9A.28.040 (1992), which holds that a person commits the offense of conspiracy when he acts with the "intent that conduct constituting a crime be performed and agrees with one or more persons to engage in or cause the performance of such conduct, and any one of them takes a substantial step in pursuance of such an agreement."
[98] Id. § 5.06 (4).
[99] Id. § 5.06 (6), (7) The conspiracy terminates when the crime or crimes which are its object are committed or the agreement that they be committed is abandoned by the defendant and by those with whom he conspired. Abandonment is presumed if none of the conspirators performs an overt act in pursuance of the conspiracy during the applicable period of limitation. If an individual abandons the agreement, the conspiracy is terminated as to him only if and when he advises those with whom he conspired of his abandonment or he informs the law enforcement authorities of existence of the conspiracy and of his participation in it.
[100] This preference is reflected in the common law rule of merger under which a lesser crime merged into a greater felony, preventing convictions for both. See Brenner, S. (1993), 'RICO,CCE and Other Complex Crimes: The Transformation of American Criminal Law?' *Wm.&Mary Bill Rts. Journal*, vol. 2, pp. 239-300,240.
[101] *Clune v. United States*, 159 U.S. 590, 595 (1895). The traditional distinction between conspiracy and substantive crimes was based on the requirement of collective action.
[102] *Pinkerton v. U.S.* 328 U.S. 640, 643 (1946) (held that conspiracy is a and extended liability to include acts committed by other conspirators in furtherance of the conspiracy, but not for acts which were not "in furtherance of the conspiracy, did not fall within the scope of the unlawful project, or was merely a part of the ramifications of the plan which could not be reasonably foreseen as an accessory or natural consequence of the unlawful agreement).
[103] Brenner, S. (1991), 'Of Complicity and Enterprise Criminality: Applying Pinkerton Liability to RICO Actions', *Missouri Law Review*, vol. 56, p. 931.
[104] *US v Alvarez*, 625 F.2d 1146 (5th Cir.1981) (D was convicted of conspiracy to import marijuana into U.S., evidence showed that several other individuals made an arrangement with an undercover agent for a marijuana shipment by air. In presence of D, one of the others told the agent that D would unload the shipment in the US and, when the agent asked D if that were so, D nodded. All alleged conspirators, including D were arrested at this moment, and even though D played a very small and isolated role in a drug trafficking operation he was charged with the crimes of much more knowledgeable and involved co-conspirators).
[105] See *Alvernaz v. United States*, 450 U.S. 333, 343 (1981) (a conspiracy to import and to distribute drugs is twice as serious as a conspiracy to do either object singly).
[106] Marcus, P. (1992), 'Criminal Conspiracy Law: Time to Turn Back from an Ever Expanding, Ever More Troubling Area', *Wm. & Mary Bill of Rts Journal*, vol. 1, p. 1.

[107] An attempt, solicitation or conspiracy to commit a (capital crime or a) felony of the first degree is a felony of the second degree. A lower grade or degree of liability can be imposed or prosecution dropped if the conduct is "so inherently unlikely to result or culminate in commission of crime that there is no public danger." Multiple convictions for conduct designed to commit or to culminate in commission of same crime is not allowed.
[108] "In the course of preparation to commit a crime, the act of combining with another is significant both psychologically and practically, the former because it crosses a clear threshold in arousing expectations, the latter because it increases the likelihood that the offense will be committed. Sharing lends fortitude to purpose. The actor knows, moreover, that the future is no longer governed by his will alone; others may complete what he has had a hand in starting, even if he has a change of heart." Model Penal Code § 5.03 comments at 388 (1985).
[109] See *State v. Johnson*, 124 Wash. 2d, 57, 68 (1994).
[110] Model Penal Code § 2.07: Liability of Corporations, Unincorporated Associations and Persons Acting, or Under a Duty to Act, in Their Behalf
[111] Model Penal Code § 2.07 (1). A corporation may be convicted of (a) the commission of an offense if (i) legislative purpose to impose liability on corporation plainly appears, and (ii) the conduct performed by an agent of corporation, (iii) acting on behalf of the corporation, (iv) within the scope of his office or employment, (v) unless otherwise designated...or (b) omission to discharge specific duty of affirmative performance; or (c) commission of offense authorized, requested, commanded, performed or recklessly tolerated by board of directors or by high managerial agent actin in behalf of the corporation within scope of office or employment
[112] Model Penal Code § 2.07 (1) - (7).
[113] RICO was enacted as Title IX of the Organized Crime Control Act, codified as 18 U.S.C. §§ 1961-1968. CCE was enacted as part of the Comprehensive Drug Abuse Prevention and Control Act of 1970, Pub.L. No. 91-513, 84 Stat. 1236 (1970), codified as 21 U.S.C. § 848 (1988).
[114] *United States v. Bledsoe*, 674 F.2d 647 (8th Cir.), cert denied, 459 U.S. 1040 (1982). See also *United States v. Turkette*, 452 U.S. 576 (1981).
[115] The Supreme Court has construed CCE as a "super-conspiracy" offense that subsumes the predicate conspiracy defined by 21 U.S.C. § 846 (1988).
[116] See 18 U.S.C. § 1962 (1988).
[117] See 18 U.S.C. § 1962(a)-(c).
[118] See 18 U.S.C. § 1961(1)(A)(1988) (listing state offenses) and 18 U.S.C. § 1961 (1)(B)-(E) (1988) (listing federal offenses). To perpetrate a substantive federal RICO offense, one must commit at least two predicate offenses within ten years of each other and use this pattern of racketeering activity against an enterprise in a way proscribed by 18 U.S.C. § 1962.
[119] See *Sedima, S.P.R.L. v. Imprex Co., Inc.*, 473 U.S. 479, 496 (1985).
[120] See *H.J. Inc.v. Northwestern Bell Tel. Col*, , 492 U.S. 229, 240 &242.
[121] The initial approach of restricting the statute to an expansion of investigative

tools was soon rejected in favor of the creation of a new, broadly worded substantive crime. See Augustine, R. (1990), 'Introduction to Reforming RICO: If, Why and How?', *Vanderbilt Law Review*, vol. 43, p. 621.

[122] Even the Smith Act, which was designed specifically for members of the Communist Party, does not target Communist party members directly but rather attempts to define in general terms the sort of organization in which membership is prohibited. See 18 U.S.C. § 2385, 2386 (1982).

[123] Lynch, G. E. (1987), 'RICO: The Crime of Being a Criminal, Parts I and II', *Columbia Law Review*, vol. 87, p. 661, 682.

[124] Id. at 681.

[125] See *United States v. Elliott*, 571 F.2d 880 (5th Cir.), cert. denied, 439 U.S. 953 (1978). In the important case of United States v. Elliott, the Supreme Court allowed diverse crimes and defendants to be joined in a single RICO prosecution despite the fact that many of the defendants did not even know each other and were engaged in very different predicate crimes, based on a finding of agreement on an overall objective to further the affairs of the enterprise.

[126] This latter concern is applicable to RICO, which allows the prosecutor flexibility in deciding whether to increase penalties by transforming ordinary offenses into RICO violations.

[127] According to Professor Bradley, "RICO has virtually never been used in a case which was not reachable by other statutes, federal or state, which were on the books prior to its passage." See Bradley, R. (1984), 'Racketeering and the Federalization of Crime', *American Criminal Law Review*, vol. 22, p. 213, 257.

[128] S.2187, 89th Cong., 1st Sess., 111 Cong. Rec. 14,680 (1965).

[129] Lynch suggests that such a departure is already evident in modern techniques of criminal investigation, particularly the investigation of organized crime, and notes an increasing conflict between "proactive" investigations and the "reactive" system of transaction-based justice. See Lynch, G. (1987), 'RICO: The Crime of Being a Criminal, Parts III & IV', *Columbia Law Review*, vol. 87, p. 920, 960 and 969. "Recognizing the importance of context to the gravity of individual criminal acts, increasing the possibility of convicting racketeers who might otherwise slip through the cracks in a transaction-based model of procedure, and utilizing the dramatic context of the criminal trial to educate the public to models of criminal activity more significant than the isolated derelictions of particular individuals are important and appropriate goals for criminal law." See also id. at 971.While he argues that the use of context in assessing guilt is not only an acceptable but "an essential part of what makes the defendant's actions particularly threatening to society," Lynch recognizes the need to consider the ability of the existing procedural framework to handle the innovations introduced by RICO style prosecutions.

[130]Id. at 663.

[131] Lynch, G. (1987), 'RICO: The Crime of Being a Criminal, Parts III & IV', *Columbia Law Review*, vol. 87, p. 920, 935.

[132] Id. at 937.

[133] Goldsmith, M. (1988), 'RICO and Enterprise Criminality: A Response to Gerard E. Lynch', *Columbia Law Review*, vol. 88, p. 774.
[134] Lynch, G. (1987), 'RICO: The Crime of Being a Criminal, Parts III & IV', *Columbia Law Review*, vol. 87, p. 920, 943.
[135] Goldsmith suggests, for example, that the "existence of an enterprise provides a basis for conceptualizing the various crimes as part of one overall conspiracy." Goldsmith, M. (1988), 'RICO and Enterprise Criminality: A Response to Gerard Lynch', *Columbia Law Review*, vol. 88, p. 774, 788.
[136] The statute has been applied to a variety of different patterns of racketeering activity, and over 40 percent of the indictments containing counts under section 1962(c) have involved illegal enterprises. See Lynch, G. (1987), 'RICO: The Crime of Being a Criminal, Parts I and II', *Columbia Law Review*, vol. 87, p. 661, 732.
[137] Se e.g. *United States v. Coonan*, 938 F.2d 1553 (2d Cir. 1991) (affirming RICO conviction of members of the Westies gang, cert denied, 112 S.Ct. 1486 (1992); *United States v. Andrews*, 749 F. Supp. 1520 (N.D.Ill. 1990) (denying motion to dismiss charges against Chicago's El Rukn gang on grounds that RICO unconstitutionally vague). But see e.g. *United States v. Aleman*, 609 F.2d 298, 311 (7th Cir. 1979) (RICO should be applied only to organized crime). See Bonney, L.S. (1993), 'The Prosecution of Sophisticated Urban Street Gangs: A Proper Application of RICO', *Catholic University Law Review*, vol. 42, p. 579.
[138] 571 F.2d 880, 884 (5th Cir.), cert denied, 439 U.S. 953 (1978).
[139] 452 U.S. 576 (1981).
[140] Lynch, G. (1987), 'RICO: The Crime of Being a Criminal, Parts I and II', *Columbia Law Review*, vol. 87, p. 661, 705.
[141] Pub. L. No. 98-473, 98 Stat. 1837 (1984). See also *Russello v. United States*, 464 U.S. 16 (1983) (forfeiture provision of RICO should be expanded to include interest in and profits from illegitimate enterprise). Both the express provision for forfeiture of the proceeds of racketeering activity and of property derived from such proceeds and the "relation back" provisions are important primarily in broadening the scope and effectiveness of forfeitures in prosecution of illegal enterprises.
[142] President's Commission. (1986), *President's Commission On Organized Crime, Report to the President and the Attorney General, The Impact: Organized Crime Today*, pp. 26-29.
[143] *United States v. Coonan*, 938 F.2d 1553 (2d, Cir. 1991).
[144] *United States v. Andrews*, 749 F. Supp. 1520 (N.D.Ill. 1990). This case concerned a gang whose primary business was the distribution of narcotics which provided a daily income ranging from $50,000 to $70,000 which they sustained through the use of violence against rival gangs. See Lesley Bonney, S. (1993), 'The Prosecution of Sophisticated Urban Street Gangs: A Proper Application of RICO', *Catholic University Law Review*, vol. 42, p. 579.
[145] 21 U.S.C. § 848.
[146] 21 U.S.C. § 853(a) (1988) provides that those convicted under § 848 "shall

forfeit to the United States...any property constituting, or derived from, any proceeds the person obtained, directly or indirectly, as the result of such violation," any property used to facilitate the operations of the CCE, and any property or contractual rights representing an interest in or affording control over the CCE. The defendant's assets can sometimes be frozen even before trial.

[147] Skalitzky, W. (1996), 'Aider and Abettor Liability, the Continuing Criminal Enterprise, and Street Gangs: A New Twist in an Old War on Drugs', *Journal of Criminal Law and Criminology*, vol. 81, p. 348, 368.

[148] The crime must be a violation of 21 U.S.C. §§ 801-972, subchapters of Comprehensive Drug Abuse Prevention and Control Act of 1970.

[149] "Series" has been interpreted as three or more related acts, and a violation has been interpreted as offense rather than conviction. In this context they must be violations of federal drug laws, the notion being that CCE is aimed at the continuing activities of a narcotics operation.

[150] "Concert" is interpreted as agreement in design or plan and has been interpreted liberally. The prosecutor is not required to establish the identities of the five individuals or show that the kingpin had personal contact with them, and they need not be active at the same time or in the same jurisdiction.

[151] See *United States v. Bond*, 847 F.2 1233, 1236 (7th Cir. 1988)(indirect supervision can satisfy the management requirement since leaders may rule indirectly in ways that leave few traces). See also *United States v. Alvarez*, 860 F.2d 801, 817 (7th Cir. 1988) (an individual's place in the hierarchy or structure of the organization may be used to establish management or supervision of five or more persons); *United States v. Sisca*, 503 F.2d 1337, 1340 (2nd Cir. 1974) (defendant was the undisputed kingpin of corporate-like criminal enterprise).

[152] Occupying a central role in the production or marketing process has been held sufficient to satisfy the managerial element. See *United States v. Oberski,* 734 F.2d 1030, 1032 n.3 (5th Cir. 1984) (although defendant did not exercise control, his role as main chemist within the organization was sufficient to satisfy organizational element for CCE conviction).

[153] Skalitzky, W. (1996), 'Aider and Abettor Liability, the Continuing Criminal Enterprise, and Street Gangs: A New Twist in an Old War on Drugs', *Journal of Criminal Law and Criminology*, vol. 81, p. 348, 361.

[154] Id. at 363.

[155] 18 U.S.C. § 2(a), Principals, has been applied to 21 U.S.C. § 848, Continuing Criminal Enterprise, in order to hold principal contributors liable for aiding and abetting the operations of an illegal narcotics network.

[156] See *United States v. Ambrose*, 740 F.2d 505 (7th Cir. 1984). In *Ambrose*, ten former Chicago policemen, known as the "Marquette 10," who had provided protection for two large narcotics dealers in exchange for money and drugs, were convicted for aiding and abetting a CCE. The conviction was upheld because the police were not "employees" but rather independent contributors.

[157] While the court in *United States v. Ambrose* adopted a test which applied to all third parties, allowing for sentencing discretion to avoid disporportionate

punishment, the court in *United States v. Pino-Perez* replaced this with a "degree of culpability" test which made the applicability of aider and abettor liability a function of the defendant's degree of culpability. According to *Pino-Perez*, an accomplice who "associated with, participated in, and, by his actions, sought to make the criminal enterprise succeed" may be punished as an aider and abettor, where purposeful intent to make the CCE succeed is a necessary element. See *United States v. Pino-Perez*, 870 F.2d 1230, 1235 (7th Cir. 1989) (drug supplier who supplied gang with substantial drug supply, court held that liability should be made a function of the defendant's degree of culpability).

158 In *United States v. Amen* the court required that all five CCE statutory requirements be met before punishing the defendant, rejecting the application of aider and abettor liability to the CCE. See *United States v. Benevento*, 836 F.2d 60 (2d Cir. 1987) (uncle who provided substantial assistance to his nephew's CCE , including provision of his home and capital to finance narcotics operations, conviction overturned because insufficient evidence of all five statutory elements for conviction).

159 Lynch, S. (1991), 'Drug Kingpins and Their Helpers: Accomplice Liability Under 21 USC Section 848', *University of Chicago Law Review*, vol. 58, p. 391, 414.(suggests a new standard for applying CCE accomplice liability which addresses the concerns lying behind the current court division on this issue).

160 Whether a threshold test of culpability and mandatory minimum sentencing (the Pino-Perez approach) is more effective than broader application of aider and abettor liability coupled with sentencing discretion (the Ambrose approach) will depend on factors such as the ability of kingpins to evade higher penalties through structural rearrangements, the ability to distinguish between independent third parties and employees, and the relative evidentiary burdens.

161 Pub. L. No. 91-513, 84 Stat. 1236 (also known as the Drug Control Act and the Controlled Substances Act).

162 See Reed, R. (1985), 'Criminal Forfeiture Under the Comprehensive Forfeiture Act of 1984: Raising the Stakes', *American Criminal Law Review*, vol. 22, p. 747; and also see Webb, D.K. and Turow, S.F. (1983), 'RICO Forfeiture in Practice, A Prosecutorial Perspective', *University of Cin. Law Review*, vol. 52, p. 404 .

163 Both provisions have been expanded. The Comprehensive Crime Control Act of 1984 expanded RICO's forfeiture provisions to include both interests in and proceeds or profits from illegitimate enterprises and provided for forfeiture of assets upon commission of the RICO violation.Pub. L. No. 98-473, 98 Stat. 1837 (1984). While application of the criminal forfeiture provision introduced under the Drug Control Act was originally restricted to convictions under the CCE statute, the statute was subsequently amended to impose forfeiture upon all defendants convicted of drug felonies. Comprehensive Forfeiture Act of 1984, Pub. L. No. 98-473, sections 301-309, 98 Stat. 1837, 2040-57. The provision is now applied under 21 U.S.C. section 853. For further discussion see Smith, S.D. (1988), 'The Scope of Real Property Forfeiture for Drug-Related Crime Under the Comprehensive Forfeiture Act', *Univ. of Penn. Law Review*, vol. 137, p. 303 (considers the use of

section 853 in the forfeiture of real property, argues that entire parcels should be forfeited even if only a potion was used directly in offense).

[164] Harvard Law Review Association. (1984), 'A Proposal To Reform Criminal Forfeiture Under RICO and CCE', *Harvard Law Review*, vol. 127, p. 1929, 1932.

[165] Id. at 1940.

[166] An alternative to looser procedural requirements for forfeiture is to reduce the scope for evasion through strategies such as an attack on money laundering.

[167] 18 U.S.C.A. § 521 (West Supp. 1995).

[168] See Anderson, D. (1995), 'Jail, Jail, The Gang's All Here: Senate Crime Bill Section 521, The Criminal Street Gang Provision', *Boston College Law Review*, vol. 36, p. 527.

[169] Block, C. and R. (1993), 'Street Gang Crime in Chicago', *National Institute of Justice, Research in Brief*, Dec. 1, p. 3.

[170] Cal. Penal Code § 186.22(a). The eight crimes specified in § 186.22(e) are: assault with a deadly weapon or deadly force, robbery, homicide or manslaughter, trafficking in controlled substances, shooting at an inhabited dwelling or occupied motor vehicle, arson, intimidation of witnesses and grand theft of any vehicle.

[171] Cal. Penal Code §186.20-.27 (Deering Supp. 1992).

[172] Section 186.22(a) of STEP provides: Any person who actively participates in any criminal street gang with knowledge that its members engage in or have engaged in a pattern of criminal gang activity, and who willfully promotes, furthers, or assists in any felonious criminal conduct by members of that gang, shall be punished by imprisonment in the county jail for a period not to exceed one year, or by imprisonment in the state prison for one, two, or three years."

[173] Cal. Penal Code § 186.21 (Preamble).

[174] Cal. Penal Code § 186.22(a).

[175] Cal. Penal Code § 186.22(e).

[176] *In re. Nathaniel C.*, 279 Cal. Rptr. 236, 244 (Ct. App. 1991).

[177] See Molina, A. (1993), 'California's Anti-Gang Street Enforcement and Prevention Act: One Step Forward, Two Steps Back?', *Southwestern University Law Review*, vol. 22, p. 457.

[178] Id. at 465.

[179] *People v. Gamez*, 286 Cal. Rptr. 894 (Ct. Ap. 1991) (STEP neither over-broad nor vague); *People v. Green.*, 227 Cal.App.3d 692 (1991) (statute prohibiting active participation in criminal street gang not unconstitutionally vague under due process clause).

[180] Molina, A. (1993), 'California's Anti-Gang Street Enforcement and Prevention Act: One Step Forward, Two Steps Back?' *Southwestern University Law Review*, vol. 22, p. 457, 471.

[181] See e.g. Illinois Street Gang Terrorism Omnibus Prevention Act, Ill St Ch 740 s 147/10; Colorado Street Terrorism Bill (similar to California's STEP Act); Florida-- F.S.A. s 874.04 (reclassifies penalties for pattern of criminal street gang activity); Georgia - GA ST 16-15-4 (prohibits participation in criminal gang activity, additional punishment on felony conviction); Missouri - MO ST 578.425

(additional punishment for crimes to promote or assist criminal conduct by gangs).

[182] Staff writer. (1996), 'Street gangs can now face added charges', *The Tampa Tribune*, Dec. 14, p. 1.

[183] Kerr, J. (1996), 'Colorado Springs Proposal Would Enhance Crackdown on Gang Membership', *West's Legal News*, Nov. 5.

[184] *State v. Johnson*, 124 Wash. 2d 57 (1994) (Johnson, a BGD member with a history of prior gang-related confrontations, fired a gun at members of a rival gang after a confrontation in which gang signs were flashed). See Rein, L. (1995), 'Washington State Exceptional Sentences for Gang Members: An Analysis of State v. Johnson', *Gonzaga Law Review*, vol. 30, p. 411.

[185] Id. at 419. Expert testimony established that gang members gain reputation within a gang by "perpetrating acts of violence upon police and rival gang members," noting that criminal conducts is an integral part of street gang activity and that its primary focus is to control a geographical area where a "group can exercise a monopoly over drug traffic."

[186] Id. at 418.

[187] Rotella, S. (1991), 'Gangs Question Their Exile From Park', *L.A. Times* (Valley Ed.), September 18, p. B3.

[188] See Ariz.Rev. Stat.Ann. § 13-2301-2308 (1992).

[189] See Nev.Rev.Stat.Ann. § 207.370 (Michie 1992).

[190] Overlap between the two will arise because the RICO predicates are a subset of the felonies that can serve as objectives for a criminal syndicate and because a syndicate could qualify as a RICO enterprise.

[191] See Brenner, S. (1991), 'Of Complicity and Enterprise Criminality: Applying Pinkerton Liability to RICO Actions', *Missouri Law Review*, vol. 56, p. 931.

[192] See Wash.Rev.Code Ann. § 9A.82.060(1), § 9A.82.903, § 9A.82.010(15) (West 1988).

[193] See N.J. Stat.Ann. § 2C:5-29g(West 1992).

[194] See generally *State v. Alexander*, 624 A.2d 48, 50 (N.J. Super.Ct.App.Div. 1993) (leading a narcotics trafficking network versus "such lesser offenses as distributing or conspiring to distribute a controlled dangerous substance").

[195] See Williamson, D. (1990), 'Loitering Law: A Day Without Winners', *Seattle Times*, July 3, p. A10.

[196] See § 8-4-015 of the Chicago Municipal Code.

[197] Chicago, Ill., Mun.Code S 8-4-015 (preamble).

[198] *City of Chicago v. Youkhana*, 660 N.E. 2d 34 (1995).

[199] Poulos, P. (1995), 'Chicago's Ban on Gang Loitering: Making Sense of Vagueness and Overbreadth in Loitering Laws', *California Law Review*, vol. 84, p. 379.

[200] Boga, T.R. (1994), 'Turf Wars: Street Gangs, Local Governments, and the Battle for Public Space', *Harvard Civil Rights Civil Liberties Law Review*, vol. 29, p. 477, 478.

[201] Staff reporter. (1996), 'Praise, court test in anti-gang fight; San Jose uses 19th Century Law', Sacramento Bee, March 4, p. 1A.

[202] *People v. Acuna*, No. H022802.
[203] West's Legal News Staff. (1996), 'Federal Judge Overturns D.C. Curfew Law', *West's Legal News*, November 1.
[204] Staff reporter. (1996), 'New laws clip wings of teenage nighthawks: Curfew violations can now mean loss of driver's licenses for teens', *Los Angeles Times*. May.
[205] West's Legal News Staff. (1996), 'Gang Sweep Tactic Includes Warrantless Searches of Probationers', *West's Legal News*, June 26.
[206] West's Legal News. (1996), 'Police Program Aims to "Knock and Talk" Gangs out of Homes', *West's Legal News*, March 4.
[207] See 1988 amendment to California Penal Code § 272.

2 Modeling Criminal Street Gangs as Organizations

A gang structure can be used to expand both the capacity and the range of criminal activities available to gang members, providing a vehicle for the development of more sophisticated and lucrative criminal business practices. In addition to expanding the criminal capacity of gang members, the gang structure can be used to satisfy a number of non-economic objectives such as status, identity and companionship. The gang operates simultaneously as a business enterprise, a club or social group, a communication network and even in some cases as an extended family. The multiplicity of functions which the gang structure performs, and the ways in which the organization accommodates potentially conflicting objectives, make it an interesting case study in group organization and behavior. This chapter investigates alternative economic approaches towards collective action and joint production that can be used to shed light on different organizational aspects of criminal street gangs. Part I provides a survey of economic approaches towards collective action and team production which can be employed to understand the structure and behavior of criminal street gangs. Understanding how to think about gangs and how to model gang decision making will improve economic modeling of criminal activities and will enhance law enforcement efforts to constrain the dangers posed by criminal gangs. Part II provides an economic model which emphasizes the importance of gangs as agreement enforcing institutions.

Part I: Survey of Economic Approaches to Collective Action with Application to Street Gangs

Street gangs can be viewed as one of many forms of social organization, and interesting parallels can be drawn between gangs and other group enterprises such as firms, social clubs, or even primitive states. Underlying general questions about how to explain the similarities and differences between alternative forms of group enterprise and how to account for the emergence of organizations in some situations but not others are a set of more basic questions concerning how groups should be understood and modeled. Treating the group either as an aggregation of individual decisions or as a single operational unit fails to capture important features of group incentives and group behavior. The search for a satisfactory intermediate position has proven difficult, impeded by the difficulties of balancing individual and social roles within the same decision making framework. This chapter begins by providing an economic perspective on the tensions inherent in collective action and how this tension may play out in different contexts.

I. In Search of an Economic Methodology for Group Behavior

Tension Between Individual and Social Roles and Values

In the traditional economic paradigm of rational decision making, individuals will choose to operate through a collectivity when it offers them opportunities to achieve objectives that could not be obtained individually. Organizations will be developed to exploit the efficiencies of joint production. The nature of the organization will be a product of the information, interests, resources and skills that each individual brings to the group and the mechanisms available for coordinating interests and exploiting synergies in a way which utilizes these skills and resources efficiently. The tension existing between individual interests and social roles determines both the scope and the limitations of the organization.

The natural limits to this endeavor are indicated by economic results which suggest that there cannot be a completely consistent meaning to social value and collective rationality. Schumpeter (1909) addresses the concept of social value at a methodological level, arguing that the notion of social value as an independent unit of analysis has no obvious or natural meaning in a non-communist society.[1] He rejects the notion that economic theory can depart from "individual wants, values and demands and their interaction."[2] It is interesting to note that Marx (1844) adopts the same view with respect to communist societies, arguing that application of the concept would produce an incoherent view of society as an abstraction vis-a-vis the individual.[3] Shumpeter's discussion highlights what continues to be a conceptual difficulty that economists face in departing from an individual-based methodology. The reliance on individual preferences as the basic unit of analysis is particularly problematic in contexts in which group behavior seems to be more than the product of individual needs and wants. In the street gang context, where group identity, status and a network of social support and respect have been identified as important objectives in and of themselves, the individual preferences-collective choice structure seems inadequate to fully capture group dynamics.

Arrow (1974) compares narrow self-interest and collective values as alternative methods of defining the role of the individual in social contexts.[4] The struggle between the exigencies of collective action and the pursuit of individualized objectives operates both at the level of individual conscience and at the level of social behavior. The impact of social norms and stigma on individual behavior provides an example of a situation in which social roles are internalized to create private payoffs from specified behavior. There have been two very different responses at the political level to the tension between individual and social roles, one calling for an idealized picture of socially defined individual roles and the other calling for a more limited role of collective action and the state in order to protect individual autonomy. The tension is reflected in debates over the role of local versus state and federal power. The same approach is applicable to a variety of other contexts, particularly those which involve economic decision making within semi-autonomous, self-regulating groups such as criminal organizations. Organization theorists (such as Cyert and March (1963)) and sociologists (such as Crozier (1967)) have laid the foundation for an organizational theory which occupies this middle ground, emphasizing the importance of individual incentives and group objectives in analyzing organizational behavior.[5]

Mechanisms for Moving from Individual Actions to Joint Outcome

An economic approach can be usefully applied to analyze the mechanisms by which individual decisions are combined to produce joint outcomes. In the neoclassical world of competitive markets, the operation of the price mechanism ensures that actions taken by self-interested, autonomously interacting individuals will have the unintended consequence of producing collective outcomes which are pareto optimal. Adam Smith's "invisible hand" operates to map individual consumption maximizing behavior into collective production and distribution outcomes. The ways in which individual decisions interact to shape collective outcomes become more complex and the consequences of interaction less straightforward as one departs from the competitive market paradigm. Once outside of a situation in which markets are complete and well-working, narrowly self-interested actions taken by individuals do not necessarily generate efficient collective action in even the minimal sense of pareto optimality, and the individual is now called upon to take a more directive role in fashioning opportunities for joint trade or production. Groups of varying size, structure and accessibility will emerge in response to different economic opportunities and distributions of wealth.

Recognizing the importance of social norms in shaping individual behavior in even competitive market situations, John Stuart Mill (1859) saw collective economic behavior as the product of competition and custom.[6] He suggested that room was required in the paradigm of laissez-faire market efficiency for different types of collective decision making and social constraints. Marx took this view to an extreme in his theory of collective economic behavior as the product of class conflict occurring in unstable institutional contexts. Economic outcomes were seen as the product of class conflicts operating within a historically driven economic and social system to shape individual actions. While "institutionalists" such as Veblen and his cohorts shared this emphasis on the formative role of institutions in shaping interaction between individuals, they shifted the focus away from historical determinism and towards the practical nature and functions of bureaucracies in channeling economic activity.

These approaches share a common view of individual choice operating within structures that define the nature of transactions. In the new institutional approach, in contrast, individual actions play an active role in shaping the nature of trading institutions within the context of a broader institutional framework. The new institutional approach focuses on the specific features of the economic problems faced by individuals with potentially overlapping and potentially conflicting interests who can benefit from working together but are limited in their ability to restrict their own and each others actions in order to obtain the benefits from a joint transaction. According to Williamson (1979), transaction costs arising from opportunism, asymmetric information and uncertainty place constraints on joint production opportunities existing between self-interested individuals.[7] Coase (1937) uses the notion of transaction costs (i.e. planning, bargaining and contracting costs) to explain the division of activities between the market and the firm, where the firm is characterized by the use of authority.[8] For transactions which are removed from the market, questions arise as to the division of authority between participants and how this division affects the incentives of each participant. Principal-agent theory focuses on the incentive problems involved in joint production in the presence of information asymmetries and divergent interests.[9] Alchian and Demsetz (1972) argue that non-separablilities in production, and the free-rider problems that they create, are key to understanding organizational design. They adopt a principal-agent type theory of the firm based on the need for independent monitoring of effort contributions in a situation of joint production.[10] Contract theory provides a related set of explanations about when and how individuals are able to form mutually beneficial agreements, and incomplete contracting theories emphasize factors such as the role of reputation in repeated play and the importance of residual control rights over productive assets in determining a priori investment patterns.[11]

Game theory introduces the role of strategic planning and use of information into group interactions. Individuals act in a self-interested manner based on the expectations they have about the actions that other members will take and the consequences of deviating from shared guidelines. The rules which constrain group interaction (e.g. information constraints and feasible choice sets) and the strategies which will promote individual interests in this interaction become the focus of the model. Cooperation, where it emerges, is the product of competition between individuals who are choosing their actions strategically to accomplish individual goals. Evolutionary theories of cooperative behavior explain the development of socially efficient norms of behavior over time based on the notion that populations are behaving "strategically" in the sense that they will develop in ways which take advantage of profitable opportunities over the long run. Binmore offers an intermediate approach that focuses on the evolution of social norms as forms of coordinating activities, viewing cooperation as an organizing principle.

Rather than exploring notions of social value and social preferences, most collective choice theorists start with the premise that social choices should depend upon individual preferences and should satisfy similar properties. The theory of collective choice focuses on ways in which individual needs, wants and interests are combined to produce social choices. Alternative methods of collective decision making are established by imposing different rules on methods of moving from individual preferences to social outcomes. The ability to establish even very basic consistency properties from collective decision making has been called into question by collective choice theorists, however. Arrow (1951) takes individuals' orderings over the set of social states to be the basic components of collective choice.[12] He focuses on collective choice rules which make the preference ordering of the society a function of individual preference orderings, and demonstrates that there is no collective choice rule (no rule that specified social orderings based on individual orderings) which simultaneously satisfies what seem to be four reasonable restrictions (i.e. conditions of unrestricted domain, the weak Pareto principle, non-dictatorship and the independence of irrelevant alternatives).[13] This "General Possibility Theorem" calls into question the coherence of moving from individual preferences to group choices without significant additional constraints on the context of and rules for decision making.

II. Application of Economic Organization Theories to Street Gangs

A criminal gang can be defined as a group of individuals who work together on a repeated basis within a set of shared guidelines or rules and use group assets to engage in income generating criminal activities. A criminal street gang is distinguished by its close connection to a particular geographic location, its visibility as a distinct group, and the multiple functions which it performs. Members are drawn from teen-agers and young adults who live in the neighborhood, and these members band together to establish territorial control over some part of their neighborhood. The gang operates as a mechanism for satisfying individual needs through joint action and interaction in an environment with substantial limitations on resources and information. It provides both economic benefits, in the form of information about and increased capacity to perform income generating crimes, and non-economic benefits, in the form of status, identity, companionship and protection. Gang members have individual interests which are partially overlapping and partially conflicting. Team problems arise when the divergence of interests leads individuals to engage in opportunistic behaviors such as under-investment in group activities which hinder the exploitation of group benefits. The problems are exacerbated by constraints on the organizational responses that street gangs have available to control opportunistic behavior. Important characterizing features of the criminal street gang as a distinctive form of organization include: (1) gang identity and membership externalities, (2) self-enforcement of agreements and punishment, (3) informal networks for communication and information transfer; (4) external threats imposed on gang activities by rival groups and law enforcement, and (5) reliance on the gang structure to perform multiple functions. These features play important roles in shaping the joint production possibilities available to criminal street gang. This section employs theories of economic organization to shed light on empirical features and patterns of gang structure and behavior.[14] The theories are organized in terms of their ability to explain particular features of the gang. Attention is paid to the ways in which the gang structure accommodates competing objectives and to the possibilities for achieving the same objective in different ways. A summary of the main theories and their role in explaining gang structure and behavior is provided in Table One. The table lists the main types of economic theories that this chapter explores and connects these theories with some general characteristics of gangs.

Table One

Summary of Theories

(1) Club Theory
(2) Membership Externalities
(3) Team Production
(4) Reputation and Commitment
(5) Common Pool Resources
(6) Group Stability
(7) Common Preferences / Utility
(8) Syndicates
(9) Social & Economic Networks
(10) Economics of Conflict

Gang Characteristics	**Theories**	**Approaches**
Identity, Membership Externalities	(1),(2)	
Self-Enforcing Systems	(3),(4),(5)	cooperative / non-coop.
(a) Commitment	(1),(4),(5)	static / repeated
(b) Punishment Schemes	(4),(5)	
(c) Group Stability	(6)	
System of Communication	(7),(8),(9)	observable /unobservable
External Threats	(6), (10)	internal /external source of of cohesion
(a) Rival Gangs		
(b) Law Enforcement		
Performance of Multiple Functions		
(a) Competing Objectives	(5)	
(b) Complementarities	(1), (2), (9)	

Gang Identity and Membership Externalities

Club Theory: Participation Benefits and Membership Restrictions

Street gangs share a number of similarities with clubs, both in terms of the use of membership restrictions to address problems of moral hazard and adverse selection, and in terms of the ways in which gang members benefit from interaction as an identifiable group. A club is characterized by membership criterion and a group-based production technology. It is composed of a group of individuals with compatible objectives who form an identifiable group from which non-members are excluded. Different groups have different matching criteria and production technologies, and club-theoretic problems take the form of concerns about the efficiency of group composition (a matching problem) and optimal group size (a technology problem). In the standard club-theoretic framework a coalition of agents assemble to engage in production, generating and distributing surplus subject to technological constraints. Club membership rules and requirements can be used to maximize the surplus generating opportunities of the group.

Iannaccone (1992) models religion as a club good that displays positive returns to "participatory crowding."[15] The analysis focuses on the collective nature of certain activities in which individual benefits are increasing in the average level of inputs and inputs are intrinsically difficult or costly to monitor. Each member's participation confers benefits on the other members, and the central problem is to ensure a sufficiently high average level of participation. The model explains costly behavioral restrictions attached to membership as a rational response to free-rider problems arising where participation is costly and generates positive externalities. Membership restrictions can be used to increase the relative cost of engaging in non-group activities and to deter entry by less enthusiastic participants.[16] In Iannaccone's model team production problems surface because people benefit from belonging to groups with average participation levels higher than their own and because they ignore external benefits when making individual input decisions. The same forces are at work in gang membership. The collective character of many gang activities, such as investment in a group reputation, can lead to free-rider problems. Costly behavioral restrictions on membership can be used as a substitute for alternative methods of monitoring and enforcing participation. Examples of such restrictions include painful initiation rituals, forcing new members to commit crimes, and use of graffiti and intra-gang fights to affirm continuing group solidarity. The visibility of gang membership plays an important role in reducing the availability and benefits of non-group activities. Group identity and commonality of interests is protected by restricting membership to individuals who live in the same neighborhood and share the same cultural and ethnic background. Gangs are both the "initiators of membership and the gatekeepers, deciding who will join and who will not."[17] The gang has an interest in ensuring that individuals who appear to be affiliated with the gang actually are gang members, since their behavior may have effects on the gang reputation.

The problem of determining optimal club size arises where there are costs as well as benefits from participation, in which case a balancing of scale economies and congestion costs is required. Cornes and Sandler

(1984) provide a description of a general, variable utilization rate club which includes an analysis of "participatory crowding" and congestion costs.[18] In the context of illegal organizations, law enforcement may operate as a constraint on group size, and the risks of individual transactions may at some point begin to increase with the size of the criminal organization. In the context of drug sales facilitated through the use of a shared reputation, the gang must compare the cost of increasing local competition with the benefits of a potentially larger reputation.

Legros and Newman (1995) adopt a model with a structure similar to those used in club theory.[19] The features of this model capture many of the structural problems arising in a criminal organization. A firm is modeled as a coalition of agents who assemble to engage in production, contributing effort and investment capital to a joint venture whose production capabilities are subject to technological and incentive compatibility constraints. Effort can only be observed if a fixed monitoring cost is incurred (creating a moral hazard problem) and borrowing is subject to a costly state verification problem (creating a problem of asymmetric information). Both of these agency problems could be resolved if agents within the firm had enough wealth to post incentive bonds and engage in self-financing. Where incentives vary with the level of an agent's wealth, the production possibilities of the firm will vary with agent type (i.e. wealth). Depending on the cost of borrowing, the firm may consist of one type of agent and inefficient organization or many types of agents and more efficient organization. Similarly, wealth constraints and imperfect screening criteria play important constraining roles in the operations of criminal organizations. Street gangs tend to be racially and ethnically homogenous and membership is typically limited to those who live in the same location even when the gang might gain from diversification. In place of performance bonds, individuals (and sometimes their immediate family members) are subject to the threat of physical punishment and are forced to undertake criminal activities in order to incriminate themselves.

Membership Externalities and Feed-back Effects

The number of people involved in gang organizations and in criminal activities can have important feed-back effects on the risks and benefits of gang membership. A larger membership expands criminal networks and illegal markets and may reduce the individual risk of apprehension where gangs expand more quickly than law enforcement capabilities. The prevalence of gangs in a particular area may also affect the risks of no gang affiliation, encouraging the formation of new gangs as a protective response. Social attitudes influence and are influenced by the level and nature of gang activity. The models of "social contagion" and "social osmosis" described below capture some of the ways in which these types of membership externalities might affect the rate of expansion and proliferation of gangs and the high concentration of gang activities in particular locations.

Minniti (1995) examines the "privileges of membership" in the Mafia by focusing on the large number of participants and the self-perpetuating character of the organization as key defining features.[20] She argues that the development of a Mafia-like organization results from a large scale shock to the social system which pushes it from a low-crime to a high-crime equilibria taken in combination with the existence of a network externality created by those belonging to the organization. A shock large enough to secure a critical membership level puts in motion a self-reinforcing dynamic captured by a non-linear path-dependent stochastic process which maps proportion of Mafia to population into probability of new membership. In this group dynamic, which she terms "social contagion", as the number of Mafia participants grows the relative influence of the Mafia goes up and the relative returns to legitimate activity decline, resulting in further membership increases. Her model suggests that policies which do not push membership in a criminal organization below a certain critical level will have only transitory effects. This phenomenon has been observed in law enforcement strategies which involve individual prosecution and targeting of specific gang locations. The limited nature of these strikes makes only a temporary dent in the operations of all but the smallest and most loosely organized gangs.

Sah (1991) introduces a model of "social osmosis" which suggests the presence of similar feed-back effects.[21] In this model the effects work through changes in probability assessments about the likelihood and expected magnitude of punishment. Individuals base their expectations about the cost of crime on the number of crimes they observe and the extent to which these crimes are punished, updating their assessments in response to new information. If entry into illegal markets increases faster than the rate of incarceration, then the expectation of punishment will fall even if the overall level of incarceration increases. Moreover, where the frequency of incarceration goes up in a particular population, the stigma and perceived cost of spending time in jail is likely to fall. Both of these models highlight the importance of the local environment in determining the perceived payoffs from gang participation and suggest the role of local concentration of gang members in perpetuating new cycles of gang activities.

The importance of concentration and feed-back effects in increasing criminal activity have been well documented by gang sociologists. The basic notion shared by most leading gang theorists is that criminal street gangs are at least in part the product of poverty and joblessness concentrated in racially, socially and economically segregated neighborhoods.[22] The feed-back effect of incarceration on gang activity can lead to an increase in the crime level of already troubled neighborhoods while simultaneously reducing the mobility of crime prone individuals out of these neighborhoods. The disproportionate effect of drug crime sentencing on racial minorities exacerbates racial hostilities and reinforces the boundaries surrounding criminal groups. Over time the economic and social networks in these areas become dominated by participants in street crimes and members of street gangs who provide role models for new generations of gang members. Because of both internal and external barriers to mobility, the local environment for many gang members consists of an isolated group of individuals in a concentrated area, and this forced interaction tends to increase the similarity of interests and the cohesion of gang members, contributing to further social breakdown.

The way in which a neighborhood gang develops will depend in part upon the degree to which the neighborhood is dependent on the economic activities of street gangs (either as supported family members or as customers) and in part on the inability of the neighborhood to exercise social control. Both of these factors are positively related to the level of gang activity.[23] Wilson (1987) has advanced the well-known argument that poverty and joblessness have contributed to a pathological and self-perpetuating process of social breakdown and the formation of a "ghetto underclass." He presents a picture of social disorganization in minority dominated inner cities which he attributes to the interaction between poverty and economic organization. According to Wilson, if "strong norms and sanctions against aberrant behavior, a sense of community, and positive neighborhood identification are the essential features of social organization in urban areas, inner-city neighborhoods today suffer from a severe lack of social organization."[24] The "ghetto underclass" is seen as the product of a changing economy which offers fewer job opportunities for unskilled workers, a polarization of labor markets into low-wage and high-wage sectors, job relocation out of inner cities, and a changing social composition in ghetto neighborhoods. These factors feed on each other to create further social breakdown via what Wilson terms "concentration effects" - negative reinforcement of conditions arising from localized poverty, joblessness and lack of role models, and the removal of "social buffers" - support for neighborhood institutions provided by a sufficient number of working and middle-class families. The presence of street gangs in these communities is seen as an inevitable response to social breakdown and an attempt to create alternative social networks.

Structuring Individual Transactions to Achieve Joint Objectives

Team Production Problems

An alternative approach is to focus on the ways in which individuals structure their transactions with each other in order to achieve a common objective. Principal-agent theories and contract theory focus on the question of how individuals with conflicting interests can organize their actions in order to exploit the benefits of joint production. Principal-agent theory focuses on the incentive problems involved in joint production in the presence of information asymmetries and divergent interests.[25] Mirllees (1976) adopts a view of the organization as a group of people (or roles) within which a structure of authority is defined.[26] He looks at the optimal structure of incentives and control over decision variables within an organization in which self-interested members who have diverse interests take independent but related decisions, exploring the consequences of uncertainties of production activity and supervision for payment structures and feasible outcomes.

Team production problems arise when there are multiple agents who produce a joint output and their actions are unobservable and inseparable. Alchian and Demsetz (1972) describe the team production problem as one of metering inputs and rewards where individual contributions to a joint output are non-separable.[27] They suggest that the solution to team production problems is to appoint a residual claimant to specialize in monitoring the inputs of team members. This approach overlooks a number of problems that are particularly likely to arise in the context of street gangs. In the absence of enforceable property rights there will be no residual control rights to confer to the monitor as incentives, and inputs are likely to be difficult and risky to measure. Penalty schemes will generally require group participation, and the danger of collusion between the monitor and individual members will further impede effective enforcement. The traditional team monitoring story is thus inadequate to account for the operations of criminal street gangs.

Holmstrom (1982) suggests that the role of the principal is one of budget breaking rather than active monitoring. He shows that a pareto-optimal outcome can be achieved by appointing a third party who breaks the budget by penalizing team members when output falls below the pareto-optimal level (or rewarding them when output reaches this level).[28] In the context of a street gang, the leader faces fewer constraints on the severity of punishments available to "break the budget constraint." These punishments will require costly group participation, however, creating problems of enforcement. Moreover, the scheme may not be immune to collusion between leader and individual gang members. Eswaran and Kotwal (1984) demonstrate that the penalty scheme may not work when the principal can make side-contracts with individual agents if he stands to gain when output falls below the prescribed level.[29] Thus, while the availability of coercion in illegal organizations can be employed as a budget breaker, this approach provides only part of the story.

Itoh (1991) studies moral hazard problems in multi-agent, multi-task situations where production of separable tasks can be performed either individually or with help from others and team production emerges as the result of interdependent incentive schemes.[30] Each agent must choose effort to devote to his own task and "helping effort" devoted to the tasks of other agents based on the incentive scheme offered, where payment depends only on task outcomes.[31] The effort choice affects the probability of success in the task. This model describes a situation in which a centralized incentive structure is necessary to exploit the benefits of cooperation and in which the ability to exploit these benefits is limited by imperfect observation. This situation is analogous to that faced by gang members who would benefit from mutual cooperation but are limited in their ability to ensure reciprocity of benefits.

While the principal-agent models discussed above provide a useful starting point for identifying incentive problems in team production and organizational responses to these problems, they are most directly applicable to situations in which there is a clear authority structure and control over assets. In the case of street gangs there are often no individual property rights over the organization's productive assets, and to the extent that monitoring or punishment occurs, it must take a form which involves self-enforceable group participation. The repeated nature of group interaction plays an important role in defining outcomes which static principal-agent models fail to capture.

Commitment and Reputation in Repeated Games

Gang members do not have access to legally enforceable contracts and must therefore rely on a system of self-policing. The problems arising from a lack of third party enforcement are compounded by the absence of clearly defined property rights over key group assets, such as the gang's reputation and market territory. With joint proprietary interests over group assets and joint control over penalty schemes, participation in punishment schemes must be individually rational for a sufficiently large sub-group. Self-enforcing agreements can be sustained in a variety of different ways. These include preserving a reputation for honest dealings in multi-market or multi-period situations, group penalties in indefinitely repeated games and mutual monitoring of performance.

Standard repeated game models focus on repeated versions of the prisoner's dilemma and search for opportunities for departing from an inefficient single period outcome. Cooperation is sustained through the use of threats to revert to a non-cooperative (nash equilibrium) outcome for a given number of periods in response to observed deviations from an agreed upon outcome. Stigler (1964) provides a general theory of self-policing collusion in which firms are able to sustain cooperative industry performance as the result of non-cooperative individual actions either by making it unprofitable for individual firms to act opportunistically or by threatening to punish deviations. Green and Porter (1984) provide an example of non-cooperative collusion in the face of demand uncertainty via the use of trigger strategies.[32] In this model the demand uncertainty faced by a cartel of firms seeking to restrict unobservable individual output levels results in periodic price wars even though in equilibrium none of the firms overproduce.

Stock Assets in Repeated Games While repeated games generally do not allow for state variables, Benhabib and Radner (1992) demonstrate that efficient resource use is obtainable in an infinitely repeated game using history dependent strategies and allowing for the presence of a stock asset which changes in response to players' actions.[33] They focus on a situation in which self-interested players jointly exploit a productive asset using trigger strategies to prevent over-exploitation. In the street gang context, gang members invest in group resources such as a reputation and a market territory, and strategies must be developed to ensure efficient use of these shared resources. Dutta and Sundaram (1993) demonstrate that history dependency is not essential in order to avoid overexploitation of resources.[34] They demonstrate that overexploitation of common property resources need not result in a Markov-Perfect equilibrium formed by strategies which are based on stock levels of the asset. The state of the asset proxies for the previous history of actions. In a situation of covert illegal activities, gang members will be able to condition their investment strategies on changes in gang reputation.

Private Systems of Monitoring While allowing for uncertainty, most repeated game models assume imperfect information about a public variable that is influenced by private actions. This assumption is problematic in the context of illegal markets which lack the same systems of information transmission. An alternative to the assumption of imperfect public information is to consider situations in which individuals receive different private signals. Ben-Porath (1996) considers a repeated game of private monitoring in which individuals operate in small teams to produce a joint output and the actions of each player can be observed and reported on only by other members of the team.[35] He shows that a cooperative outcome can be sustained through private monitoring and reporting as long as there are at least three team members. Accurate reporting is achieved by punishing both reporting players when the reports made are incompatible, and cooperative actions are sustained by punishing observed deviations. The private monitoring scheme presumes that there exists an enforceable penalty structure. Private monitoring schemes will play a key role in illegal organizations. Peer monitoring can be used to reduce the cost of acquiring and transmitting information. The feasibility of the system will depend upon the ability to provide incentives to make truthful reports and the existence of self-enforcing penalty systems for those who cheat or make inaccurate reports.

Reputation as a Commitment Device Gang identity can be viewed as a renewable and depreciable group controlled asset which persists in the face of membership turnover. Street gangs devote substantial resources to establishing a group identity. This includes establishing membership criteria and systems of recruitment and adopting distinctive patterns of dress, code words and hand signals. Group activities are generally centered around a particular location, or "turf", and these activities, which include loitering and socializing, enhance the visibility of group identity. Investing in an identity provides the basis for a reputation which is visible to potential entrants, competitors and illegal market participants. The group reputation serves as a commitment mechanism which facilitates illegal market transactions and deters entry. Reputation plays an important role in repeated game settings where previous history can be used to determine current actions. Bull (1987) provides a useful model of self-enforcing implicit contracts in the context of labor markets which can be generalized to the gang setting.[36] In this model, implicit wage contracts which promise last period bonuses to hard workers are sustained through intra-firm labor market reputations in situations where third party enforcement is unavailable due to information asymmetries. The situation is complicated by the relatively short employee life-span and the relatively long duration of the firm. In the context of gangs, reputation plays a key role in sustaining illegal agreements in the absence of third party enforcement. Reputation effects may operate through uncertainty about gang characteristics (such as degree of toughness) or simply through the effect of internalizing the future costs of current actions (such as selling high quality products) on current period payoffs. The relatively longer life-span of the organization in comparison to the membership life-span of individual members makes group investments in a group reputation more profitable, particularly if some sort of extended reward system can be established for gang members who exit.

Self-enforceability The self-enforceability of punishment schemes is a key requirement in illegal organizations. Bernheim and Peleg (1987) develop a sufficient condition for self-enforceability of agreements made in non-cooperative environments by individuals who cannot make binding commitments but who can communicate.[37] They argue that while the Nash best-response property (i.e. agreements in which each player is doing the best he can taking the actions of others as given) is necessary for self-enforceability, it is not sufficient because of the scope for mutually beneficial deviations by groups of individuals. They introduce the concept of a coalition-proof nash equilibrium in which the resulting agreement is required to be pareto efficient within the class of self-enforcing agreements (i.e. agreements from which deviation will not be profitable for any coalition).[38] Only deviations which are themselves self-enforcing are considered. This type of restriction is appropriate in environments such as those characterizing illegal organizations, where the scope for internal communication is broad but the ability to bind individual actions is limited.

Limitations Standard repeated games are sensitive to assumptions about the expected time horizon of play and do not easily accommodate changing time horizons. Their reliance on trigger strategies to induce cooperation in the presence of uncertainty further limits their applicability to street gangs. A structure which is based on reversion to a minimum non-cooperative outcome for a certain length of time in response to cheating does not fit easily into a context in which trigger strategies may produce permanent costs. It also presumes the existence of a non-cooperative nash equilibrium outcome and the presence of a self-enforcing penalty structure to punish deviators. The standard literature on repeated games can be employed to show that cooperation can be sustained through the threat of sanctions in an indefinitely repeated game of full information as long as discount rates are sufficiently low or the probability of future interaction is sufficiently high. In illegal organizations the discount rate is likely to be high, due to the risk of apprehension by law enforcement or attack by rival gangs, and the probability of future interaction is likely to be low due to limitations on the ability of criminals to make themselves easily identifiable and to commit to remaining in a particular location. Thus, while repeated interaction plays a key ingredient in gang organization, more explanation is needed as to how cooperation is sustained.

The specter of a "tragedy of the commons" situation surfaces where there is unregulated social use of limited natural resources or "local commons" such as forests, water and fish stocks. In the absence of private property rights to limited resources, uncoordinated individual usage based on narrow self-interest could lead to the degradation and even the extinction of the resource despite the fact that all of the users would be better off by jointly restricting their usage. The notion that a "tragedy of the commons" is somehow inevitable where local commons are neither privately owned nor appropriated or regulated by the government has been challenged on both empirical and theoretical grounds. There are a large number of case studies documenting cooperative management of local commons.[39] Examples include the informal management of Maine lobster fisheries by local fishermen through the use of private (and often illegal) enforcement actions designed to keep out outsiders, as documented by J. M. Acheson (1993), and the management of common forests and pastures by Himalayan villagers in India using local counsels and informal social norms and customs backed by social disapproval of violations, as described by Somanathan (1991).[40] Given the prevalence of situations in which there is sustainable use of local commons, interesting questions arise as to when and how such situations occur. The basic ideas can be applied to explain the ability of criminal street gangs to coordinate the use of and investments in shared resources such as gang "turf" and market contacts. The gang structure is designed to ensure concentrated interaction with at least a sub-group of other gang members, and this repeated interaction provides the basis for developing and enforcing group norms regarding joint investments and resource use. Repeated game strategies offer little in the way of specific predictions about the form of group coordination and the type of agreement which will emerge, however, and they are overly sensitive to assumptions about the time horizon of the game, the information available to group members and the feasibility of penalty schemes.

Ostrom (1990) adopts an institutional approach to self-organization and self-governance in "CPR" (common pool resource) situations and tries to identify certain factors which facilitate cooperative resource use.[41] She frames the problem as one of understanding how "a group of principals...can organize themselves to solve the problems of institutional supply, commitment, and monitoring." Ostrom argues for the need to connect theories of collective action with instances of collective action in CPR situations using a framework of institutional choice which rests upon a set of design principles illustrated by long-enduring CPR institutions and a set of variables which influence the scope for successful design and implementation of a CPR institution.[42] These variables include the number of decision makers, the minimum number of participants necessary to derive the group benefits, the discount rate in use, similarities of interests, and the presence of participants with substantial leadership or other assets.[43] Participants have the choice of pursuing existing norms or introducing changes that will alter the CPR structure. Their choices are shaped by a number of different situational variables that include monitoring and enforcement technologies, shared norms, information about other opportunities, legitimacy of existing rules and benefits of proposed rules. The criminal street gang can be seen as a CPR situation in which the common resource takes the form of a joint reputation, a shared location, community support (if any) and any other resources available in a demarcated geographical area. Street gangs must manage the use of jointly owned assets (here construed as a reputation) in the absence of private property rights and legally enforceable agreements, relying instead on their own set of rules and norms of behavior. The gang structure increases the probability and the intensity of repeated interaction between relatively small groups of individuals, features which Ostrom (1990) identifies as important factors in establishing social norms for efficient resource use. Vigil and Yun (1996) emphasize the importance of the local community and the role of ethnic and cultural forces in shaping gang behavior.[44] The situational factors that Ostrom identifies can be applied to these contexts to analyze the process of institutional development and change within specific types of communities.[45]

Sethi and Somanathan (1996) examine the problem of cooperative use of common pool resources within an evolutionary-game-theoretic framework in which long run gains are exploited through evolutionary selection of higher payoff strategies.[46] They demonstrate that cooperative behavior guided by norms of restraint and punishment may be stable even in the face of narrowly self-interested behavior. By assuming that the proportion of individuals choosing a particular behavior increases when the payoff to that behavior is larger than the average payoff in the population and decreases otherwise, they are able to demonstrate the existence of a stable cooperative equilibrium in which cheats are deterred . The stability of the outcome depends upon initial proportions of cheats and enforcers in the population and upon the cost of adhering to cooperative norms given different resource stock levels and other factors. This framework suggests a way of viewing the development of group norms over time which may be helpful in understanding how street gangs have been able to sustain cooperative outcomes, although some of the assumptions made are in conflict with traditional ways of thinking about rational individual choice. The discussion of threshold effects is relevant in situations where the ability to sustain cooperative outcomes via a reputation is dependent upon the proportion of gang members who are likely to cheat and the initial value of the reputation "stock." Group penalties which affect the stock variable could have long lasting effects. Below a certain reputation level it may be impossible for the gang to attract new members and withstand attack from rival gangs, and the net benefits from cooperative investments will drop, leading to further disinvestment. These threshold effects could explain the variable mortality rate observed for different street gangs.

Coalitions and Collusion

Group Stability

D'Aspremont and Gabszewicz (1985) provide an abstract framework for collusive arrangements which tries to capture the effects on the stability of cooperative arrangements of two opposing tendencies, the first arising from "the recognition by individual participants of the collective advantage of co-ordination" and the second "from the evidence that this co-ordination may not be immune against advantageous recontracting by some of the participants."[47] A collusive arrangement is created when a set of individuals form a group and delegate decision making rights to a single decision unit which represents their interests. An effective group is one in which outcomes reflect the decisions made by this single unit. The stability of a collusive scheme can be evaluated by examining the outcomes associated with alternative feasible schemes, including both "internal" comparisons of payoffs for a given collusive scheme and "external" comparisons between alternative schemes.[48] Institutional factors and the nature of the group decision process will determine the feasible set, and a stable group in this context is one in which the cooperative outcome does not leave any sub-group with the ability and incentive to deviate and form its own agreement and does not leave any outsiders with the ability and incentive to enter and disturb the existing coalition.[49] D'Aspremont et. al. (1983) examine the emergence of a stable coalition in the oligopoly context, introducing the concept of a stable cartel and providing a framework for examining the endogenous formation of coalition structures in a price leadership model, demonstrating the existence of a stable cartel.[50] This corresponds to the observation of both gangs and independent sellers operating simultaneously in illegal markets and suggests a framework for analyzing gang size. Thoron (1995) looks beyond the formation of a cartel to examine coalition deviations, using a "coalition-proof nash equilibrium" concept to define and identify conditions under which a coalition-proof stable cartel will emerge as the unique equilibrium of the game.[51]

This same approach could be applied to analyze the stability of a drug selling gang. Maintaining the cohesion of the gang is an ongoing problem where enforcement schemes must be self-enforceable, opportunities for opportunistic behavior are extensive, and important decisions must be made covertly. The relationships between different sub-groups of gang members and between the gang and other groups must be examined in light of the relative payoffs from alternative feasible coalitions.[52] Cultural differences, including relationships between gang and community and degree of territoriality, may influence the set of feasible mechanisms and can account for some of the observed structural differences between gangs of different ethnic and racial origins.

Since they are involved in illegal activities, gang members do not have recourse to legally enforceable contracts or property rights over resources connected with their membership or their criminal activities. The group must therefore develop its own system of rule making and its own methods of enforcement. The range of penalties available for use in enforcement is not limited in the same way as legal penalties are, and physical coercion plays an important disciplinary role. The potential for strong coalitions within the gang to form and expropriate the resources of marginal gang members may lead to internal instability. The effects of this instability become evident in situations in which the existing pattern of authority within a gang, or between rival gangs, is disturbed, as suggested by observations of escalating violence during periods of leadership turnover and shifts in the balance of power between local gangs.

Organizational design must be sensitive not only to the scope for opportunistic behavior by individuals, but also to the opportunities available to sub-groups within the organization. Tirole (1986) suggests that organizations can be seen as "a network of contracts that interplay."[53] He presents a three-tier principal/supervisor/agent model which illustrates the danger of collusion between the agent and his supervisor where they can exploit an informational advantage to the detriment of the principal.[54] Tirole searches for a coalition-proof final allocation, defined as a final allocation resulting from the optimizing behavior of parties given all contracts and side contracts such that the coalition cannot increase its aggregate payoff by changing a variable under its control. This model reflects the more general point that coalitions emerge between parties that can influence the information received by the rest of the agency to their own advantage. Multi-agent models raise the additional concern of collusion among agents against the principal. It can be shown that where side contracting does not introduce new information, it will never leave the principal better off since it adds additional incentive constraints without increasing the set of feasible contracts. Collusion based on shared information not held by the principal may increase the set of feasible outcomes, however, by opening up opportunities for peer monitoring and mutual insurance.[55] They can be formed in a variety of ways, including the use of covert transfers of money, manipulation of information and manipulation of outcomes. Collusion is driven by reciprocity of benefits between members of an organization who can exploit the organizational design to the advantage of the collusive sub-group. The presence of coalitions has important effects on organizational structure and on the stability and efficiency of the organization.

The premium on information transfer and the presence of covert transactions increases the likelihood of collusion in larger street gangs. Organizational responses include restrictions on discretion in individual decision making and the use of multiple systems of monitoring. Emphasis on internal systems of achieving status and respect within the organization, particularly those which involve some degree of competition between members, can be used to reduce the risk of collusion. The danger of collusion can explain the prevalence of cliques within the larger gangs. Tasks that involve substantial discretion can be left to sub-units where monitoring and policing will be easier and the scope for colluding smaller.

Systems of Communication and Information Use

Common Preferences or Joint Utility

One approach to the study of joint production is to focus on groups of individuals who have common preferences. This approach was developed by Marschak and Radner (1972), who provide a "theory of teams" based on groups of individuals with common preferences.[56] Marschak and Radner concentrate primarily on the consequences of the diversity of information available to members of a team who have common preferences. Marschak (1955) and Bowers (1965) consider the case of a team in which members have a joint utility function and examine circumstances under which this utility function satisfies certain efficiency and consistency properties.[57] Ways of factoring diverse market information into group decisions will be of importance to gang members over at least a limited range of decisions affecting group survival.

The gang structure can be employed to increase the range of decisions over which gang members have common preferences. Street gangs devote resources to the creation of a team-like structure, investing in a group identity and culture and using dress codes and other methods to make membership visible and clearly defined. Gang identity narrows the divergence between individual and group interests by increasing interdependence of actions and interests through time spent together performing similar activities and through the development of group norms and shared resources. An internal status system provides one way of increasing the overlap of preferences.[58] Prominent gang researcher Spergel (1995) emphasizes the central role played by the need for recognition, identity and status in driving gang membership, arguing that this need "is achieved through delinquent or violent activity that must be based on gang norms, involve group support and contribute to or grow out of group cohesion...(e)ach gang member seeks status through types of behavior that must be meaningful to members of his gang and members of opposing gangs."[59] This method of organizing internal relationships and providing internal incentive schemes can enhance the ability of the gang to function as a team. Competition engendered between rival street gangs reinforces the team identity.

Reliance on a shared objective function as an explanation of group activity imposes an artificial unity of interests on individual players which is unlikely to hold in most settings, however, including that of the criminal street gang. In the context of a sports team, for example, the rules of the game impose a common objective on team members which can be achieved only by cooperative actions. The rules are designed to provide members with a common ranking of alternative actions and the discontinuity in the payoff function (i.e. the win or lose outcome) increases the weight placed on cooperative actions. But the mobility and the divergence in prestige and pay of different team members and the private costs of generating team benefits drive a wedge between individual and group interests which the assumption of common preferences cannot accommodate. Similarly, while members of a street gang share the common objective of protecting their territory and reputation, this shared interest is insufficient to protect against opportunistic behavior in situations where being the first to deviate is profitable or being the last to deviate is very unprofitable. Moreover, when the decision becomes one of how much costly investment to make in a joint outcome, rather than how to rank a set of alternative outcomes, unified decision making breaks down. Team theories are most useful in the negative sense of illustrating problems inherent in joint decision making under uncertainty and in the normative sense of exploring the implications of complete identity (via joint utility) for decision making.

Syndicates

Theories of "syndicates" are targeted at loosely associated groups of individuals with their own preferences and independent utilities who engage in common decision making. Syndicate models are designed to address the question of how individuals with imperfect information who must take actions that produce a joint outcome should structure their decision making, and to examine the ways in which methods of distributing the surplus affect ex ante decision making. By employing the diverse information provided by its members to structure local market activities, the criminal gang operates as a syndicate in illegal markets. The gang structure substitutes for public systems of coordination and information transfer.

Syndicate models center around the construction of sharing rules and surrogate group utility functions that satisfy certain consistency and efficiency properties. Wilson (1968) defines a "syndicate" as a group of individual decision makers who must make a common decision under uncertainty which produces a joint payoff which they must share between them.[60] Rather than looking at conflicting interests, his approach focuses on pareto optimal decision making by a group whose members have diverse information about and/or diverse risk tolerances concerning uncertain events that affect a common payoff. The nature of the sharing rule is shown to be an important factor in determining the decision process since the relative merits of alternative decisions will turn on the way in which the output is shared.[61] The model examines conditions under which sharing rules which generate pareto optimal behavior by the group will produce decision making under uncertainty which satisfies certain consistency properties. The pareto optimal criterion is based on a notion of the syndicate as a cooperative but loosely organized and static group whose primary concern is the immediate welfare of the members. The longer term concerns of gang members, and the greater cohesion existing between group members, can be partially accommodated through a different choice of criterion.

Legros (1987) looks at the issue of whether forming a syndicate in a mixed market will be advantageous to members of the syndicate.[62] He shows that incentives for collusive behavior decrease with the relative scarcity of the commodity that its members own, and introduces conditions under which a syndicate will be advantageous for its members.[63] A syndicate is advantageous if and only if its members initially own the abundant commodity because in this case the syndicate can make a credible threat which individual members could not. Stability is determined by employing a Nash concept for coalitions (i.e. no group of players wants to change its status from syndicate to non-syndicate or to a different syndicate), and stability is linked to whether or not the syndicate is advantageous. The notion that syndicates will confer greater advantage to their members where the resources they have available are not relatively scarce corresponds to the idea that the gang structure is most beneficial in situations where individual members have no bargaining power.

Social and Economic Networks as Systems of Communication

Social and economic networks play an important role in the organization of many economic relationships. They provide informal systems of information transfer and trade that are particularly important for distribution of goods and services which are not or cannot be traded in legitimate markets. Concepts of social and economic networks have been applied by sociologists such as Wilson (1987) to explain the development of the American "underclass" and Iacobucci and Hopkins (1992) to explain communication patterns among consumers.[64] They have been employed by economists in contexts such as the internal organization of firms and employment search, and have also been used in more formal game theoretic models involving communication structures.[65]

Rather than focusing on incentive problems within organizations, network theories look at the importance of information processing and communication costs. This approach maps into an analysis of issues such as optimal degree of centralization and span of control within an organization. Positioning in this network will determine effects on productivity and bargaining power in the allocation of benefits. Economic "network" models focus on the different ways in which individuals within the system (nodes) can be linked and different ways of allocating the value created by this connection between the nodes. The connection generally involves transfer of information, with the number of nodes connected providing a measure of the benefit and the distance between nodes provides a measure of the cost of transmission. Williamson (1975) suggests the efficiency benefits of a simple wheel network consisting of a controlling center linked with many peripheral participants.[66] This is compared to an all channels network which performs well in situations of repeated interaction by small numbers. Zusman and Rausser (1991) present the move from an all channel network to a wheel network as a shift from an n person prisoner's dilemma game to an n+1-person bargaining game played by the center and the peripheral participants.[67] They argue that collective action requires organization by participants and that in the presence of multiple participants the structure which tends to emerge will lead to suboptimal decision making. The organization is modeled as a nexus of contracts in which the "influence equilibrium" structure of the organization is the result of an n+1 person bargaining game between an authoritative center which internalizes group interests and narrowly self-interested peripheral participants who exert social control on the center. The failure of collective action stems from this "particular intraorganizational influence structure."[68]

Jackson and Wolinsky (1996) examine the stability and efficiency of social and economic networks when individuals can form and sever links with each other.[69] They demonstrate the tension which can exist between stability and efficiency where self-interested individuals can choose to maintain or sever relationships based on the relative profitability of alternative relationships. Their analysis can be applied to analyze the informal communication and marketing networks that are employed in illegal markets and criminal organizations. The criminal street gang can itself be modeled as a social and economic network which plays a significant role in structuring the internal and external relationships of its members. The need to coordinate covert transactions requires informal communication, but the risk of detection places a premium on information transfer. The efficiency of the gang structure will depend in part on its efficiency as a communication system.

Arrow (1974) emphasizes the importance of information "channels" in shaping the contours of the organization, emphasizing the lack of uniformity of information costs in different directions.[70] Learning may be cheaper in different types of relationships with different types of people, and communication may be easier with individuals who share a common approach, language or set of experiences. Viewing the structure and operation of criminal street gangs as the result of differential information costs involved in coordinating individual actions focuses attention on patterns of information transfer both within and between different groups.

This idea of information channels can be linked to Hirschman's notion of commensality. Hirschman (1996) emphasizes the important public functions of widely shared private activities.[71] Private activities such as eating and drinking can be used to foster what he terms "commensality." The shared activities, and the rituals which develop around them, help to define a group identity. Shared activities may lead to improved forms of communication as well as contributing to the development of a shared set of norms and expectations. This type of commensality will be of particular importance when there is no legal apparatus to organize interactions and where society has not provided a clearly defined set of socializing principles with which to structure relationships.

American society has traditionally drawn boundaries along racial and ethnic lines, and one can argue that street gangs have merely internalized existing boundaries. It may be cheaper and easier to adopt existing patterns of differentiation as a means of establishing group boundaries, and once these boundaries are established they will tend to be self-perpetuating. Moreover, the group can rely on external pressures and stereotyping to police these boundaries. The racial and ethnic homogeneity of gangs is in part a function of the geographical segregation of different racial and cultural groups in the United States, particularly in the big cities where street gangs are most prevalent. Hagedorn, a well-known gang sociologist, suggests that "gang" has always been a code word for race in this country.[72] Media stereotyping also facilitates group identity, leading individuals to place themselves and others in culturally and socially predetermined groups. The geographical basis of gang membership can be explained in similar terms. Close proximity and familiarity lead to reduced costs of information transfer and increased paths of communication. Moreover, a similarity of interests and background facilitates group identity and increases the likelihood of overlapping interests. Drawing membership from the neighborhood also ensures that gang members are less mobile and easier to punish if guidelines are violated. The gang can impose costs on family members and friends as a means of extending punishment beyond gang membership, preventing fleeing to avoid punishment and increasing exit costs. The fact that gangs tend to be racially and ethnically homogenous is attributable in part to segregated residential patterns. Communication costs are likely to be lower when interacting with individuals who have a shared background and experiences, and this has a concentrating effect on local interaction which reinforces existing group boundaries.

The importance of networking in explaining the success of gangs as organizations is evidenced by the perverse effects of the current U.S. crime policy on gang activity. The U.S. war on drugs and, more recently, on gang members, has taken the form of a policy of incarceration.[73] The U.S. now incarcerates a higher proportion of its population than any other industrialized country, and its incarceration policies have had disproportionate effects on low income neighborhoods and minority groups.[74] Tough new laws have been enacted to penalize drug related and gang related crimes, and many of those incarcerated are serving time for such activities. One important and unintended consequence of this approach has been a noticeable increase in the number and influence of prison gangs.[75] Both gang and non-gang members are recruited to prison gangs and many retain affiliations with prison gangs upon release. The flow of money and drugs between prison gangs and gangs on the street allows gangs to continue their activities while incarcerated and provides opportunities for disciplining deviant street gang members who are arrested. Once incarcerated, prison provides an opportunity for learning new skills and developing criminal networks that will prove useful upon release. This criminal networking effect is exacerbated by the disproportionate impact of incarceration on low income, high crime neighborhoods. Individuals who have expanded their criminal network with prison and non-prison gang members while in jail are released into the same communities with stronger criminal ties, reduced legitimate opportunities, and greater hostility towards figures of authority.[76] Released prison gang members have come to dominate the drug markets in some cities. The local concentration of individuals who have spent time in jail may reduce the stigma and the fear associated with arrest for members of these communities, leading to a further escalation in crime. Incarceration of gang members opens up opportunities for new entrants, thus potentially increasing the number of individuals involved in street gangs.

External Threats

Absence of Property Rights and the Economics of Conflict

To the extent that organizational theorists have used economics to model gangs, the tendency has been to compare the gang to a primitive state whose primary activity is the use of violence. This is not a particularly useful approach towards what are typically relatively small, multi-functioned organizations which participate in illegal market activities. Gangs operate in a constrained environment and their actions are determined in part by external pressures. The notion of an authoritarian leadership that exercises control is unrealistic, since most gangs have a much less centralized structure and no such well-defined leadership. Moreover, the exercise of coercion is a group activity which requires group support. While gangs do employ violence both defensively, in conflicts with rival gangs, and coercively, to obtain resources, the use of violence is often best explained as part of a broader theory of gang activity.

Although the focus of these theories of conflict is too narrow to capture the nature of a criminal street gang, they are helpful in highlighting some of the trade-offs involved when allocating resources between purely coercive and productive activities. Gang membership is drawn from the teen-agers and young adults who live in the same neighborhood, and for many gang members the gang becomes their primary system of governance. The gang is able to exercise coercive power over a particular geographic area and domain of criminal activity. This power is used to exploit income opportunities. Violence or the threat of violence is used to establish property rights and to defend gang resources from rival gangs. Fagan and Chin (1990) suggest that gang violence performs the function of regulating the illegal drug business, functioning as a means of maintaining social control.

In standard theories of conflict, organizational decisions include the allocation of resources between productive and expropriative activities, investment in defense technologies, and the effects of alternative forms of coercive taxation. Three types of theories have been suggested. The first is based on the notion of the gang as a primitive state which has been able to achieve a monopoly over a particular territory through the use of force. These groups establish monopolistic control over a certain area and range of activities through the use of force. They establish and enforce their own systems of rules and taxation within this territory. Although this view was originally aimed at organized crime, it has limited applicability for smaller and less formally organized criminal groups. Olson (1993) presents a model in which the emergence of the state is the result of an individual who gains monopolistic control of an area through force and rationalizes theft through taxes, and Schelling (1967) examines the use of force by a criminal group to gain monopolistic control and taxation power over a territory.[77] Participation in the drug trade creates profits which need to be protected and agreements which need to be enforced. Where normal means of policing business practices, controlling monopolies, and regulating product quality are unavailable, gangs must rely on private enforcement through the use of private power. Violence becomes the mechanism by which drug transactions are regulated, and a reputation for violence becomes a profitable asset which is needed in order to participate in the drug trade. A gang may try to gain a comparative advantage in this market by recruiting individuals with a proclivity to violence. This parallels theories of strategic delegation in the firm, where delegating production or pricing decisions to a "crazy" individual who has a reputation for selecting non profit-maximizing acts may actually result in higher profits by allowing the firm to make credible threats against business rivals.[78]

The second view focuses on the "economics of conflict", examining the allocation of resources between productive and coercive activities. The "economics of conflict" is developed in a growing body of literature which focuses on the self-generation and destruction of property rights by investments in defensive and offensive capabilities.[79] For example, the potential for multiple equilibria involving different levels of investment in violent activity is discussed by Skaperdos (1989) in the context of a game theoretic model involving allocation of resources between productive and appropriative activities. The third approach is to provide a contractual account of the formation of the street gang. "Social contract" theories view the state as the product of voluntary agreements by individuals who stand to benefit from establishing a state policing mechanism to protect individual productive activities. The emergence of street gangs could be seen as the product of a social contract between members of a neighborhood who can increase their ability to exploit the resources offered by their environment through economies of specialization and scale in the formation of a centralized defense system.

Models of military conflict and arms races may have a limited role in explaining escalating gun use among gang members. The increase in gang violence over the past decade can be attributed in part to the increased availability of guns and gang participation in the drug trade. The U.S. has more federally licensed gun shops than it does public high schools, one in every three firearms is used at some time in the commission of a crime, and gang members are more likely to have and use guns than are non-gang members.[80] The prevalence of guns in gangs creates a coordination problem which results in escalating gun use. An individual will feel the need to have a gun if he thinks that his rivals have guns, and he will want to use it in order to let rivals know that he is armed and dangerous to interfere with. The danger of being the last, rather than the first, to end a confrontation with a gun leads to an escalation of non-lethal fights into homicides. The Blocks (1995) argue that gang violence often follows an escalating pattern of hostile events ending in a lethal shooting. While all of the gangs would be better off without guns, unilateral deviations from an "arming" equilibrium would be extremely disadvantageous. One of the more successful reductions in gun homicide rates among gangs has been achieved by establishing a forum for large rival gangs to bargain with each other for a coordinated reduction in gun use between large rival gangs. This method was applied with success in Chicago to reduce gang homicide rates via a truce established between the Vice Lords and the Black Gangster Disciples. Other examples include work done by Jesuit priests in Los Angeles and Milwaukee in uniting adult members of rival gangs to reduce conflict.[81] The stabilizing effect of age-integrated gangs and the control exerted by older and more business oriented drug gangs on drug markets may be one reason for recent decreases in the country's national level of homicides.

III. Conclusion

In Part I of this chapter it has been argued that in order to model group behavior it is necessary to move away from the simple economic paradigm of individual choice to encompass different forms and levels of interaction between individuals. An economic approach offers a number of advantages for those interested in controlling criminal street gang behavior. It can be used to amalgamate diverse theories about the source and nature of street gang activity, providing a more coherent and consistent picture of contemporary street gangs. Identifying stable patterns of behavior provides the basis for testable inferences about future gang responses to changes in social and economic conditions. This endeavor is premised on the notion that viewing street gangs as rational organizational responses to economic and social conditions will promote a more effective and informed policy approach towards criminal street gangs. Once an economic basis for group action is identified, efficiency criteria can be applied to alternative group processes to predict the range of likely outcomes in response to policy changes. An economic framework can also be used to focus law enforcement efforts by isolating the mechanisms through which gang members are able (or unable) to sustain cooperative outcomes.

Although economics does not yet have a satisfactory answer to the question of how to capture group dynamics in economic models, the complexity of group behavior can be approached indirectly by identifying the multiplicity of mechanisms which are at work in shaping organizational structure and group action. Alternative theories of group organization can be used to shed light on particular aspects of a given organizational structure. Part I of this chapter has suggested a number of different economic approaches to group decision making and collective action which can be used to shed light on the structure and function of criminal street gangs. Part II expands on a central aspect of criminal street gang organization, focusing on the role of street gangs as agreement enforcing institutions.

Part II: Criminal Street Gangs as Institutions for Enforcing Agreements

Criminal street gangs have been depicted by various experts as juvenile delinquent play-groups, extended families, social clubs, and criminal enterprises. While theories vary in terms of their explanations and descriptions of street gangs, they generally begin from a common starting point in which gangs are seen as mechanisms for satisfying group needs in the absence of mainstream organizational structures. One of the central aspects of criminal gangs is their ability to function as institutions for enforcing agreements in the absence of legally enforceable contracts, a function which is essential to the commercial activities of the gang. The need for secrecy and mobility in illegal markets prevents individuals from establishing the extended trading relationships and reputations which are needed in order to sustain trade in the absence of legally enforceable contracts. Participants in illegal markets will be unable to make credible commitments to satisfy the terms of their agreements if their current actions have little or no impact on future trading opportunities. The gang structure provides a vehicle for increasing the profitability of trade in illegal markets by increasing the probability that the same seller will be able to re-identify the same seller or group of sellers. If a buyer, or group of buyers who share information, can re-identify the same seller, or group of sellers, then they will be able to avoid engaging in trade with those sellers who have reneged on their agreements in the past. Criminal street gangs are distinguishable from other types of criminal gangs by their connection to a specific geographic area or "turf", their visible and distinctive identity, and the multiple functions for which the gang structure is employed.[82] By allowing sellers to operate as a single identifiable unit (generally with a specific geographic location), the gang serves as a device for increasing the frequency of interaction both between gang members and between members and their trading partners. It also operates as an information saving device for buyers, who can base their trading relationships on trade with the same gang rather than the same individual seller. Gangs thus become mechanisms for signaling product quality and reliability in illegal transactions. Where the cost of breaking an agreement with a buyer is imposed on the gang, members will have an incentive to monitor and enforce the agreements made by other gang members.

The commercial opportunities which the gang structure creates are evidenced by the proliferation and economic success of gangs in different domains of illegal market activity. While membership in a street gang provides opportunities for expanding trade, exploitation of joint benefits is limited by the inability to control narrowly self-interested behavior. Gang members will prefer to minimize the effort they devote to gang activities and will shirk in the absence of direct incentives or enforcement. Members face the risk of external penalties if their criminal activities are discovered, making information about individual activities costly to obtain and risky to transmit. Membership turnover is high, there are no formal insurance markets, and shares in gang "assets" are non-tradable. This chapter looks at how criminal street gangs can enforce agreements in the face of these constraints. While attention is focused on criminal street gangs, the analysis can be extended to other types of criminal groups and, more generally, to situations in which there are opportunities for joint production and trade which will remain unexploited in the absence of private enforcement.

I. Self-enforceable Agreements in Extended Relationships

The ability to exploit the benefits offered by group production and trade is often limited by the inability of individuals to commit themselves to take cooperative actions. The Prisoner's Dilemma provides a paradigm example of the "commitment problem" which arises when self-interested individuals acting independently are unable to exploit the benefits available from cooperative action because of their inability to commit themselves ex ante to take certain costly actions ex post. Diagram 1 illustrates the commitment problem which arises in a trading game in which the quality of the trading good is a function of investment by the seller and the buyer is unable to ascertain the quality of the good before purchasing it.

Diagram 1

	Buyer Trades	**No Trade**
Seller Invests	10, 10	0,-5
No Investment	-15, 15	0, 0

In this trading game, the only single period nash equilibrium outcome is a situation of no trade, even though both the seller and the buyer would gain from trade.

Repeated interaction provides opportunities for sustaining cooperation among self-interested individuals in situations that allow for short-term gains from opportunistic behavior.[83] The potentially wide scope for cooperative behavior in extended relationships is suggested by the "folk theorems" for repeated games, which assert that if players are sufficiently patient then any set of feasible, individually rational payoffs can be obtained as the equilibrium of an indefinitely repeated game.[84] The ability to sustain efficient trade has been shown to hold for virtually all repeated games as long as cheats can be identified and penalized with sufficient speed and severity and the rate at which future gains are discounted is not too high.[85] This result has been extended to situations in which players change partners often, provided that there is some means of sharing information about previous trading histories.[86] The benefits available from extending trading relationships provides buyers and sellers with incentives to organize their trading activities in ways which maximize the opportunities for repeated interaction.[87] The gang structure provides one way of obtaining the benefits of repeated interaction in situations where extended trading relationships are difficult and costly to establish and future profits are likely to be heavily discounted.

The gang structure provides an interesting case study in opportunities for private monitoring and use of group reputation to sustain trade in an environment which places a premium on keeping transactions hidden. The reputation model is motivated by the notion that history-dependent strategies can substitute for contracts to sustain cooperative outcomes in situations of repeated play. Individuals will be prevented from cheating by the fear that they will foreclose profitable future trading opportunities.[88] One of the limitations of the reputation literature is the lack of attention paid to the nature of the "reputation" and the manner in which it is communicated to the relevant parties. Exceptions include Milgrom and Weingast (1990), Grief (1993), and Grief, Milgrom and Weingast (1994), who provide historical examples of self-enforcing systems of trade based on reputation and explore the nature and structure of these systems in detail.[89] The cost and availability of information channels for communicating information about reputations are also an important but often neglected component of reputation games. The complex nature and multi-faceted role that reputation plays in the criminal gang context, and the restrictions imposed on communicating information about this reputation, provide new challenges for the existing economic framework.

An essential component of cooperative reputation models is the underlying system of enforcement by which cheating can be detected and punished by the group which is affected. The basic folk theorems obtained for repeated games refer to situations in which each player has full information about the actions of all of the other players, in which case monitoring cheating is not a problem. Where imperfect information is introduced, it is typically introduced in the form of public uncertainty about a publicly observed variable, and most of the work on imperfect monitoring has focused on situations in which group members observe an imperfect public signal which depends upon random shocks and the profile of actions taken.[90] Systems of private monitoring have been relatively neglected in the literature despite their practical importance in many settings. Exceptions include Radner (1986), who considers a situation in which production is performed by teams, and Ben-Porath and Kahneman (1996), who consider repeated games in which each player can be observed by only a subset of other players who can then make public reports about the behavior they have observed.[91] These models focus exclusively on the ability of a group to establish a private monitoring scheme and do not extend the analysis to consider how this facilitates the trading opportunities of the group. The effect of costly enforcement of punishment for those who do cheat is also typically ignored, either by focusing on equilibrium conditions in which no cheating occurs or by assuming that punishment is costless.[92] Where monitoring and punishment are costly, questions arise as to how participation in the enforcement scheme required to prevent cheating will be enforced. In the street gang context, the gang must rely upon a system of private monitoring of private activities in which it is individually rational for gang members to participate. In the presence of unexploited gains the group must also consider its ability to commit to punishments where there is room for re-negotiation.[93]

It should be noted that while criminal organizations may face special problems in sustaining cooperation and enforcing agreements, commitment problems and the use of reputation mechanisms to address them occur in other settings. Trade associations provide a contemporary example of an institutional response to the commitment problem created by difficulties in the ability to commit ex ante to satisfy the terms of an agreement ex post where satisfaction of the terms is costly and confers no additional benefit. Macaulay (1963) comments on the use of non-legal sanctions in different business settings, and notes the importance of "reputation" and the threat of loss of future business in sustaining relations between market participants.[94] Klein and Leffler (1981) describe the use of reputation to sustain trade in high quality goods in consumer markets.[95] Bernstein (1992) describes a particular industry in which large transactions are regularly performed using non-legal methods within a tightly knit community of traders.[96] Given that many of these transactions could be performed using legally enforceable contracts, questions arise as to whether self-enforcing systems may provide cost savings and related benefits even when legal enforcement is available.

The Gang as an Institution for Enforcing Agreements

The criminal street gang can be viewed as an institution that provides a group of individual sellers of illegal goods who occupy the same geographic area with a common seller identity. Illegal markets are characterized by high information costs, mobile participants and covert transactions. The risk of detection and the absence of public mechanisms for transferring market information force buyers to rely primarily on their own trading history and informal methods of communication about market opportunities.[97] Sellers are likewise constrained in their ability to publicize their location, identity and the high quality of their goods, and cannot rely on third party enforcement as an alternative way of committing to product quality. These factors contribute to high search costs that impede the ability of buyers to find and re-identify the same seller in repeat transactions.

Gangs can take advantage of economies to scale in the creation and use of reputation. By increasing the size and identifiability of the trading unit above a critical size, the gang is able to employ a reputation device that is unavailable to independent sellers.[98] Methods of creating a distinctive and visible gang identity include particular dress codes, hand signals and control over a geographic location from which non-member sellers can be excluded. Membership in a criminal street gang can be used to signal involvement in illegal activities and attachment to a particular trading location without the same risk of detection as would accompany individual attempts to establish a seller identity and market location. Other sellers can be excluded from the territory, allowing buyers to associate a gang with a particular geographical location. The gang structure provides a means of increasing the profitability of trade by reducing search costs and increasing the ability of gangs to commit to the terms of their agreements. In addition to facilitating trade with non-gang members, the gang structure will increase the incentive to be "helpful" to fellow gang members by increasing the likelihood of repeated interaction between individual members of the group and the interdependence of pay-offs.

Gang members have an incentive to discipline cheats because of the negative effect of cheating on a shared gang reputation, and this threat of punishment induces honest behavior. This allows gang members to make credible commitments to fulfill their obligations. Control over a particular trading location provides the gang with a local monopoly power which, taken in combination with the premium available from a reputation for honest dealing, can be used to increase profits. Where there is a premium associated with gang membership, the threat of exclusion from this territory can be used as a disciplining device for gang members. Increases in the premium may lead to increases in the gang's enforcement capacity, which may in turn lead to further increases in the value of the gang reputation.

A prerequisite for such a system is the ability of the gang to identify cheats. Interesting features of the street gang as an organization include the ways in which the structure facilitates peer monitoring. Individuals interact with each other repeatedly in a well-defined physical area, and all of the gang members will interact on a repeated basis with at least a sub-group of other gang members. Even if individual actions may not be observable to the gang as a whole, it is likely that they will be observed by neighboring gang members. The negative externalities that cheats impose on their neighbors and penalty schemes based on mis-reporting or failure to report can both be used to motivate gang members to monitor the actions of their neighbors. The ease with which gang members are identifiable and distinguishable from non-members and their geographic concentration enhances the ability to sustain peer monitoring. The use of an internal status system built upon distinctive group norms serves as an additional mechanism for ensuring peer monitoring and as a means of reducing the payoffs available from opportunistic behavior. An increased importance is attached to actions which are good for the group since these actions will lead to higher status and more control rights within the organization.[99]

Section two presents a model of the criminal street gang as a mechanism for sustaining trade through repeated interaction in illegal markets. The gang employs a combined reputation and penalty scheme for sustaining trade, the success of the system turning on the ability of the gang to establish self-enforceable monitoring and penalty schemes to support the group reputation.

II. Economic Model of a Gang as an Institution for Enforcing Agreements

Consider an illegal drug market in which there are N sellers whose primary interest is to maximize income from retail drug selling. The value of the good is determined by the effort that the seller has invested in product quality, but the buyer is unable to assess the value of the good before buying it and cannot make payment contingent on the value of the product received. While repeated trade might allow for sustainable agreements between buyers and sellers, the nature of illegal markets imposes limits on the ability of buyers and sellers to establish continuous trading relationships. Drug sales must be performed covertly and without the aid of legally enforceable contracts, and sellers must maintain a certain degree of mobility and anonymity. In the extreme case, buyers will be unable to re-identify the sellers they have dealt with in the past and will be unable to trade information with other buyers. In this case the seller will have no incentive to invest in product quality, and no trade will occur. Forming a gang provides a way of increasing the frequency of trade between a buyer and the new "selling unit" and facilitates information transfer among buyers. This repeated interaction can be used to sustain trade via history-dependent strategies (i.e. reputation effects). Control over a particular physical territory will increase the buyer's ability to relocate the gang and to identify members of the same gang. The increased frequency of transactions between sellers and buyers allows buyers to impose a cost on sellers who cheat by refusing to trade with them in future periods.

The Trading Game

The key to profitable trade lies in increasing the likelihood of repeated trade with a buyer who can re-identify sellers who have performed badly in the past. Only then will sellers have an incentive to perform their ends of the agreements made. By way of illustration, consider an illegal market in which there are N risk neutral buyers and N risk neutral sellers of illegal goods who must trade with each other in the absence of legally enforceable agreements. The seller provides a good whose value is determined by the amount of effort (e) that he invests in product quality.[100] The market value of the good is given by R(e). The buyer is willing to pay the seller an amount equal to the expected market value of the good, given by $ER(e)=R(e^e)$. Expectations are assumed to be rational. The seller receives this payment and then chooses effort. The seller can select $e \in \{0,e_l,e_h\}$ at effort cost C(e).

Assumption 1: $0 = C(0) < C(e_l) < C(e_h) < \infty$

After the payment is received, the seller provides the buyer with a good which is worth R(e). If the seller selects e=0 and the buyer anticipates this and sets ER(e)=R(0) then no trade will occur.

Let $\Pi_h = R(e_h)\text{-}C(e_h)$ and $\Pi_l = R(e_l)\text{-}C(e_l)$.

Assumption 2: $0<\Pi_l<\Pi_h<\infty$

Efficient trade occurs when the buyer offers payment for and the seller provides a good of value $R(e_h)$. The mark-up of price over cost reflects the seller's local monopoly power (due, for example, to the search costs incurred in finding alternative sellers, or to a risk premium). The timing of a single transaction is as follows:

|-------------------------|-------------------------|- -------------------------|

buyer j matched with seller i	buyer pays ER(e)	seller selects e, buyer gets R(e)

Since this is an illegal market, the buyer and seller do not have access to legally enforceable contracts and the buyer cannot condition payment upon the actual value of the good received. He can condition payment upon the information that he has about his own and the seller's trading history. The buyer chooses a payment strategy and the seller chooses an investment strategy which maximize the discounted sum of their respective expected future profits. The discount factor, which reflects the rate of time preference and expectations about whether trade will continue, is given by ∂.[101] Individual i's history of transactions prior to date t is given by h_{it}. Both buyers and sellers expect to stay in the market for an indefinite amount of time, and they trade with each other according to a matching rule M.

Define: $M_j(h_{jt}, \beta h_{it}, i)$ gives the probability that seller i will be matched with buyer j in period t

In a decentralized market where buyers and sellers trade with a different partner each period, if buyer j trades with seller i in period t then M_j=0 in all future periods. In a bilateral trading model M_j=1 in every period. In most cases trade will occur intermittently, with $0<M_j<1$. The analysis extends easily to any matching rule which assigns a positive probability of recurrent trade with buyer j to all sellers.[102] M_j specifies the information that buyer j has about his own trading history (h_{jt}) and seller i's trading history (βh_{it}) at time t, where $0\leq\beta\leq1$. If β=1 then there is full information about all transactions occurring before time t, and if β=0 then buyers know only their own trading history. Imperfect communication between buyers would lead to $0<\beta<1$. The covert nature of illegal transactions and the high cost of information transfer suggests that β will be close to zero.

Assumption 4: β=0

The seller's expected profit evaluated at time t is given by:

$$\sum_{i=0}^{\infty} \partial^{t}[ER_{t+1}(e) - C(e_{t+1})]$$

The buyer's expected profit evaluated at time t is given by:

$$\sum_{i=0}^{\infty} \partial^{t}[R(e_{t+1}) - ER_{t+1}(e)]$$

Define: Efficient trade is trade that yields the maximum surplus for buyer and seller combined. Given assumption 2, trade is efficient when the high quality good is produced and traded. Trade is inefficient when the low quality good is traded, and joint surplus is lowest when there is no trade.

The ability of buyers and sellers to sustain efficient trade will depend upon the matching rule (M), the number of buyers and sellers (N), and the rate at which future profits are discounted (∂), which will itself depend upon the level of risk and probability of exit from the market. Strategies in the repeated game are based on a tit-for-tat strategy in which current actions are based on actions taken in previous periods. This simple strategy does just as well as more complicated history-dependent strategies.

Define: Trading Strategies - the buyer chooses strategies e_0 for the first period and $e_t^e=e_{t-1}$ and the seller then decides whether to select $e_t= e_t^e$ or to deviate and select a lower effort level.

Independent Sellers in a Large Market (M=0)

Repeated trade will not occur where N is very large or where sellers are difficult to re-identify or relocate.[103] If the probability of trading with the same buyer again is close to zero and each buyer knows only his own trading history, then the seller will maximize expected profits by selecting e=0. Knowing this, the buyer will not be willing to pay a positive amount for the good and trade will not occur.

Proposition 1: The unique sub-game perfect nash equilibrium of the trading game when $M_j=0$ is no trade.

For a proof of this see Appendix One. The no trade outcome occurs because independent sellers in a large market with no communication between buyers are unable to commit to supplying quality goods.

Bilateral Trade (M=1)

If the buyer and seller trade only with each other, then the trading game becomes a simple repeated game in which trade can be sustained through history dependent strategies as long as the future is not discounted too heavily. A tit-for-tat strategy in which current actions are based on actions taken in the previous period does just as well as more complicated history-dependent strategies.

Proposition 2: Efficient trade can be sustained when there is bilateral trade as long as the discount rate is sufficiently high.

i.e. The strategies $e_0=e_h$ and $e_t^e=e_{t-1}$ for the buyer and $e_t= e_t^e$ for the seller are a sub-game perfect Nash Equilibrium of the game when $C(e_h)-C(e_l) / R(e_h)-R(e_l) \leq \partial$. Inefficient trade is a sub-game perfect Nash Equilibrium but efficient trade is not when $C(e_l)/R(e_l) \leq \partial < C(e_h)-C(e_l) / R(e_h)-R(e_l)$. No trade is the unique Nash Equilibrium of the trading game if $C(e_l) / R(e_l) >\partial$

See Appendix One for the proof.

Infrequent Interactions (N large)

Individual sellers and buyers may be unable to trade in the face of infrequent interaction and limited information transfer. Consider a sequential matching rule M_N in which a seller i is matched with a buyer j once every N periods.[104] The results extend easily to any matching rule that results in a positive probability of trade with multiple sellers, including random matching rules in which there is a positive probability of being matched in each period (e.g. $M_j=1/N$). The buyer is restricted to history-dependent strategies based on his own trading history, and given this restriction a simple tit for tat strategy performs as well as any other strategy.

In the first period of trade with Seller i, Buyer j offers $ER(e_o)$ and in all subsequent trades with Seller i the buyer offers a price $ER_t(e) = R(e_t^e)$ where the expected effort level $e_t^e=e_{it-N}$. In response, Seller i decides whether to behave honestly, choosing $e_{it}=e_o$ in the first period and $e_{it+N}=e_{it+N}^e$ for all subsequent periods, or to cheat, choosing $e_{it}<e_o$ and $e_{it+N} = e_{it+N}^e$ in future periods.[105]

The following proposition suggests that there will be no trade if N is very large or ∂ is very small, where N is the interval between periods of trade with the same buyer and ∂ will depend in part on the probability of continuing trade in the same market in future periods. When sellers operate independently, they will be unable to sustain efficient trade where interaction with the same buyer is too infrequent and the future is heavily discounted (due, for example, to high risk of imprisonment by law enforcement).

Proposition 3: In a market where the frequency of repeated interaction is low, no trade is the unique sub-game perfect equilibrium of the trading game. i.e. there is no trade if:

$$C(e_l) /R(e_l) > \partial^N$$

Inefficient trade is sustainable (but efficient trade is not) where there is a moderate trading frequency, i.e. $e_o=e_l$ and $e_t^e=e_{t-1}$ for the buyer and $e_t=e_t^e= e_l$ for the seller are sub-game perfect nash equilibrium strategies of the game if:

$$C(e_l) /R(e_l) < \partial^N< C(e_h) -C(e_l) / R(e_h) -R(e_l)$$

Efficient trade is sustainable as a sub-game perfect nash equilibrium of the game if:

$$C(e_h) -C(e_l) / R(e_h) -R(e_l) < \partial^N$$

See Appendix One for the proof.

Sellers Joining a Gang

Sellers can increase the range of market parameters for which trade can be sustained by becoming members of a gang. A gang consists of a group of individuals who have a well-defined set of entry and exit criteria, a visible identity and a system for enforcing gang rules. Gang members conduct repeated illegal transactions according to group guidelines in a specific market territory from which non-member sellers can be excluded. Membership life-span is indefinite and members cannot predict their last period of membership. By investing effort in a group identity, individual sellers can create a joint reputation that allows buyers to treat gang members as interchangeable. The gang structure functions as an information saving device for buyers in illegal markets by increasing the size of the trading unit and by signaling member involvement in illegal trade and information about a member's previous trading history.

If the seller operates independently then he has an individual reputation (i.e. trading history) that is determined by his previous actions and the matching rule M_N.

The seller's reputation with Buyer j who he trades with in period t is given by:

$$e_{it} = e_{it-N}$$

If the seller is a member of a gang, then his effort choice in period t determines the reputation that this buyer assigns to the gang during the next period of trade with the same gang. For a gang of size N and matching rule M_N this will be:

$$e_{gt} = e_{gt-1}$$

The gang effectively creates a new matching rule $M_g = \sum_{i=1}^{N} M_{iN}$ for the N gang members. Where the gang does not control the entire local market (i.e. when the gang consists of K<N sellers), the reputation depends upon the last period of trade with any gang member. While the gang structure will always provide the opportunity for improving upon the outcome obtainable by independent sellers, the ability to sustain trade will depend upon the matching rule and upon K/N, which can be interpreted as a measure of local market power.

If a gang member cheats and selects an effort level lower than that he is being paid to take, the expected profits of other gang members will be lowered via the effect on the gang's reputation in the next period of trade. This provides the gang with an incentive to punish the cheat. It is assumed initially that the gang can observe cheating and can impose a penalty Y without cost on an individual who cheats, although these assumptions are re-examined below.[106] Buyers use the same tit-for-tat strategy, with the difference that they treat gang members as a single seller. Buyer j offers a price based on $e^e=e_o$ in the first period and $e_t^e=e_{t-k}$ in all future periods, where k is the interval between periods of trade with a gang member, here assumed to be equal to 1. Seller i chooses between dealing honestly, selecting $e_t=e_t^e$, and cheating, selecting $e_t<e_t^e$, subject to punishment Y. When the gang member does not expect to deal with the same buyer again, the only cost of cheating is Y, and the optimal deviation will be given by e=0. If the gang member expects to deal with the seller again in N periods, then his loss includes the lower expected profit in period N, and the optimal deviation may involve positive effort. The time-line is as follows:

|-------------------------|----------------------------|--------------------------------|

1: Agreement buyer offers $ER_t(e)=R(e_{t-1})$	2: Effort Choice seller selects et, which determines $ER_{t+1}(e)$	3: Penalty Y if seller has cheated chosen $e_t<e_{t-1}$

Proposition 4: Gang membership increases the range of market parameters for which trade can be sustained, i.e. the ability to trade for gang members is extended beyond that of individual sellers to include: (1) low level trade (i.e.$e_0=e_l$ and $e_t^e=e_t=e_l$) when: (i) $(\partial^N/1-\partial^N) < C(e_l)/\Pi_l < (\partial/1-\partial)$ and (ii) $Y> C(e_l) - \partial^N R(e_l)$ (or $Y > C(e_l)$ where no repeat trade is expected); and (2) efficient trade (i.e. $e_0=e_h$ and $e_t^e=e_t=e_h$) when: (i) $(\partial^N/1-\partial^N) < (C(e_h) -C(e_l)) /(\Pi_h-\Pi_l) < (\partial/1-\partial)$ and (ii)$Y > C(e_h) -C(e_l) - \partial^N(R(e_h)-R(e_l))$ (or $Y > C(e_h)$ where no repeat trade is expected).

See Appendix Two for the proof. The first condition ensures that the loss to the gang is greater than the gain to the individual member (an enforcement compatibility constraint), and the second condition ensures that individual members will not cheat (a no-cheating incentive constraint). This model offers a way of thinking about the basic relationships between market parameters, the structure of the gang (i.e. penalties available and ability to punish), and the possibility of trade in illegal markets.[107] These relationships are investigated in more detail below by relaxing the assumptions of perfect observability of effort and costless punishment.

Premium from Gang Membership

Where membership confers benefits, cheating can be deterred through the threat of exclusion from the gang. When gang members control a particular market territory from which non-gang sellers of illegal goods can be excluded, the gang can use its local monopoly power to increase the benefits of membership, allowing sellers to charge higher prices because of the quality control and reduced search costs which accompany trade with the gang. Where buyers are willing to pay higher prices, seller access to the territory provides the seller with a positive "reputation premium" which is given by the difference B(e) between the reputation attached to a gang member, given by the expected value of the good $ER_g(e)$, and that generated by an independent seller, given by the expected value of the good $ER_i(e)$:

$$B(e) = ER_g(e) - ER_i(e)$$

Where this premium is positive, the gang can use the threat of exclusion to deter cheating. If gang member i cheats, he can be excluded from the gang and is left to operate as an independent seller in another market location. In other words, the penalty for cheating becomes $Y = B(e)$.

Proposition 5: A reputation premium from gang membership allows gang members to sustain trade for a broader range of market conditions than they could sustain as independent sellers. Gang membership extends the range of trade to include:

(i) efficient trade when

$$(\partial^N/1-\partial^N)(\Pi_{ih}-\Pi_{il}) < C(e_h) - C(e_l) < (\partial/1-\partial)(\Pi_{gh}-\Pi_{il})$$

$$\text{i.e.} \partial^N < C(e_h) - C(e_l)/ ER_i(e_h)-ER_i(e_l)$$

$$\text{but } \partial > C(e_h) - C(e_l) / ER_g(e_h)-ER_i(e_l)$$

(ii) inefficient but not efficient trade (i.e. trade of $R(e_l)$) if

$$(\partial^N/1-\partial^N)\Pi_{il} < C(e_l) < (\partial/1-\partial)\Pi_g$$

See Appendix Two for the proof. Where an individual seller is unable to engage in trade (as identified in Proposition One) and gang members are able to sustain efficient trade (as identified in Proposition 5), the gang premium is given by $B(e) = \Pi_h$. When inefficient trade is possible by an individual seller and efficient trade is sustainable by a gang member, $B(e) = \Pi_h - \Pi_l = R(e_h) - R(e_l) + C(e_l) - C(e_h)$. Since the conditions for sustainable trade by gang members are a function of K and N, with trading opportunities increasing in K, B(e) is an increasing function of K and N.

Corollary: A gang with market power (i.e. where K/N is large) is better able to sustain efficient trade.

The efficiency gains from group enforcement make membership a valuable asset, and the more valuable this asset is the easier it is to sustain group enforcement.[108]

Self-enforceability of Punishment

The gang structure has several features that are conducive to self-enforceable penalty schemes. Where punishment is costless to inflict, group punishment schemes can be based on voluntary participation since members will wish to prevent deviations that will harm the shared reputation. Where detecting and punishing cheats is costly, however, gang members face a free riding problem in which each individual will prefer to rely on monitoring and enforcement by other gang members. In this situation, the gang must rely on an additional layer of penalty schemes designed to punish those who fail to participate in group monitoring and punishment schemes. If participation is observable, then it can be enforced through the threat of penalties for non-participation, although once again a question arises as to how the gang will enforce this penalty scheme where enforcement is costly. The localized nature of the market, and the close proximity of other sellers with inter-dependent payoffs, also provide opportunities for peer monitoring and reporting schemes. Where the costs of cheating are borne disproportionately by neighboring gang members, the incentives for local monitoring will be even higher.

Expectations of participation in a group penalty scheme by others can lead to a self-enforceable multilateral punishment scheme. If a gang member expects other gang members to participate in penalty schemes, then it will be in his interest to do so as well, but if he does not expect other gang members to enforce the scheme, then he will have no incentive to do so. As a simple example of such a system, suppose that a cheating gang member is punished by exclusion from the gang territory, at a cost of X to the gang. Each remaining gang member i must invest effort x_i, at a cost of $x_i= X/N-1$, in order to enforce exclusion. This effort might include communication costs to neighboring sellers and buyers and the use of physical coercion. A gang member who fails to exclude cheats will himself face exclusion by other gang members, at a now higher cost of $x_i=X/N-2$ to the remaining gang members. Note that as the number of deviators increases, the cost of punishing also increases, making cooperation more costly to sustain. In a situation of efficient trade, gang member i will have an incentive to punish a cheater j if he expects the other (N-2) gang members to participate in the punishment and if the future gain from preserving a no-cheating equilibrium outweighs the current cost of punishment (i.e. if $(\partial/1-\partial)\ (\Pi_{gh}-\Pi_{il})>2X/(N-2)$).

Proposition 6: Full participation in penalty enforcement by the N-1 gang members is a sub-game perfect nash equilibrium of the game as long as $(\partial/1-\partial)(\Pi_{gh}-\Pi_{il})>2X/N-2$. No participation is also a sub-game perfect nash equilibrium of the game.

This reflects the notion that failure to participate in punishing will not be profitable as long as the individual member expects other members to participate, but will be profitable if the individual member does not expect others to participate.[109]

Observability and Peer Monitoring

Since illegal activities must be performed covertly, the gang must develop a self-enforceable system of private monitoring. The gang structure is conducive to a system of peer monitoring in which neighboring gang members are responsible for observing each other's activities. The effectiveness of peer monitoring will depend upon the matching technology. It will be most effective where the matching rule has a local bias (i.e. where buyers are more likely to trade in subsequent periods with sellers who are located close by) since the costs of cheating will be borne disproportionately by neighbors of the cheater and since the source of cheating will be easier to pin-point.

Even if the matching technology is such that cheating imposes the same expected cost on all gang members (i.e. $M=1/N$), peer monitoring can be sustained through a team reporting system as long as each gang member has two neighbors who can observe his actions and the two neighbors cannot collude. Suppose, for example, that each period a gang member has two new neighbors and can observe only who his neighbors are and what actions they take. Each gang member is required to report the effort levels taken by his two neighbors, at a personal cost of $c>0$. If there is no way of verifying the report, and gang member i expects other gang members to perform accurate monitoring, then his best response is to cheat and report honest dealing. Where two gang members report on the same individual, and these two cannot compare their reports, the threat of a large penalty (Y) in the event of conflicting reports can be used to increase the expected cost of inaccuracy above the monitoring cost c. Thus, where observations are costly, peer monitoring without local effects can be sustained by a reporting system which imposes a large penalty on inaccurate reports as long as at least two reports are made about each individual's effort choice and there is no collusion between the reporting gang members.

III. Conclusion

One of the central difficulties of trading in illegal markets is the absence of third party enforcement. Where payment for goods and services cannot be made contingent on the value of the goods and services actually received, trade will not occur in the absence of some form of commitment device. In the absence of legal enforcement, agreements between buyers and sellers in illegal markets must be self-enforceable and, in particular, sellers must be provided with adequate incentives to carry out their promises. Reputation can be employed as a commitment device in markets where there is communication between buyers or repeated transactions between buyers and sellers. In order to ensure continuity of trading relationships, transactions must involve localized, repeated relationships rather than anonymous market trades. The ability to ensure repeated transactions on an individualized basis in illegal markets will be limited, however, by the difficulties of re-identifying and re-locating individual sellers.

Employing the gang structure as a commitment device provides a potentially cheaper and more effective mechanism for trading in illegal markets. By investing effort in a group identity, individual sellers can create a joint reputation that allows buyers to treat gang members as interchangeable. The gang structure functions as an information saving device for buyers in illegal markets by increasing the size of the trading unit and by signaling member involvement in illegal trade and information about a member's previous trading history. The gang structure provides members with the benefits of being identifiable without the corresponding increase in risk associated with investing in an individual criminal identity. Group monitoring and punishment can be used to support the group reputation by deterring cheating by individual gang members and by exclusion of non-gang members. The above discussion serves to highlight the ways in which the gang structure can be employed as an institution for enforcing agreements. The effectiveness of this institution will depend upon structural factors such as the monitoring and enforcement technologies the gang has available and market parameters such as the size of the market and the nature of trade.

Appendix One

1. Independent Sellers in a Large Market (M=0)

Proposition 1: The unique sub-game perfect nash-equilibrium of the single period trading game which occurs when $M_j=0$ is no trade.

Proof:

Since the seller receives payment ER(e) before making his effort choice, and the payment he receives is not contingent upon his effort choice, the seller has no incentive to choose positive effort in a one shot game. The seller chooses e_i to maximize $[ER(e)-C(e_i)]$, which yields $e_i=0$.

Since the effort choice of the seller is not affected by the payment offered by the buyer, the buyer maximizes his expected profit, given by $[R(e_i)-ER(e)]$, by choosing $ER(e)=ER(0)=0$.

2. Bilateral Trade (M=1)

Proposition 2: Efficient trade can be sustained when there is bilateral trade as long as the discount rate is sufficiently high. i.e. The strategies $e_0=e_h$ and $e_t^e=e_{t-1}$ for the buyer and $e_t= e_t^e$ for the seller are a sub-game perfect Nash Equilibrium of the game when $\partial \geq C(e_h)-C(e_l) / R(e_h)-R(e_l)$. Inefficient trade is a sub-game perfect Nash Equilibrium, but efficient trade is not, when: $C(e_l) / R(e_l) \leq \partial < C(e_h)-C(e_l) / R(e_h)-R(e_l)$ and no trade is the unique Nash Equilibrium of the trading game if: $\partial < C(e_l) / R(e_l)$.

Proof:

In a bilateral trading game the buyer and seller trade with each other each period and have full information about the actions taken by each other in the past. This is a standard repeated one-sided prisoner's dilemma game.

The buyer can condition his strategy only on his prior trading history. Consider tit-for-tat strategies $e_0=e_h$ and $e_te=e_t-1$ for the buyer and $e_t=e_t^e$ for the seller. Using the optimal deviation principle of repeated games, we can focus on single period deviations.[110]

For $e_0=e_h$ the seller does not gain from a deviation from this strategy where:

$$C(e_h) < \partial/1-\partial\ \Pi_h \text{ and } C(e_h)-C(e_l) < \partial/1-\partial\ (\Pi_h-\Pi_l)$$

Given that the seller has not cheated, the buyer will maximize his profits by offering a price based on $e_{t+1}^e=e_h$ in the next period. If he offers $e_{t+1}^e= e_l$ he will receive a good worth $R(e_l)$, which makes him strictly worse off, and if he offers $e_{t+1}^e=0$ then no trade will occur, which makes him strictly worse off.

For $e_0=e_h$ the seller will gain from a deviation when:

$$C(e_h) > (\partial/1-\partial)\ \Pi_h \text{ or } C(e_h)-C(e_l) > \partial/1-\partial\ (\Pi_h-\Pi_l)$$

The optimal deviation is given by el when the buyer will set $e_{t+1}^e=e_t$ and:

$$C(e_l) < (\partial/1-\partial)\ \Pi_l$$

The buyer's best response to $e_t=e_l$ is to set $e_{t+1}^e=e_l$. The threat to cease trade if the seller cheats is not credible since once cheating has occurred, the buyer gets a higher payoff from trading at the new lower level than he would from no trade. The threat to punish by refusing to trade where trade is profitable and sustainable is not credible.

The seller will always find it profitable to cheat and select zero effort when:

$$C(e_l) > (\partial/1-\partial)\ \Pi_l \text{ and } C(e_h) > (\partial/1-\partial)\ \Pi_h$$

Knowing this, the buyer will never find it profitable to offer a positive price and will not trade with the seller.

Proposition 3: In a market where the frequency of repeated interaction is low, no trade is the unique sub-game perfect equilibrium of the trading game, i.e. there is no trade if:

$$\partial^N < C(e_l)\ /R(e_l)$$

Inefficient trade is sustainable (but efficient trade is not) where there is a moderate trading frequency, i.e. $e_o=e_l$ and $e_t^e=e_{t-1}$ for the buyer and $e_t=e_t^e= e_l$ for the seller are sub-game perfect nash equilibrium strategies of the game if:

$$C(e_l)\ /R(e_l) < \partial^N < C(e_h)\ -C(e_l)\ /\ R(e_h)\ -R(e_l)$$

Efficient trade is sustainable as a sub-game perfect nash equilibrium of the game if:

$$\partial^N > C(e_h)\ -C(e_l)\ /\ R(e_h)\ -R(e_l)$$

Proof:

We know from the optimality principle of repeated games that attention can be focuses on the profitability of a single period deviation from equilibrium strategies. Cheating in this model takes the form of $e_t<e_o$. The buyer can

offer a first period price ER(e)=0 where $e_o=\{0,e_l,e_h\}$. If the buyer selects $e_o=0$, then no trade will occur. If the buyer selects $e_o=e_h$, then the seller chooses e_t to maximize the following:

$$R(e_h)-C(e_t)+\sum_{t=1}^{\infty}\partial^t[ER_{t+1}(e) - C(e_{t+1})]$$

Following the same argument as in Proposition 2, the seller, and therefore also the buyer, will not find it profitable to deviate when:

$$C(e_h) < (\partial^N/1-\partial^N)\Pi_h \text{ and } C(e_h)-C(e_l) < (\partial^N/1-\partial^N)(\Pi_h-\Pi_l)$$

Similarly, the seller will find it profitable to deviate from e0=eh, selecting el instead, but will not find it profitable to deviate from $e0=e_l$ when:

$$C(e_l) < (\partial^N/1-\partial^N)\Pi_l \text{ but } C(e_h)-C(e_l) > (\partial^N/1-\partial^N)(\Pi_h-\Pi_l)$$

The seller will always find it profitable to deviate when:

$$\partial^N< C(e_l) /R(e_l)$$

and no trade will occur.

Appendix Two

Proposition 4: Gang membership increases the range of market parameters for which trade can be sustained, i.e. the ability to trade for gang members is extended beyond that of individual sellers to include: (1) low level trade (i.e.$e_0=e_l$ and $e_t^e=e_t=e_l$) when: (i) $(\partial^N/1-\partial^N) < C(e_l)/\Pi_l < (\partial/1-\partial)$ and (ii)$Y > C(e_l) - \partial^N R(e_l)$ (or $Y > C(e_l)$ where no repeat trade is expected), and (2) efficient trade (i.e. $e_0=e_h$ and $e_t^e=e_t=e_h$) when:
(i) $(\partial^N/1-\partial^N) < (C(e_h) -C(e_l)) /(\Pi_h-\Pi_l) < (\partial/1-\partial)$ and
(ii)$Y > C(e_h) -C(e_l) - \partial^N(R(e_h)-R(e_l))$ (or $Y > C(e_h)$ where no repeat trade is expected).

Proof:

Consider the tit-for-tat strategies $e_0=e_h$ and $e_t^e=e_{t-1}$ for each of the buyers and $e_t= e_t^e$ for each of the gang members. The conditions specified in Proposition 3 continue to hold for sellers who become gang members as long as there is repeat trade within the gang or Y is at least as large as the Nth period profit loss (i.e. $Y \geq \partial^N(R(e_h) -R(e_l))$.

Gang membership provides an increase in the frequency of trade between the buyer and the group of sellers taken as a unit, which means that the cost of cheating for the gang occurs in the next period rather than in the Nth period, i.e. the loss of cheating by seller i to the gang is given by:

$$L= (\partial/1-\partial)(\Pi_h-\Pi_l)$$

The benefits of cheating accrue solely to the individual gang member, who, if he expects to trade with the same buyer every N periods, receives a net benefit of:

$$B_i=C(e_h) -C(e_l)-Y- (\partial^N/1-\partial^N)(\Pi_h-\Pi_l)$$

Note that if this gang member does not expect to trade with the same buyer again, and the gang is unable to restore trade with the seller, then this becomes:

$$L = (\partial/1-\partial)\Pi_h \text{ and } B_i=C(e_h) -Y$$

The range of parameters for which cheating is profitable from the gang's point of view is smaller than for the individual seller. Given $e_0=e_h$, the gang has an incentive to punish cheats when:

$$(C(e_h) - C(e_l)) / (\Pi_h - \Pi_l) < (\partial/1-\partial)$$

Once a buyer has been cheated, he will readjust his expectations, and trade will continue to occur at the new lower level given that each gang member continues to set $e_t = e_t^e$. Where the buyer deals with the same gang member every N periods, the gang member bears both the cost of lower profits and the penalty Y when he cheats. Where there is no repeat trade within the gang, the seller bears only the cost Y. Assuming that trade within the gang occurs according to MN, no gang member will have an incentive to cheat when:

$$Y > C(e_h) - C(e_l) - \partial^N (R(e_h) - R(e_l))$$

Similarly, for $e_0=e_l$, the gang has an incentive to deter cheating when:

$$(\partial^N/1-\partial^N) < C(e_l) / \Pi_l < (\partial/1-\partial)$$

and gang members will not cheat when:

$$Y > C(e_l) - \partial^N R(e_l)$$

Using an argument similar to that in Proposition 2, it can be shown that where the seller has no incentive to deviate, neither does the buyer.

Proposition 5: A reputation premium from gang membership allows gang members to sustain trade for a broader range of market conditions than they could sustain as independent sellers.
i.e. Gang membership extends the range of trade to include:
(i) efficient trade when:

$$(\partial^N/1-\partial^N)(\Pi_{ih}-\Pi_{il}) < C(e_h) - C(e_l) < (\partial/1-\partial)(\Pi_{gh}-\Pi_{il})$$

$$\text{i.e. } \partial^N < C(e_h) - C(e_l) / ER_i(e_h) - ER_i(e_l)$$

$$\text{but } \partial > C(e_h) - C(e_l) / ER_g(e_h) - ER_i(e_l)$$

(ii) inefficient but not efficient trade (i.e. trade of $R(e_l)$) if

$$(\partial^N/1-\partial^N)\Pi_{il} < C(e_l) < (\partial/1-\partial)\Pi_g;$$

Proof:

The gang member compares the following payoffs:

For $e_o=e_t=e_h$ and $e_{t+1}=e_t$:

$$E\Pi_i=Rg(e_h) -C(e_h)+ (\partial^N/1-\partial^N)(ERg(e_h)-C(e_h))$$

For $eo=e_h$, $et=e_l$ and $e_{t+1}=et$:

$$E\Pi_i=Rg(e_h) -C(e_l)+ (\partial^N/1-\partial^N)(ER_i(e_l)-C(e_l))$$

For $e_o=e_h$, $e_t=0$ and $e_{t+1}=et$:

$$E\Pi_i=R_g(e_h)$$

A similar comparison can be done for $e_o=e_l$ and $e_o=0$. Efficient trade is sustainable within a gang but is not sustainable by independent sellers where

$$(\partial^N/1-\partial^N)(\Pi i_h-\Pi i_l)<C(e_h) -C(e_l)<(\partial^N/1-\partial^N)(\Pi g_h-\Pi i_l)$$

Trade at an inefficient level (e_l) is sustainable with a gang member but not with an independent seller when:

$$(\partial^N/1-\partial^N)\, \Pi i_l < C(e_l) < (\partial^N/1-\partial^N)\Pi g_l$$

Appendix Three

Proposition 6: Full participation in penalty enforcement by the N-1 gang members is a sub-game perfect nash equilibrium of the game as long as $(\partial/1-\partial)(\Pi_{gh}-\Pi_{il})>2X/N-2$, and no participation is also a sub-game perfect nash equilibrium of the game.

Proof:

For cost X/N-1 of excluding the cheat and cost 2X/N-2 of excluding both the cheat and any gang member who does not participate in cheating, gang member i will have an incentive to punish a cheat j if and only if the following conditions hold:

$$(1)\ - X/(N-1) + (\partial/1-\partial)\ \Pi_{gh} > (\partial/1-\partial)\ \Pi_{il}$$

This condition ensures that the cost of being punished for not participating in group penalty schemes is larger than the benefit in terms of effort saved.

$$(2)\qquad -2X/(N-2) + (\partial/1-\partial)\ \Pi_{gh} > (\partial/1-\partial)\ \Pi_{il}$$

$$\text{i.e.}\qquad (\partial/1-\partial)(\ \Pi_{gh} -\Pi_{il})> 2X/(N-2)$$

This condition ensures that the threat of other gang members to punish a cheat is credible. Where gang members do not expect other gang members to participate in the penalty scheme, individual members will not expect to be punished and will have no incentive to participate. In this case, the no cheating outcome is not sustainable.

Notes

[1] Schumpeter, J.A. (1909), 'On the Concept of Social Value', *Quarterly Journal of Economics*, pp. 213-232.
[2] Id. at 4.
[3] Marx, K. (1844), *Economic and Philosophic Manuscript of 1844*, Foreign Languages Publishing House, Moscow, 1959 edition.
[4] Arrow suggests that "some sense of rational balancing of ends and means must be understood to play a major role in our understanding of ourselves and our social role". Arrow, K.J. (1974), *The Limits of Organization*, W.W. Norton & Company, New York, p.1.
[5] See Crozier, M. (1967), *The Bureaucratic Phenomenon*, University of Chicago Press. Chicago; Cyert, R. and March, J. (1963), *A Behavioral Theory of the Firm*, Prentice-Hall, Englewood Cliffs, N.J.
[6] Mill, J.S. (1859), *On Liberty*, Gateway, New York.
[7] Williamson, O.E. (1979), 'Transaction-Cost Economics: The Governance of Contractual Relations', *Journal of Law and Economics*, vol. 22, pp. 233-61.
[8] See e.g. Coase, R. H. (1937), 'The Nature of the Firm', *Economica*, vol. 4, pp. 386-405.
[9] See e.g.Holmstrom.,B. (1979), 'Moral Hazard and Observability', *Bell Journal of Economics*, vol. 10, p. 74.
[10] See Alchian, A. and Demsetz, H. (1972), 'Production, Information Costs and Economic Organization', *American Economic Review*, vol. 62, p. 777.
[11] See Grossman, S. and Hart, O. (1986), 'The Costs and Benefits of Ownership: A Theory of Vertical and Lateral Integration.', *Journal of Political Economy*, vol. 94, no. 4, pp. 691-719.
[12]An ordering is a ranking relationship which satisfies transitivity, reflexivity and completeness. It provides a ranking of all alternatives in a specified set. See Sen, A. K. (1979), *Collective Choice and Social Welfare*, University of Oxford, Oxford.
[13] Arrow, K. J. (1951), *Social Choice and Individual Values*, Wiley, New York. See also Sen, A. K. (1979), *Collective Choice and Social Welfare,* University of Oxford, Oxford.
[14] One way of side-stepping the conceptual issue of how to characterize group behavior as distinct from individual behavior is to begin with an analysis of organizational structure and a comparison of the mechanisms which emerge in different contexts.
[15] Iannaccone, L. R. (1992), 'Sacrifice and Stigma: Reducing Free-Riding in Cults, Communes and Other Collectives', *Journal of Political Economy*, vol. 100, no.2, pp. 271-291.
[16] Iannaccone comments on the relative success of those religious groups which make comparatively strict demands on the behavior of their members and suggests that the explanation lies in the collective nature of religious activity and the need to address free-rider problems in situations of collective action.

[17] Jankowski, M. (1991), *Islands in the Street. Gangs and American Urban Society*, University of California Press, Berkley, CA, at p. 47.
[18] Cornes, R. and Sandler, T. (1984), 'Easy Riders, Joint Production, and Public Goods', *Economic Journal*, vol. 94, pp. 580-98.
[19] Legros, P. and Newman, A. (1996), 'Wealth Effects, Distribution, and the Theory of Organization', *Journal of Economic Theory*, vol. 70, pp. 312-341.
[20] Minniti, M. (1995), 'Membership Has Its Privileges: Old and New Mafia Organizations', *Comparative Economic Studies*, vol. 37, no. 4, pp. 31-47. New entrants must select between honest work and mafia membership based on a return technology which is a function of individual characteristics and the ratio of the population who have chosen to be in the mafia. The process is modeled as a non-linear path-dependent stochastic process in which the probability for an event being repeated is a function of its relative share of previous realizations and the process generates multiple equilibria of varying stability.
[21] Sah, R. (1991), 'Social Osmosis and Patterns of Crime', *Journal of Political Economy*, vol. 99, no. 6, pp. 1272-1295.
[22] A theory of street gangs as organizational responses to existing social and economic conditions can be used to explain the gender divisions in gang activity in terms of differences in the conditions which males and females have been confronted with. In the past young women have relied on the family unit as their support structures and have regarded child rearing, as opposed to employment, as their defined role. Association with gang members or gang activities had more of a stigmatizing effect on females in their later life. Female gang activity is becoming more prominent, due in part to changes in perceptions of gender roles, reductions in government support and the continuing lack of male financial support in poor communities. As a generalization, female gang members tend to be much less violent and more risk averse in their choice of illegal activities than male gangs and tend to age out of the gang at an earlier age. Fagan (1993) suggests that in a world of limited opportunities for poor singe mothers, drug dealing has become one way to avoid prostitution as a means of supporting themselves and their families. This pattern reinforces the connection between joblessness, now perceived as a female as well as a male condition, and gang activity.
[23] "The story of male gang involvement with drug sales at the end of the 1980s has been repeated by studies in Detroit (Taylor, 1989), San Francisco (Waldorf et. al. 1991), Chicago (Padilla, 1992; Venkatesh ,1996), New York (Fagan, 1989), Los Angeles (Vigil, 1988), St. Louis (Decker and Van Winkle, 1996) and Milwaukee (Hagedorn 1996) among other cities." See Hagedorn, J. (1996), 'Gang Violence in the Post-Industrial Era', Working Draft, University of Illinois-Chicago, p.23. According to Hagedorn, Milwaukee male gang members made an average of about $2400 a month selling drugs but made less than $700 in legitimate jobs, but nevertheless spent more months in these low wage legitimate jobs. Taylor (1992) notes the development of "corporate gangs" as a substitute for business enterprises in devastated Detroit neighborhoods, for example, and Venkatesh (1995) describes the conflicting support and hostility of residents in some of Chicago's large, extremely poor housing projects towards the drug related activities of gangs.

Hagedorn's Milwaukee research (Moore and Hagedorn, 1995) supports the view that the lack of social controls and the importance of the economic dimension in extremely poor, job-less communities contribute to gang development.

[24] Wilson, W. J. (1987), *The Truly Disadvantaged*, University of Chicago Press, Chicago.

[25] The principal-agent literature centers around the conflict between risk sharing and incentive problems which arise in situations where an individual delegates tasks which are performed in return for compensation of some form. In the most basic form of the principal-agent model the principal and agent have conflicting objectives and either the agent's action or his information is not directly observable. This creates problems of moral hazard in the case of hidden actions or post-contractual hidden information which the principal must address through choice of incentive schemes. In the standard model, the principal employs the agent to perform actions in accordance with his own interests, but is limited in his ability to control the agent's objectives and actions because of hidden information and uncertainty. See e.g. Hart, O. and Holmstrom, B. (1987), 'The Theory of Contracts', in T.F. Bewley, *Advances in Economic Theory, Fifth Wold Congress*, Cambridge University Press, Cambridge, pp. 71-155, 76.

[26] Mirllees, J. A. (1976), 'The Optimal Structure of Incentives and Authority Within an Organization', *Bell Journal Of Economics*, vol. 7, no. 1, pp. 105-131.

[27] Alchian, A. and Demsetz, H. (1972), 'Production, Information Costs, and Economic Organization', American Economic Review, vol. 62, pp. 777-795, 779.

[28] See Holmstrom, B. (1982), 'Moral Hazard in Teams', *Bell Journal of Economics*, vol. XII, pp. 324-40. Individuals with too little incentive to invest if their only incentive to perform is provided by a partial share of the joint output. Holmstrom (1982) shows that the first best is not obtainable with budget balancing and unobservable individual actions. This solution depends on risk neutrality and the absence of wealth constraints.

[29] Eswaran, M. and Kotwal, A. (1984), 'The moral hazard of budget-breaking', *Rand Journal of Economics*, vol. 15, no.4, pp. 578-581.

[30] Itoh, H. (1991), 'Incentives to Help In Multi-Agent Situations', *Econometrica*, vol. 59, no. 3, pp. 611-636.

[31] Id. Where tasks are similar and agents care only about effort, the cost function for implementing effort levels increases discontinuously as agents move from zero to positive help. Since the expected revenue function is continuos, this introduces a non-convexity result. Teamwork will be optimal where own and helping efforts are complementary or where the decrease in own effort substantially reduces the payment required to induce own effort.

[32] Green, E. and Porter, R. (1984), 'Non-cooperative Collusion Under Imperfect Price Information', *Econometrica*, vol. 52, no. 1, pp. 87-100.

[33] Benhabib, J. and Radner, R. (1992), 'The Joint Exploitation of a Productive Asset: A Game Theoretic Approach', *Economic Theory*, vol. 2, no. 2, pp. 155-90.

[34] Dutta, P. and Sundaram, R. (1993), 'The tragedy of the commons?' *Economic Theory*, vol. 3, pp. 413-426.

[35] Ben-Porath, E. (1996), 'Communication in Repeated Games with Private

Monitoring', *Journal of Economic Theory*, vol. 70, pp. 281-297.

[36] Bull, C. (1987), 'The Existence of Self-Enforcing Implicit Contracts', *Quarterly Journal of Economics*, pp. 147-159.

[37] Bernheim, D., Peleg, B. and Whinston, M. (1987), 'Coalition-Proof Nash Equilibria I. Concepts', *Journal of Economic Theory*, vol. 42, pp. 1-12.

[38] "An agreement is coalition proof if and only if it is Pareto efficient within the class of self-enforcing agreements. In turn, an agreement is self-enforcing if and only if no proper subset (coalition) of players, taking the actions of its complement as fixed, can agree to deviate in a way that makes all of its members better off." Id. at 3.

[39] G. Harden was the first to joint the phrase "tragedy of the commons", using it to refer to situations in which the absence of private property rights and governmental regulation of limited natural resources leads to an overexploitation and, potentially, the destruction of the resource by individuals acting in a narrowly self-interested manner. See Hardin, G. (1968), 'The Tragedy of the Commons', *Science*, vol. 162, pp. 1243-48.

[40] Certain lobster fishing territories in Maine are protected by group s of fishermen who engage in private and sometimes illegal enforcement actions designed to keep out outsiders. The result has been a stable catch-to-effort ratio for over 25 years. See Acheson, J.M. (1993), 'Capturing the Commons: Legal and Illegal Strategies', in T. L. Anderson and R. T. Simmons (eds), *The political economy of customs and culture: Informal solutions to the commons problem*, Rowman and Littlefield, Lanham.

[41] See Ostrom,E. (1990), *Governing the commons: The evolution of institutions for collective action*, Cambridge University Press, Cambridge, p. 29.

[42] These design principles are: (1) clearly defined boundaries; (2) congruence between appropriation and provision rules and local conditions; (3) collective-choice arrangements; (4) monitoring; (5) graduated sanctions; (6) conflict-resolution mechanisms; (7) minimal recognition of rights to organize. Id at p. 90.

[43] Id at p. 188.

[44] This pattern is linked to and perpetuated by the unequal distribution of economic resources and economic opportunities among different groups, which contribute to social isolation and a lack of internal mobility.

[45] She suggests, for example, that monitoring and enforcement costs are affected by the physical attributes of the resource, the exclusion and appropriation technology available, marketing arrangements, proposed rules and legitimacy of rules in use. Situational variables affecting internal norms and discount rates include proximity to the resource, scope of interaction, and information available about alternative opportunities. Id at p. 203.

[46] See Sethi, R. and Somanthan, E. (1996), 'The Evolution of Social Norms in Common Property Resource Use', *American Economic Review*, vol. 86, no. 4, pp. 766-788.

[47] d'Aspremont, C. and Gabszewicz, J. (1985), 'On the Stability of Collusion', in J. Stiglitz and G. Mathewson (eds), *New Developments in the Analysis of Market Structure*, MIT Press, Cambridge, pp. 243-264, 244.

[48] The "collusive scheme", denoted by C, is given by a partition of a set of N individuals into subsets Nk, with all individuals in Nk acting as a collusive "group" or single decision making unit. The stability of a collusive scheme can be evaluated by examining the outcomes associated with alternative feasible collusive schemes, including both "internal" comparisons of payoffs for a given collusive scheme and "external" comparisons between alternative schemes. The full agreement collusive scheme is given by Cf = {N}, where N denotes the entire set of individuals, and at the other end of the spectrum the disagreement collusive scheme is given by Cd={(1),(2),...,(n)}.
[49] Id. at p. 245.
[50] See d'Aspremont, C., Gabszewicz, J., Jacquemin, A. and Weymark. J. (1983), 'On the Stability of Collusive Price Leadership', *Canadian Journal of Economics*, pp. 17-25. In their model there are a fixed finite number of firms (n) producing homogenous output with identical differentiable cost functions and industry demand function. k of these firms combine to form a cartel and the remaining n-k firms constitute competitive fringe. Given the definitions of internal and external stability imposed, they show that with a discrete number of firms there is always a stable cartel but with continuum of firms there is no internally stable cartel.
[51] Thoron models the formation of coalitions in oligopolies as a non-cooperative game in which firms' strategies consist of the binary decision to cooperate or not and demonstrates that the Nash equilibrium of this game corresponds to the existence of a stable cartel. Thoron, S. (1995), 'Formation of a Coalition-Proof Stable Cartel', Working Paper, University of Toulon.
[52] Interesting questions arise as to why some gangs are able to persist over time whereas others have very short life-spans.
[53] Tirole, J. (1986), 'Hierarchies and Bureaucracies: On the Role of Collusion in Organizations', *Journal of Law, Economics and Organization*, vol. 2, no. 2, pp. 181-213.
[54] In this model it is the supervisor's task to monitor the effort choices of the agent and report his observations to the principal, and the supervisor and agent can gain by misreporting observed effort choices.
[55] Tirole, J. (1986), 'Hierarchies and Bureaucracies: On the Role of Collusion in Organizations', *Journal of Law, Economics and Organization*, vol. 2, no. 2, pp. 181-213.
[56] Marschak, J. and Radner, R. (1972), *Economic Theory of Teams*, Yale University Press, New Haven.
[57] Marshak, J. (1955), 'Elements for a Theory of Teams', *Management Science*, vol. 1, pp. 127-137. See also Bower, J. L. (1965), 'The Role of Conflict in Economic Decision-Making Groups: Some Empirical Results', *Quarterly Journal of Economics*, vol. 79, no. 2, pp. 263-277.
[58] The importance of structuring jobs and work environments in ways which provide employees with a sense of corporate loyalty and job satisfaction has been documented in the business literature. Empirical evidence has suggested that factors which interfere with the conception of "team" production, such as salary differentials between closely associated workers, can lead to lower productivity and

that factors which increase individual participation in group processes can lead to higher productivity.

[59] See Spergel, I. (1995), *The Youth Gang Problem*, Oxford University Press, Oxford, p. 99.

[60] Wilson, R. (1968), 'The Theory of Syndicates', *Econometrica*, vol. 36, no. 1, pp. 119-132.

[61] The nature of the sharing rule plays a central role in Wilson's model. The syndicate makes a common decision α which, depending on the realization of a random variable , results in a payoff given by $x=p(\varepsilon,\alpha)$ that is shared among the members.

[62] Legros, P. (1987), 'Disadvantageous Syndicates and Stable Cartels: The Case of the Nucleolus', *Journal of Economic Theory*, pp. 30-49, 42.

[63] In Legros' model there are two types of players and two commodities. He develops a side-payment game in which the allocation of profits is given by the nucleolus (i.e. the allocation which minimizes the dissatisfaction of any coalition as measured in a way which tries to minimize deviations from preferred outcomes for all possible coalitions).

[64] See Wilson, W. J. (1987), *The Truly Disadvantaged*, University of Chicago Press, Chicago (talking about the importance of social and economic networks in enabling individuals to obtain education and jobs and other forms of socio-economic mobility); Iacobucci, D. and Hopkins, N. (1992), 'Modeling dyadic interactions and networks in marketing', *Journal of Marketing Research*, vol. 29, pp. 5-17 (looking at informal patterns of communication among consumers).

[65] See Bolton, P. and Dewatripont, M. (1994). 'The firm as a communication network', *The Quarterly Journal of Economics,* vol. CIX, no.4, pp. 808-839; Keren, M. and Levhari, D. (1983), 'The internal organization of the firm and the shape of average costs', *Bell Journal of Economics*, vol. 4, no.1, pp. 474-486.

[66] See Williamson, O. (1975), *Markets and hierarchies: Analysis and antitrust implications*, Free Press, New York.

[67] Zusman, P. and Rausser. G. (1991), 'Intraorganizational influence relations and the optimality of collective action.' *Journal of Economic Behavior and Organization*, vol. 24, pp. 1-17.

[68] Id. at 3.

[69] Jackson, M. and Wolinsky, A. (1996), 'A Strategic Model of Social and Economic Networks', *Journal of Economic Theory*, vol. 71, pp. 44-74.

[70] Arrow suggests that "(a)t any moment the individual is a bundle of abilities and accumulated information. He may easily find it cheaper to open certain information channels rather than others in ways connected with these abilities and this knowledge."Arrow, K. (1974), *The Limits of Organization*, W.W. Norton and Co., New York, p. 41.

[71] Hirschman, A.O. (1996), Harvard Political Economy Lecture, November 1996, Harvard University. Also see Hirschman, A.O. (1970), *Exit, Voice and Loyalty*, Harvard University Press, Cambridge.

[72] "Gangs have been largely, but not wholly, tied up with the experience of ethnic groups trying to make it in America. The vast majority of today's gangs are

African American, Latino, or Asian just as gangs in the past were largely composed of European immigrants." Hagedorn, J.M. (1996), 'Gang Violence in the Post-Industrial Era', Working Draft, University of Illinois-Chicago, October, 21. "By the 1990s, the movies "Colors," "Scarface," and "New Jack City" had popularized a different image: cold-blooded minority gangsters shooting it out in drive-bys or disputes over drugs." Id. at 1.

[73] Drug dealers, gang members, immigrants, and welfare recipients seem to be the most recent "folk devils" in U.S. domestic policy. Hagedorn, J. (1996), 'Gang Violence in the Post-Industrial Era', Working Paper, University of Illinois-Chicago, Chicago, p. 36.

[74] See Moore, J. (1996), 'Bearing the Burden: How Incarceration Policies Weaken Inner-City Communities' in K. Fulbrighted (ed), *The Unintended Consequences of Incarceration*, Vera Institute of Justice. New York; Clear,T. (1996), 'Backfire: When Incarceration Increases Crime' in K. Fulbrighted (ed), *The Unintended Consequences of Incarceration*, Vera Institute of Justice. New York. Tough sentencing for those selling crack cocaine has resulted in a substantial increase in the arrest of small time minority drug dealers, since most of the crack cocaine sellers are black and most of the buyers are white.

[75] See e.g. Camp, G. and Camp, C. (1985), *Prison Gangs: Their Extent, Nature, and Impact on Prisons*, U.S. Dept. of Justice, Washington, D.C.

[76] See e.g. Fulbrighted, K. (ed), *The Unintended Consequences of Incarceration*, Vera Institute of Justice, New York.

[77] See Olson, M. (1993), 'Dictatorship, Democracy, and Development', *American Political Science Review*, vol. 87, no.3, pp. 567-76; and Schelling, T.C. (1967), 'Economics and Criminal Enterprise', *The Public Interest*, vol. 7, pp. 61-78. Moselle and Polak (1995) present an interesting model based on a view of the state as imposed by a self-interested ruler. In their model the division between productive and non-productive activities is endogenous, and they contrast the outcomes achieved under three different stages of state-formation: disorganized crime, organized crime and extortionary state. Their results suggest that the middle stage may generate the least inefficiency. Moselle, B. and Polak, B. (1995), 'Anarchy, Organized Crime and Extortion: A Cynical Theory of the State', Working Paper, Harvard University.

[78] Blumestein (1995) points out the dramatic increases in homicide rates occurring to male teenage African Americans, particularly by the use of a firearm, which are unmatched by corresponding increase in other groups. Homicide rates for 16 year olds nationally increased 138% from 1985-92, for example, and gun related homicides for juveniles 10-17 tripled from 1984-90. Blumstein, A. (1995), 'Youth Violence, Guns, and the Illicit-Drug Industry', *Criminology*, vol. 86, pp. 10-36. See also Blumestein, A. (1993), 'Making Rationality Relevant', *Criminology*. Vol. 31, pp. 1-16.Hagedorn (1996) notes that "homicides in African American communities across the country jumped at the same time that large numbers of young males, including gang members, began selling cocaine. Hagedorn points to studies which suggest that more centralized and structured cocaine selling operations will be more likely to use violence to control and intimidate rivals, employees and customers.

[79] See Garfinkel, M. R. (1990), 'Arming as a Strategic Investment in a Cooperative Equilibrium', *American Economic Review*, vol. 80, no.1, pp. 50-68; Grossman, H. I. (1991), 'A General Equilibrium Model of Insurrections', *American Economic Review*, vol. 81, pp. 912-921; Haavelmo, T. (1954), *A Study in the Theory of Economic Evolution*, North-Holland Publishing House, Amsterdam; Hirshleifer, J. (1991), 'The Paradox of Power', *Economics and Politics*, vol. 3, pp. 177-200; Skaperdas, S. (1992), 'Cooperation, Conflict and Power in the Absence of Property Rights', *American Economic Review*, vol. 82, pp. 720-39; Skaperdas, S. and Syropoulos, C. (1995), 'Competing For Claims to Property', Working Paper, Brown University, June.

[80] See Hagedorn, J. (1996), 'Gang Violence in the Post-Industrial Era', Working Paper, University of Chicago, Illinois, p. 44; Shelley, J. and Wright, J. (1990), *In the Line of Fire: Youth, Guns and Violence in Urban America*, Aldine de Gruytr, New York.

[81] Fremon,C (1996), *Father Greg and the Homeboys: The Extraordinary Journey of Father Greg and his work with the Latino Gangs of East L.A.*

[82] In addition to its economic role as a way of expanding income earning opportunities, the gang often operates as an extended family, a means of protection, a source of information and skill development (albeit crime related skills) and a source of social status and identity. Other types of criminal gangs tend to focus on a narrower set of activities and involve less socialization between group members.

[83] The threat of a stream of future losses counter-balances the finite single-period gain from deviation. Factors identified as important in facilitating cooperation include the speed and cost of detecting and punishing cheats, the expected length and value of the relationship between actors, the distribution of information about private actions and the monitoring technologies available in the absence of perfect information, and the rate at which individuals discount future costs and benefits.

[84] Feasible, individually rational payoffs are defined by a player's minmax value, or best response to the payoff minimizing actions taken by his opponents. See Fudenberg, D. and Tirole, J. (1991), *Game Theory*, MIT Press, Cambridge. The standard version of the Folk Theorem asserts that in an infinitely repeated n-person game with finite action sets at each repetition, any combination of actions observed in any finite number of repetitions is the unique outcome of some subgame perfect equilibrium for a sufficiently large discount factor as long as the set of individually rational payoff combinations in the extended game is n-dimensional.

[85] See e.g. Fudenberg and Maskin (1986) who show that cooperation is sustainable in virtually all repeated games regardless of the magnitude of the payoffs and the number of players and strategies available.

[86] Milgrom, P , North, D. and Weingast. B. (1990), 'The Role of Institutions in the Revival of Trade: The Law Merchant, Private Judges, and the Champagne Fairs', *Economics and Politics*, vol. 2, no. 1, pp. 1-23.

[87] The cooperative results obtained in standard repeated games are sensitive to assumptions of perfect information, enforceability of punishments and limited impatience, however, and provide little guidance in determining which of many feasible outcomes will be selected.

[88] The reputation mechanism may operate by providing information about the type of player involved where there is hidden information about player type or may operate by directly affecting the incentives faced by a player with known characteristics who is planning to engage in other transactions which will be affected by his current actions.

[89] See e.g. Greif, A., Milgrom, P. and Weingast, B. (1994), 'Coordination, Commitment, and Enforcement: The Case of the Merchant Guild', *Journal of Political Economy*; Grief, A. (1989), 'Reputation and Coalitions in Medieval Trade: Evidence on the Maghribi Traders', *Journal of Economic History*, vol. XLIX, no. 4, pp. 857-882; North, D.C. and Weingast, B. (1989), 'Constitutions and Commitment: The Evolution of Institutions Governing Public Choice in Seventeenth Century England;, *Journal of Economic History*, vol. 49, pp. 803-832.

[90] See e.g. Fudenberg, D., D. Levine and E. Maskin . (1994), 'The folk theorem with imperfect information', *Econometrica*, vol. 62, pp. 997-1040. Green and Porter (1984) apply this type of scenario to explain temporary price wars in a model of imperfect collusion where there is uncertainty about market demand. Green, E. and Porter, R. (1984), 'Noncooperative Collusion Under Imperfect Price Information', *Econometrica,* vol. 52, no.1, pp. 87-100.

[91] See Radner, R. (1986), 'Repeated partnership games with imperfect monitoring and no discounting', *Review of Economic Studies*, vol. 53, pp. 43-58.; and Ben-Porath, E. and Kahneman, M. (1996), 'Communication in Repeated Games with Private Monitoring', *Journal of Economic Theory*, vol.70, pp. 281-297.

[92] A punishment scheme increases the expected cost of cheating through the threat of individualized punishment (e.g. a fine or physical punishment), group punishment (e.g. trigger price strategies leading to price wars), or the presence of social norms which are costly to violate (e.g. moral constraints and the use of social norms and stigma).

[93] In the tit for tat strategy, players begin by cooperating and then proceed by matching the actions of their opponent in the preceding period.

[94] Macaulay, S. (1963), 'Non-Contractual Relations in Business: A Preliminary Study', *American Sociological Review*, vol. 28, no.28.

[95] Klein, B. and Leffler, K. (1981), 'The Role of Market Forces in Assuring Contractual Performance', *Journal of Political Economy*, vol.89, no.4, pp. 615-41.

[96] Bernstein, L. (1992), 'Opting Out of the Legal System: Extralegal Contractual Relations in the Diamond Industry', *Journal of Legal Studies*, vol.XXI.

[97] It is interesting to consider the implications of making the purchase of drugs (rather than just the selling of drugs) illegal. This would further constrain buyer communications and would increase the value of seller reputation mechanisms.

[98] The gang structure provides members with the benefits of being identifiable without the corresponding increase in risk associated with investing in an individual criminal identity. Where the probability of detection by law enforcement is decreasing in the size of the market, gang membership provides a way of addressing the problems of decentralized trade while leaving the individual risk of detection by law enforcers the same. Moreover, the gang is able to develop a reputation based on features which are not directly associated with the sale of

illegal products (e.g. by adopting characteristics of a stereotypic "street gang", with beepers, dress codes and hand signals) whereas individual sellers must rely on more direct, and therefore more risky, signaling.

[99] The use of gang identity for business purposes parallels the use of corporate image to pursue economic objectives. A corporate image grounded on non-corporate variables may confer advantages in commercial circles because of the strategic effect of alternative objectives on incentives to perform particular actions. This notion is captured in the economics literature on strategic delegation and the empirical evidence on corporate firms engaging in public interest activities to improve corporate image.

[100] This investment could take the form of ensuring that the transaction is discreet, that the market location is secure, or that the product is of high quality, for example.

[101] The discount rate can be interpreted as an indicator of time preference (α) and expectations about escaping detection and continuing on with criminal activities in the next period ($1-\beta$), both of which are assumed to be constant, with $\partial=1-\beta/1+\alpha$

[102] Define M_C as the class of matching rules which assigns an equal probability of trade to all sellers and buyers in the market every N periods. M_C includes M_N and M_R, where M_N.is a sequential matching rule which matches seller i with buyer j once every N periods in a market with N buyers and N sellers, and M_R is a random matching rule according to which seller i has a probability (1/N) of being matched with buyer j in each period. Adopting these two types of matching rules simplifies the calculations and illustrates the implications of random interaction for trading opportunities.

[103] This corresponds to the Townsend (1981) matching rule in the context of an infinite number of traders. See Townsend, R. (1981), 'Models of Money With Spatially Separated Agents', in J.Kareken and N.Wallace (eds.), *Models of Monetary Economics*, Federal Reserve Bank, Minneapolis. Similar results could be obtained for a random matching rule in which each individual in the market expects to deal with a given buyer with probability (1/N).

[104] Within the class of matching rules such that each seller has an equal probability of trading with buyer j at least once during N periods of trade, there are two basic types of matching rules - random (e.g. each seller has a probability (1/N) of being matched with buyer j in each period), and sequential (e.g. seller i trades with buyer j once every N periods). The results extend to include other types of matching rules which assign a positive probability of trade with buyer j to all sellers within N periods of trade.

[105] Attention can be restricted to situations in which the seller chooses the same effort level in each subsequent period since if the seller's optimal choice in period t is e_t, it will not be profitable for individual i to choose $e_{tN}>e_t$ in future periods. This result is based on the optimal deviation principle applicable to repeated games.

[106] Note that the threat of punishment is only credible if the loss to the gang as a whole is larger than the gain to gang member i, since otherwise the cheating gang member could bribe the other gang members to avoid punishment, and that it is only effective if the punishment is larger than the gain from cheating.

[107] Where there is a delay in imposing penalties for cheating, expectations about the likelihood of future gang membership play an added role in determining the gang's ability to deter cheating.

[108] Factors which might influence the value of this premium include the expected time horizon of membership (intergenerational transfers allow the reputation mechanism to function more effectively), the time discount rate, alternative opportunities outside of gang membership and abilities to trade with other groups.

[109] An additional difficulty with costly self-enforceable punishment systems is the problem of credibility where cheating does not affect the future propensity to cheat. Cheating gang members can renegotiate by offering payment to avoid a punishment that gang members find it costly to inflict. If the gang is structured in such a way as to make the propensity to cheat an increasing function of the number of times a gang member has cheated then the problem of renegotiation will be lower.

[110] See e.g. Abreu, D. (1988), 'On the Theory of Infinitely Repeated Games With Discounting', *Econometrica*, vol. 56, no. 2, pp. 383-96.

3 The Economic Organization of Drug Selling Gangs

A substantial variation exists in the organizational structure of criminal groups across regions and within the same region of the United States. This chapter is based on the premise that the nature and structure of an income generating gang can be explained as an efficient response to economic conditions and that as these conditions change the organization will adapt to fit the new environment. While gangs may be formed to serve a variety of non-economic functions and membership may be influenced by socio-economic and cultural factors, it is argued that the organizational structures of gangs that focus on income generating crimes such as drug dealing are influenced by and evolve in response to economic factors. In the case of illegal narcotics sales, important determinants of gang structure and behavior include the demand and supply conditions of narcotics markets, product characteristics, alternative income sources available to gang members, and the risks associated with gang activities stemming from law enforcement, rival gangs and other gang members. Differences in economic factors can be used to explain the diversity of organizational forms among well-established American street gangs such as the Chicago based Vice Lords and Black Gangster Disciples, which are large vertically organized enterprises, and the equally infamous Los Angeles based Crips and Bloods, which are horizontally organized umbrella organizations comprised of small and loosely affiliated sub-groups. These same factors can be employed to gain a better understanding of the substantial differences in organizational form across gangs of different ethnic origin.

In this chapter an economic model similar to those employed in the industrial organization literature is developed to explain differences in the organization of criminal street gangs. This approach is based on the premise that variations in the organizational structure of criminal street gangs can be explained in economic terms as profit-maximizing responses to market conditions. A stylized model of organizational choice by a criminal street gang is used to connect a particular aspect of gang structure - the degree of centralization of decision making - with characteristics of the economic environment. Applying simple economic models to explain observed differences in the organization of drug dealing gangs provides a way of testing the assumption that drug dealing gangs function as economically rational business enterprises designed to exploit the income opportunities offered by illicit drug markets. In addition, it illustrates the importance of considering the organization of a gang when designing law enforcement policies. By highlighting the importance of economic factors as determinants of gang activity and the adaptability of gang structure to changing environments, the "crime and economics" approach has important implications for law enforcement policy.[1] The chapter begins with an overview of existing theories of gang organization. A model of gang structure is developed in the second part of the chapter, and its ability to account for observed differences in the organizational structure of gangs in the United States is examined in part three.

I. Contemporary Theories of Gangs and Gang Organization

There has been much debate about the extent to which street level drug selling gangs have adopted a "rational model of organization."[2] The debate has often been framed in terms of a distinction between "organized" and "free lance" activity, with a failure to distinguish between organization and centralization and a tendency to associate rational models of organization with conventional models of hierarchical criminal organizations.[3] By focusing their search on traditional models of organized crime, policy makers have shared in a general tendency to underestimate the degree of organization currently existing in local drug markets.[4]

Contemporary research on drug dealing street gangs can be divided into three categories. Researchers in the first category tend to focus on the group dynamics of gangs, often narrowing their study to a particular gang or group of gangs located in the same area. Researchers in the second category focus on the general characteristics of illegal drug markets. The third category includes research which tries to integrate the study of illegal enterprises and the markets within which they operate, searching for appropriate paradigms drawn from economic theories of firms, governments and markets.

The Organizational Approach to Street Gangs

Jankowski (1991) adopts the first methodology.[5] He studies gangs as organizations, looking at 37 "business" gangs in three cities over a period of 10 years. He identifies three types of gang organization (vertical, horizontal, and influential) and posits that these structures are developed by gang members with little influence from their environment. Jankowski envisions stages of development in which gang members are able to establish an increasingly more cohesive, tightly organized and profit-focused form of organization. He associates organization with degree of centralized decision making and control. Although his work is innovative and comprehensive, it has some important limitations. The first is a failure to look at the interaction between organization and environmental conditions. Second, the notion that loose organizations will be unsuccessful over time is assumed rather than demonstrated. Third, Jankowski attributes a substantial amount of rationality to individual decision makers without specifying the nature of this "rationality" or providing a means of testing the assumption.

Hagedorn (1994) applies contingency theory, which focuses on the ability of a group to adapt to changes in its environment, to explore the sources of variation in drug-selling organization of gangs from Milwaukee.[6] He argues that "in the turbulent environment surrounding drug selling, inflexible vertically organized drug businesses are unlikely to be successful," and finds that neighborhood-based drug-selling organizations vary according to the lucrativeness and stability of the drug market and the extent to which markets are local or external. "Contingency theory would predict successful organizations formed under these (rapidly changing and risky) conditions would be non vertical, decentralized, flexible, and loosely or even barely structured operations. Gang drug selling, it could be predicted, would more likely be similar to Waldorf's freelance drug sales than to Jankowski's cohesive organizations or structuralist notions of organized crime. Gang drug sales, it could be hypothesized, may be relatively more organized and successful in environments (i.e. neighborhoods) where competition is curtailed, surveillance low, and where there is access to a stable, more affluent customer base. "Tightly organized" gang forms of the Jankowski mode would be "rare in nature" and likely to fail."[7] Hagedorn (1996) makes the same point at a greater level of generality by suggesting ways in which the nature and actions of contemporary gangs reflect the consequences of deindustrialization and economic restructuring.[8] These changes include a more business oriented approach to drug dealing by young adults in concentrated areas of high unemployment and a low level of social control and a higher level of violence, instrumental and otherwise. While the results in this chapter are consistent with Hagedorn's claim that gang organization is dynamic and evolves in response to conditions in its environment, the model is based on the premise that these factors can be usefully incorporated into a rational choice model of gang structure.[9] While Hagedorn demonstrates that different kinds of neighborhoods have produced different kinds of drug-selling organizations, this chapter seeks to provide an economic rationale for some of these differences.

According to Padilla (1992), the activities of more highly organized drug dealing gangs are driven to a large extent by economic concerns, and members of these gangs perceive their organizations as businesses.[10] Members of the group tend to be involved in similar types of economic crimes, individual actions are coordinated and functional roles assigned in order to exploit the income opportunities of a demarcated area. Padilla traces the development of one particular Latino youth gang in Chicago into a wholesale business establishment during the 1970s and 80s, a time in which Chicago was becoming a central distribution point for the international drug trade. He widens his study to include noticeable trends in gang and drug activity in the Chicago area, noting in particular the relatively cooperative relations that rival Chicago gangs were able to establish between themselves in the early 1980s. Padilla interprets this method of inducing cooperation, based on a division of city areas into two gang nations, or alliances, as an indication of the growing concern for business. Organizing gangs into one of two nations (the People and the Folks) "contributed immensely to solidifying the business operation of the gang. "Respect for each other's territories" also came to mean the sharing of the larger consumer drug market. Each gang could now run its business operations within a relatively safe turf, or marketplace, selling only to those customers who voluntarily frequented it. No longer was the gang involved in efforts to take over other hoods, hoping to expand its business boundaries beyond its immediate neighborhood settings."[11] Unfortunately, substantial coordination problems have subsequently undermined this truce. It is interesting to note that New Orleans experienced the same type of phenomenon in the 1970s and 80s when the local drug market became dominated by one particular group. Upon the arrest of the ringleader by federal prosecutors, violence in the area escalated as less established groups vied for control of the "liberated" market.

Sullivan (1989) focuses on the role of economic opportunities and social organization in shaping patterns of youth crime.[12] He sees individual choices as taking place within socially bounded spheres of interaction and looks to local variations in economic process across localities to explain patterns of criminal activity. He suggests that an understanding of the economic aspects of criminality must take into account the important connections between social and economic processes at the local level. Sullivan examines the relationship between criminality and local economic opportunities through analysis of comparative ethnographic data collected in New York inner-city communities during the mid-1980s.[13] Block and Block (1993) provide empirical evidence which demonstrates the substantial variation in street gang activities across neighborhoods and population groups in their analysis of geographic patterns of street gang activity in Chicago.[14]

Taylor (1990) shares Sullivan's concern with the link between the decline of social, educational and economic structures in concentrated areas of poverty and unemployment and gang activity in these areas.[15] He observes that "cocaine and crack cocaine have provided goals, jobs, and economic realities that African-American communities in Detroit had never seen before."[16] Unsupervised black youths learn to survive on the streets by attaching themselves to semi-organized groups involved in illegal activities. According to Taylor's observations of the evolution of street gangs in Detroit, these groups develop from "scavenger" groups into "turf" gangs and, in some cases, into "corporate" gangs who use drug dealing as a "unifying economic force" and a "vehicle for social mobility."[17]

Spergel (1995) provides a comprehensive rethinking of general gang policy, program experience and research findings which emphasizes the need for an integrated organizational approach to street gangs.[18] He argues that social disorganization provides the basic stimulus for the formation of youth gangs, and that the lack of legitimate alternatives and the availability of illegitimate ones shapes the character and scope of gang behavior. The gang provides a vehicle for organizing the interests and needs of its members, with the idea of gang territory and social control as the primary organizational purpose and a close link between gang organization and increasing criminal and decreasing legitimate sources of economic opportunity and social status. While Spergel suggests that the gang develops in increasingly complex, rational and specialized ways over time, he argues that the gang "always resembles more a collectively, clan, or social movement with strong symbolic concerns than a typical bureaucratic or business organization. Each local community seems to provide a somewhat different context for the development of the gang, particularly with regard to race/ethnicity, class, community organization, and cultural traditions."[19]

Wilson (1987) goes even further than Sullivan and Taylor in emphasizing the importance of the role that socio-economic constraints have played in shaping individual patterns of behavior.[20] He focuses on the tremendous constraints that many disadvantaged residents of poor communities face and suggests that participation in criminal activities is fueled by real and perceived limitations on economic and geographical mobility. Along these lines, gangs could be seen as providing an alternative "network" for individuals who have been shut out of main-stream social and economic networks. Massey and Denton (1993) focus on the importance of race-based residential segregation as a major determinant of the development and perpetuation of the black American "underclass."[21] They emphasize the crucial connection between social and spatial mobility and the importance of geographically defined structural variables in creating the underclass ghetto neighborhoods which gang researchers have identified as conducive to the emergence of African-American street gangs. They argue that the ghetto, with its high levels of crime, violence, gangs and drug activity, is maintained by a set of deeply embedded American institutions, attitudes and practices designed to localize and isolate these problems.[22]

Fagan (1989,1990) focuses on the social processes of delinquency and group violence.[23] He adopts a group specific notion of gang development which places more emphasis on the internal nature and structure of the social process than Wilson does. He examines the use of violence by gang members as a means of regulation and maintaining social control and the importance of initiation and membership rituals in defining the social process. This approach to gang development as a special social process with discernible group-specific characteristics can be contrasted with the community-based approach that Vigil and Yun (1996) adopt.[24] They emphasize the importance of ethnicity and community structure in shaping gang structure and function. Vigil concentrates on describing the social organization of Latino "barrio gangs" in Southern California and Texas and the relationship of these barrio gangs to their (typically ethnically homogenous) neighborhoods. He explains the relative territoriality and strong codes of loyalty and honor which bind many of the barrio gang members as an extension of community values and culture.

Klein (1990, 1993, 1994,1995a) focuses on the relationship between the internal dynamics of the gang and the broader social dynamics of which they are a part, looking at issues such as "street gang cycles" and the relationship of trends in gang activity to broader economic and social trends, the role of socio-economic conditions in shaping gang organization, and distinctions between internally and externally defined groups and gang cohesiveness.[25] He suggests that despite its considerable variety over time, across locations, and even in its internal substructures, the American street gang is unique and distinguishable from other types of groups. Gang cohesiveness is identified as the key organizing concept, with territoriality and a criminal orientation as factors shaping group identity (primarily via the fostering of self-recognition).[26] Klein emphasizes the importance of territoriality to gang definition, contrasting this "recognizability by default" with the deliberate recognizablility employed and/or narrow range of activities engaged in by other groups, such as skinheads, bikers and terrorist groups. Street gangs are also distinguished from prison gangs (such as the Mexican Mafia, Nuestra Familia, and Aryan Brotherhood) which maintain group cohesiveness principally through offering protection from rival groups, strict rules and vicious sanctions. Changes in gang structure and behavior over the past three decades, including their violence, proliferation[27] and changing age, gender and ethnic characteristics, are discussed and linked to broader social and economic changes.[28] Klein's work is based in part on direct experience acquired from working with Los Angeles street gangs and law enforcement activities for over three decades.

The Illegal Markets Approach

Kleiman (1995), Reuter and Caulkins, and Moore (1990) are among the few to engage in a systematic study of illicit drug sales as economic transactions occurring within drug markets.[29] They begin by pointing out the similarities that drug markets share with other markets and go on to examine the markets' distinguishing features, some of which stem from the illegality of the transactions and some of which are peculiar to the specific features of the products being sold. Different market practices have been adopted by sellers of different types of drugs. Powder cocaine and crack markets involve a large number of small transactions, and dilution of the product is relatively easy to perform and hard to detect, for example, whereas marijuana markets involve larger but less frequent transactions of a product which is more difficult to adulterate. The typical cocaine sale occurs on the street corner, whereas sale of marijuana tends to occur more often in secluded places. Many of the differences in market practices are attributable to differences in the habits and preferences of buyers for particular drugs. Externally imposed market differences include tougher sentencing and enforcement activity for certain drugs, such as crack cocaine. While in the past gangs have tended to specialize in the marketing of a single drug, there has been a trend in some gangs towards the marketing of multiple drugs. The market for illegally diverted prescription drugs is growing rapidly, for example, as is the market for manufactured drugs such as P.C.P. There has also an increased involvement of drug gangs in other income generating activities, both legitimate and illegitimate.

Despite the differences in market practices for different types of drugs, some common features of drug markets can be identified. Important features include very high prices as judged by licit market standards, extremely high retail mark-ups, product dilution, high search costs, and geographic concentration of sellers.[30] The high prices can be attributed in part to what Reuter labels "structural consequences of product illegality", such as restrictions on ability to advertise, obtain credit, write enforceable contracts and patent inventions, and in part to risk imposed by law enforcement. Much of the price of illicit drugs is added at the retail level, and retail conditions play an important role in determining sales volume and prices. In the cases of heroin and cocaine, most of the price paid by the final buyer represents markups in the last two or three transactions. A study of cocaine pricing performed by Caulkins (1988) suggests that the mark-up pricing on cocaine is multiplicative rather than additive. Based on 1980 figures for drug prices, the mark-up for heroin at the domestic distribution stage was estimated to be 8.3 times the wholesale price, and for cocaine it was estimated at thirteen times the wholesale price.[31] The price of cocaine at the farm gate, per pure kilogram, ranged between $1,300 and $10,000, while the approximate retail price amounted to $ 650,000.

Product quality is an important and highly variable element in the illicit drug trade. Changes in effective price often take the form of changes in purity rather than changes in nominal price because these changes are less observable and difficult to monitor. Empirical studies of heroin and cocaine markets over the past few decades have shown that product purity in many cases tracks changes in wholesale price. Kleiman notes that the heroin content of retail "street heroin" averaged about 4 percent in the 1970s and early 1980s, but has been on the increase as wholesale prices have fallen. Retail cocaine was generally about 1/8 pure cocaine during the 1970s, rising to about 70% in 1988 and then beginning to fall with the subsequent rise of wholesale prices.[32] Variance in quality and consistency is much lower for chemically engineered drugs, and the potential for synthetic substitutes to drugs such as cocaine could have interesting implications for retail marketing and consumption patterns.

Geographic concentration of sellers within different localities can be explained as a natural response to the risks which accompany drug dealing. Geographic concentration reduces search costs for buyers and spreads the risk imposed by law enforcement over a larger number of transactors. There are scale economies to protecting a local market from intrusion by competing groups and positive externalities associated with initiating business. Reputation substitutes for legally enforceable contracts as a commitment device and substitutes for advertising as a means of attracting consumers. Economies of scale and scope in the development of a reputation help to explain the prevalence of gangs in the retail drug market. Sellers tend to concentrate in areas that are downwardly mobile, thus minimizing the social pressure on law enforcers to move them out. On the other hand, concentration increases the competitive pressure between drug dealers and reduces the secrecy of transactions. A market that becomes too large may also attract additional law enforcement resources and may induce competing gangs to band together in self-defense.

A derivative feature of illicit markets is the reliance placed on personal contacts when performing market transactions. "The combination of enforcement risks and the lack of legal recourse create high information costs for buyers and sellers. Not only is it difficult to find a potential transaction partner, but the cost of doing business with that person depends strongly on one's evaluation of his sincerity and integrity...."[33] Risk can be reduced by minimizing the number of participants involved in a transaction and by accumulating "relational capital" from frequent dealings with the same people. The model developed in this chapter emphasizes the benefits available from minimizing the number of participants involved in wholesale drug transactions.

Empirical evidence suggests that retail level drug dealing can be regarded as a profitable activity even with substantial allowances made for the high risk involved. While returns for controlling players in the retail drug market are huge, decent returns are available for even the base-line "street level" dealers. Efforts have been made to estimate the risk adjusted return from retail level drug dealing in different locations. According to a recent study, retail cocaine (largely crack) dealers in Washington D.C. earned about $30 per hour in cash, plus additional compensation in drugs. Someone who worked full-time as a retail drug dealer would, on average, take home about $35,000 per year in cash earnings and spend about four months per year in prison.[34] Where the base-line level of risk for local residents (particularly young, black males) is high and the social stigma associated with prison is low, engaging in drug trafficking may impose little additional cost. Moreover, for many of the participants their opportunity cost is low because of a lack of legitimate employment opportunities and because of the perceived undesirability of (and social stigma associated with) menial minimum wage jobs such as a McDonald's employee.

Law enforcers have recognized the business opportunities offered by the drug trade, and the profits available have induced a number of police to become active market participants. Investigations such as the Mollen investigation of New York City police departments have uncovered massive corruption among police in precincts characterized by an active drug trade and poor monitoring procedures. It is interesting to note that, according to the Mollen Report, police officers organized themselves in a manner similar to that of their street gang counter-parts, the structure of these gangs varying by precinct depending upon market conditions and monitoring practices. Membership in these groups was determined by the territory they controlled, and interference with their activities often met with a violent response. The similarities in organizational structure lend support to the notion that drug gang organization is shaped by economic considerations.[35]

The Economic Organization Approach to Criminal Organizations

The traditional law and economics approach towards criminal activities has centered around the individual rational choice paradigm introduced by Becker (1968), which focuses on the individual's choice between legal and illegal activities in the face of different opportunity costs and penalty systems.[36] While there is substantial empirical evidence to suggest that economic factors play a role in shaping individual choices, attempts to provide exhaustive models of individual choices have proven unfruitful, particularly from the perspective of law enforcers seeking to understand and regulate criminal activities. An alternative approach is to focus on the organizational structure of the production unit (here, the criminal organization) rather than on individual decision making. Fiorentini and Peltzman (1995) use economic theory to analyze different aspects of organized crime.[37] The "crime and economics" approach that they adopt uses ideas drawn from industrial organization and game theory to model the emergence, internal organization and market structure of criminal groups. Attention is focused on the internal structure of organized crime and on the constraints limiting their activities.

The theoretical, institutional and empirical studies which Fiorentini and Peltzman have collected exhibit a basic tension between two competing views of organized crime. The first approach emphasizes the similarities between organized crime and governments, focusing on the monopolistic, coercive and expropriative aspects of organized crime. Proponents of this view suggest that the core activities of criminal groups are oriented towards gaining control and rule making authority over a region in order to exploit its resources. Schelling (1971) focuses on exclusive control and expropriation as the defining features of organized crime.[38] Criminal groups act as governments within their sphere of control, engaging in governmental activities such as taxation, regulation of private behavior and the coercive provision of public goods. Hirshleifer (1988) and Baumol (1990) focus more generally on how institutions allocate resources between appropriative and productive activities, basing their approach on rent-seeking and rent-seeking conflicts. Skaperdas and Syropulos (1995) follow in their foot-steps, focusing on redistributive activities which take the form of a military conflict between different gangs (viewed as primitive states) enmeshed in a battle over control of resources.[39] The competing view focuses on the similarities existing between criminal organizations and business organizations, suggesting that criminal organizations can be modeled as firms competing for market share in illegal markets. In order to carry out their market activities, criminal organizations require some form of control over territory (geographical or functional) and some means of enforcing their agreements. They make investment decisions, including investment in military technology and reputation, and engage in competition with other criminal organizations in an effort to capture a larger share of the illegal market. Polo (1995) looks at internal cohesion and competition among criminal organizations, focusing on investments in military technology.[40] Related studies look at oligopolistic competition in illegal markets and the emergence of illegal cartel agreements as methods of increasing the rents available from legal business activities. Fiorentini and Peltzman suggest that the appropriate framework for studying criminal organizations probably lies somewhere in between these suggested approaches.[41] Although they fail to identify a model which integrates the two types of models, they do suggest a number of factors which influence the degree of central coordination and coercion existing in a particular region or market.[42]

II. Economic Model of Gang Organization

Economic Approach to the Study of Criminal Gangs

This chapter presents an approach to the economics of criminal activity which differs from the traditional law and economics approach, as exemplified by Becker (1968), in two ways.[43] First, it focuses on the choices made by a group of criminals rather than on the behavior of an isolated criminal. Attention is directed to the form of economic organization which a group of rational gang members interested in generating revenue would adopt, given the constraints imposed by the market environment.[44] While not all of the "gang activities" may fit neatly into a model based on economic rationality, basic decisions about control over economic variables are more likely to fall within this paradigm, and market forces will tend to favor those which are able to make rational business decisions. Note that rational decisions may include the strategic deployment of irrationalities and constraints on individual activities.[45] Second, the model in this chapter focuses on the cost and availability of information rather than the absence of legally binding contracts as the distinguishing feature of illegal transactions. Participants in organized crime must find ways of acquiring information about potential trading partners and arranging transactions in the absence of the market price mechanism and other methods of accumulating and dispersing information. The illegality of criminal activities increases the risk of sharing information with multiple transactors and reduces the avenues along which information can be transmitted and/or verified. Methods of economizing on information thus assume substantial significance. The high cost of information can be used to account for the central role of territoriality in shaping gang organization. Neighborhood boundaries provide an easy way of segmenting the market and a method of determining group membership that economizes on information and maximizes the overlap of private interests.[46]

Defining a market as a physical location has advantages for buyers as well as sellers, since physical boundaries provide a useful guide as to which sellers are part of the same organization and which areas are most likely to yield quality products. The absence of legally enforceable contracts is less important in comparison, particularly in the context of markets where participants are likely to work together over an extended period of time.[47] The minimal use of legal sanctions in many legitimate business arrangements, such as trade associations, adds support to the claim that information structure rather than the absence of legally enforceable contracts is the determinative factor in group organizations. As pointed out by Macauley (1963), business-men seldom use legal sanctions to adjust their exchange relationships or to settle disputes.[48] In a comprehensive study of the diamond industry, Bernstein (1992) also finds a systematic rejection of state-created law in favor of an elaborate, internal set of rules and institutions to handle disputes.[49]

Economic Model of a Drug Dealing Street Gang

Starting from the premise that gangs organize themselves in a way which is most effective at exploiting the resource opportunities that their territory offers, attention is focused on criminal gangs whose primary objective is the generation of income through drug trafficking.[50] A gang is composed of individuals who engage in similar types of criminal activities in a specific territory and act together to exclude non-gang members. A criminal group is considered to be "organized" if it establishes an ongoing operation that performs similar types of activities repeatedly and has a method of establishing membership and basic guidelines for coordinating group activities. In the context of this model, a gang's mode of "organization" refers to the division of control over key decision variables.[51] In this model the form of organization is implemented through strategic investment in information. Authority comes from control over information that is required in order to engage in a particular transaction, and the dispersion of information is determined a priori through investment in information.[52] Once initial investments in acquiring information have been made, it will be too costly for individual parties to deviate unilaterally from the form of organization selected.[53] While the gang is able to create its own source of authority, this authority is limited by constraints on the ability to observe and monitor decision variables.[54]

For the purpose of this chapter, a drug gang is defined as a group of N identical people who control a physical territory within which they, and only they, can sell illegal drugs. The actions of a gang member are governed by three main sets of constraints - those stemming from competition for market share, competition to acquire or protect market territory, and law enforcement measures designed to control illegal activities. While risk of attack by rival gangs and risks imposed by law enforcement activities are not explicitly introduced in this model, they provide the underlying motivation for assuming that sellers will be geographically concentrated and that information will be limited and costly to disperse. Gang members act as monopolistic competitors in the retail drug market, purchasing quantities of an illegal drug from wholesale drug suppliers and investing effort in obtaining and protecting consumer demand.[55] The quantity sold by each gang member has a negative effect on the demand for drugs faced by all gang members, while the effort invested in marketing has a positive effect on the demand faced by other gang members.[56] Individuals act to maximize their own welfare and do not take into account the externalities associated with their actions. The quantity that is purchased and sold in any given transaction is observed only by participants of the transaction, and effort level is not observable or verifiable.[57] Thus, gang members are both competitors and partners in a joint business enterprise. They must allocate resources between activities designed to increase market demand and activities designed to satisfy existing demand in an environment in which monitoring is difficult, transactions must be covert, and agreements are difficult and costly to enforce.[58]

Drug dealing street gangs must choose between two forms of organization, a vertical form of organization in which the quantity which each gang member has to sell is selected by a gang leader, and a horizontal form of organization in which individuals make their own quantity and effort choices. The organizational choice is accomplished through strategic investment in information about wholesale suppliers. In a horizontally organized gang individuals establish their own connections with high level drug distributors, make their own marketing decisions and earn their own profits.[59] In a vertically organized gang, there is centralized control over the quantity of drugs sold. Gang members are unable to acquire more than the quantities given to them by the leader because they do not know the identity or location of wholesale drug suppliers.[60]

The gang leader is compensated for the extra work and risk involved through lump sum payments from the rest of the gang members of an amount which leaves the leader indifferent between occupying the leadership role and appointing another leader. It is assumed initially that cheating by the leader, including collusion between the leader and other gang members, can be prevented and that the leader can be replaced if he tries to extract additional rents based on his private information about suppliers.[61] In a model where demand and cost conditions are non-stochastic and identical, deviations from the equilibrium can be inferred from observations of individual demand conditions. Once these assumptions are relaxed, opportunities for cheating may arise and the relative costs and benefits of different forms of organization must be reassessed.

Model 1: Sequential Choice of Quantity and Effort

The gang is composed of N identical, risk neutral gang members indexed by i. For simplicity, let N=3.[62] The gang is identified by the physical territory that it occupies, and membership is taken as given. At time 0 the gang selects between a vertical and a horizontal form of organization through strategic investment in information about suppliers. The leader is appointed and assumes his administrative role in return for compensation amounting to $(N-1)\times T$, where T is the cost that each gang member would incur if he had to locate and purchase his own supply of drugs. Allocation of decision making is enforced through selective investment in information about wholesale drug suppliers and is implemented through delegation of quantity choices. Gang members will select the form of organization that will yield them the highest expected profits. At time 1, gang members select quantity of drugs (q_i) and level of effort (e_i) to exert in market sales on the basis of non-stochastic demand and cost conditions. Under a vertical form of organization the gang leader makes quantity purchases from wholesale suppliers, and the gang members then choose effort levels taking supply as given. Under a horizontal form of organization each gang member makes his own private quantity and effort choices. Profits are realized and the leader is compensated at time 2.[63] The chronology of events is summarized below.

```
        Time 0                          Time 1                          Time 2
|------------------------|---------------------|-------------------|------------------- ----|
Invest in organization   Quantity Selected    Effort Selected     Realization of profits
```

Individual i seeks to maximize his profit, which is given by:

$$\Pi_i = p_i(q,e)q_i - c(q_i) - r(e_i) - T$$

Define:

p_i = price (demand) faced by gang member i
q_i = quantity of drug sold by gang member I
q = vector of quantities
e_i = level of effort exerted by gang member i,
e = vector of effort levels
c = cost of drugs purchased from wholesale supplier
r = cost of effort
T = fixed cost involved in wholesale drug purchase

With no loss of generality, we can assume for now that T=0.[64] Gang members act as monopolistic competitors selling differentiated but competing goods. Demand is given by the function $p_i(q_1,q_2,q_3,e_1,e_2,e_3)$.

Assumption 1: $p_i(q,e)$ is a continuos, differentiable function $p_i(q,e)$ which satisfies the following properties: (i) $dp_i/dq_i<0$, $dp_i/dq_j<0$; (ii) $d^2p_i/dq_i^2<0$; (iii) $dp_i/de_i>0$, $dp_i/de_j>0$; (iv) $d^2p_i/de_i^2<0$; (v) $d^2p_i/de_idq_i=d^2p_i/dq_ide_i=0$; (vi) p(.) is negative definite in the positive orthant of real numbers.

Demand is strictly concave in quantity and effort levels, and is increasing in effort and decreasing in quantity sold.[65] Quantity and effort have independent effects on price. In order to highlight the trade-off that occurs between dealing with incentive problems and market externalities, it is assumed that both quantities and effort levels are strategic substitutes.[66]
The cost of drugs purchased from wholesale suppliers is assumed to be a constant unit cost of c where c>0, and all gang members face the same known unit cost.[67] The cost of effort is given by $r(e_i)$.

Assumption 2: $r(e_i)$ is a twice differentiable, continuos function which has the following properties: (i) $r(e_i)\geq 0$; (ii) $dr/de_i>0$; (iii) $d^2r/de_i^2\geq 0$.

Individual i's profit is thus given by a continuous, strictly concave function:

(1) $\Pi_i = [p_i(q,e)-c]q_i - r(e_i)$

First Best Outcome The first-best outcome is obtained by choosing q and e to maximize joint profits, as follows:

$$\text{Maximize } \{q_1,q_2,q_3,e_1,e_2,e_3\} = \sum_{i=1}^{N} \Pi_i = [p_i(q,e) - c]q_i - r(e_i)$$

subject to, for i=1,2,3

$q_i\geq 0$, $e_i\geq 0$

This yields the solution $(q_1^F, q_2^F, q_3^F, e_1^F, e_2^F, e_3^F)$ and profits for each gang member given by $\Pi_i^F(q_i^F, e_i^F)$. See Appendix One.

Horizontal Organization Under a horizontal form of organization, each individual chooses his own quantity and effort levels to maximize profits, taking the actions of the other gang members as given.[68] Gang member i solves the following:

$$\text{Maximize } \{q_i, e_i\} \quad \Pi_i = [p_i(q,e) - c]q_i - r(e_i)$$

subject to

$$q_i \geq 0, \ e_i \geq 0$$

In equilibrium each gang member selects (q_i^H, e_i^H) to satisfy the conditions for a non-cooperative Nash Equilibrium, i.e. (q_i^H, e_i^H) satisfy:

$$\Pi_i(q_i^H, q_j^H, q_k^H, e_i^H, e_j^H, e_k^H) \geq \Pi_i(q_i, q_j^H, q_k^H, e_i, e_j^H, e_k^H)$$

for all $q_i \neq q_i^H$ and $e_i \neq e_i^H$. Since each profit function is strictly concave in the decision variables, this problem has a unique equilibrium given by $(q_1^H, q_2^H, q_3^H, e_1^H, e_2^H, e_3^H)$ and profit $\Pi_i^H(q_i^H, e_i^H)$. See Appendix One.

Vertical Organization Under vertical organization, the leader selects quantities q_1, q_2 and q_3 to maximize the sum of profits. Given these quantities, gang members select effort levels to maximize their individual profits. The leader solves the following problem:

$$\text{Maximize } \{q_1, q_2, q_3\} \sum_{i=1}^{N} \Pi_i = \sum_{i=1}^{N} [p_i(q,e) - c]q_i - r(e_i)$$

subject to

$$i \text{ maximizes } \{e_i | q_i\} \ \Pi_i = [p_i(q,e) - c]q_i - r(e_i) \quad i = 1,2,3$$

$$q_i \geq 0, \ e_i \geq 0$$

Solving this problem yields a unique sequential (Stackelberg) equilibrium $(q_1^V, q_2^V, q_3^V, e_1^V, e_2^V, e_3^V)$ in which the leader selects quantities which, together with the effort levels they induce, maximize joint profits and each gang member chooses his own profit maximizing level of effort given the quantity he is allocated. The leader is able to exploit his first mover advantage to influence effort choices through his quantity choices. From the first-order conditions, the leader chooses q_i^V to satisfy (ii) based on the first-order conditions for the gang member's choice of effort given in (i):

(i) $q_i \times dp_i/de_i - dr/de_i = 0$

(ii) $\sum_{k=1}^{3} [q_k \times dp_k/dq_i] + (p_i - c) + \sum_{k=1}^{3} [q_k \times dp_k/de_i] de_i/dq_i - dr/de_i \times de_i/dq_i = 0$

This yields a profit for gang member i given by $\Pi_i^V(q_i^V, e_i^V)$.

Under the assumptions of Model 1, vertical organization will always be preferable to horizontal organization because it will generate total profits for the gang which are at least as large as those obtainable under horizontal organization.[69] The leader can use his first-mover advantage to improve upon the non-cooperative outcome, selecting quantities strategically based on the trade-off between increasing output above the monopoly level and inducing higher effort. The first best outcome is unobtainable when there are externalities associated with effort choices, however, since the leader must distort quantity choices to induce higher effort levels. The results of Model 1 are summarized in the following two propositions, the proofs of which can be found in Appendix One.

Proposition 1: When quantity and effort choices are sequential, vertical organization dominates horizontal organization. Vertical strictly dominates horizontal organization if gangs compete for market share and/or investments of effort benefit all sellers in the market.

i.e. $\Pi_i^H(q_i^H, e_i^H) \leq \Pi_i^V(q_i^V, e_i^V)$, holding with strict inequality when $B>0$ and $C<0$ and $B \neq -C$, where
$B = [q_i \times dp_i/de_i + q_j \times dp_j/de_i + q_k \times dp_k/de_i - dr/de_i] de_i/dq_i$ and
$C = q_j \times dp_j/dq_i + q_k \times dp_k/dq_i$

Vertical organization does not yield the first best outcome where there are positive externalities arising from individual effort choices, and horizontal organization does not yield the first best outcome where there are market share and/or effort externalities.

i.e. if $B>0$ and $C<0$ and $B \neq -C$ at q_i^H, e_i^H, then
$\Pi_i^H(q_i^H, e_i^H) < \Pi_i^V(q_i^V, e_i^V) < \Pi_i^F(q_i^F, e_i^F)$.

An increase in quantity has competing effects on the gang's total profit.

Product competition increases as quantity increases, but so does the level of effort devoted to increasing the profitability of the market. Under vertical organization the leader will weigh the relative benefits of restricting quantity and inducing higher effort and may choose to distort quantity choices in an upward direction in order to induce higher effort or to restrict quantity to a level closer to the monopoly level.

Proposition 2: When negative market share externalities have a larger effect on the gang's total profit than positive effort externalities, quantity and effort choices will be lower under vertical organization than under horizontal organization, and where the reverse conditions obtain quantity and effort choices will be higher.

Price will depend not only on product quality, but also on the risk associated with the consumer purchase. Where penalties are imposed on consumers who purchase illegal products, these consumers will be willing to pay more for goods that are less risky to obtain. Under vertical organization, the leader can induce higher investment in market "security" by increasing the quantities each gang member has to sell.

Corollary 1: Enforcement policies which increase the risk of consumer transactions may have the perverse effect of increasing the level of criminal activity in vertically organized gangs if choice of quantity and effort is sequential.

One of the disadvantages of horizontal organization is the inability of gang members to restrict their joint output to the monopoly level. External restrictions on output can have the same positive effect on gang profits that internal coordination of quantity choices would where the restriction in output does not substantially increase wholesale prices. Law enforcers should take this perverse effect on the profitability of horizontally organized gangs into account when selecting between alternative enforcement measures.

Corollary 2: Law enforcement policies that restrict the quantity of drugs sold may improve the profitability of horizontally organized gangs.

Model 2: Simultaneous Choice of Quantity and Effort Levels

This scenario differs from the first only in the timing of effort and quantity choices. It is now assumed that effort and quantity choices are made simultaneously rather than sequentially. The chronology of events is illustrated below.

Time 0	Time 1	Time 2
Choice of organization	Quantity and Effort Selected	Profits earned

First Best Outcome This yields the same outcome as in Model 1.

Horizontal Organization This yields the same outcome as in Model 1.

Vertical Organization Under vertical organization, the leader selects quantities to maximize the sum of profits taking effort choices as given, and gang members simultaneously select effort levels which maximize their individual profits taking the supply and the effort level of their competitors as given. The leader solves the following:

$$\text{Maximize } \{q_1,q_2,q_3\} \sum_{i=1}^{N} \Pi \ [p_i(q,e)-c]q_i - r(e_i)$$

subject to, for i=1,2,3

$q_i \leq 0,\ e_i \leq 0$

Gang member i solves:

$$\text{Maximize } \{e_i\}\ \Pi_i=[p_i(q,e)-c]q_i - r(e_i)$$

Solving this problem yields a Nash Equilibrium $(q_1^V,q_2^V,q_3^V,e_1^V,e_2^V,e_3^V)$ in which each gang member chooses his own profit maximizing level of effort given his quantity and the effort and quantity levels of the other gang member and the leader selects quantities which maximize joint profits given the effort levels selected.[70] From the first-order conditions, q_i and e_i are chosen to satisfy, respectively:

$$dp_i/dq_i \times q_i+(p_i-c)+dp_j/dq_i \times q_j+dp_k/dq_i \times q_k=0$$
$$dp_i/de_i \times q_i-dr/de_i=0$$

This yields a profit for gang member i given by $\Pi_i^V(q_i^V, e_i^V)$.

The benefits of vertical organization are lower when decisions are made simultaneously.[71] Under vertical organization the leader will always have an incentive to reduce the quantities selected if total quantity is above monopoly level. The leader will be unable to induce higher effort through the promise of higher quantity allocations since he cannot commit to quantity choices which are above the monopoly level for a given investment of effort. Thus, where the positive externalities associated with effort are substantial and the negative externalities associated with an increase in quantity are relatively small, horizontal organization will dominate vertical organization. The results of the model are captured by the following propositions, the proofs of which are provided in Appendix Two. Under the assumptions of the model the efficient organizational form will depend upon the relative impact of effort and quantity changes on total profit.

Proposition 3: Where investments in quantity and effort are made simultaneously, quantity and effort levels will be lower under vertical organization than under horizontal organization. They will be strictly lower where there are externalities associated with both choices (i.e. when $d\Pi_i/dq_j<0$ and/or $d\Pi_i/de_j>0$).

Proposition 4: When quantity and effort choices are made simultaneously, horizontal organization will be more profitable than vertical organization if positive effort externalities (i.e. investment) dominate negative market share (i.e. competition) effects, and vertical organization will be more profitable where the opposite conditions obtain.

Application of Model to Market Context

Under the assumptions of this model, choice of organizational form turns on whether quantity and effort choices are made simultaneously or sequentially and on the relative size of quality and quantity externalities. These basic determinants can be mapped onto a broader set of market factors in order to predict which form of organization will be most profitable for a gang located in a particular type of market. The results are summarized in the following table.

Table One

	Positive Effort Externalities	Negative Quantity Externalities
Simultaneous	Horizontal	Horizontal/Vertical
Sequential	Vertical	Vertical

	Sequential	**Simultaneous**
Large Markets	X	
Young Markets		X
New Entrants		X
Concentrated Structure	X	
Fragmented Markets		X
Volatile Conditions		X
Quality Fluctuations		X
Frequent Consumer Purchases	X	
Predictable Consumer Purchases	X	

	Positive Effort Externalities	**Negative Quantity Externalities**
Product Variation	X	
Quality Fluctuation	X	
Price Variation with Respect to Quality	X	
High Price Elasticity		X
Competitive Market		X

Factors that will affect the timing of decisions include size and maturity of the market, location of the market, volatility of market conditions and type of product. Sequential decision making will predominate where transactions between wholesalers and retailers are larger and less frequent than consumer transactions and where advance planning and credit arrangements are possible. Factors that will affect the magnitude of quality and quantity externalities include the degree of competition in the market, the extent and observability of product quality variation, scope for product differentiation, and the degree of market fragmentation.

Sequential decision making is easier to sustain in mature markets. Established relationships between wholesalers and retailers and the scope for informal credit arrangements will allow a separation in time between wholesale and retail transactions and will allow for larger wholesale transactions. Sequential decision making is more likely to emerge in larger markets, particularly where the markets are strategically located. First, established organized crime groups will be more likely to locate in markets that serve as source locations for retail operations in other locations. The larger and more sophisticated an organization is, the greater the control it will have over the timing of its investments. Second, transactions between wholesalers and retail level sellers will tend to be larger and less frequent than transactions with consumers in larger markets. Sequential decision making is also more likely to occur in more highly concentrated drug markets where wholesale transactions will be larger and the relationships between dominant players will tend to be more stable. A concentrated market will facilitate the development of implicit understandings among market players, and this will allow for more sophisticated credit arrangements and for calculated investments of effort in market security and reputation. Markets that are relatively stable, with low price volatility and low risk of confiscation of profits, will be more conducive to sequential decision making. Investments of effort in protecting the market can be made at discrete intervals, utilizing current market information, rather than being required on a continuous or unpredictable basis.

The nature of the product will affect both the timing of decisions and the relative magnitude of quantity and effort externalities. Gangs which sell products that vary substantially in quality will face substantial gains from ensuring higher product quality where consumers are unable to verify the quality for themselves prior to purchase. The motivation to cheat on product quality will depend in part upon the ease with which the product can be diluted or otherwise altered and upon the ease with which such changes can be detected. Product type will also determine frequency of transactions. Cocaine markets typically involve frequent repeat customers purchasing relatively small amounts of cocaine, whereas marijuana transactions tend to be less frequent and more bulky. The relative importance of quality externalities will vary positively with the frequency of the transaction, variation in product quality, and the extent to which the market involves repeat customers. Sequential decision making will predominate where expenditures in effort are required primarily at the retail stage, either because of higher risks involving consumer transactions, the relative importance of reputation as a means of attracting customers, or because there is substantial room for adulteration or modification in the product at the retail stage. If decision making is simultaneous, then vertical organization will be less prevalent in markets where product quality, advertising and reputation are relatively important, and will be more prevalent where price is very sensitive to changes in quantity. Applications of the results in this section are examined in Part III.

Leadership and Incentive Problems

In the previous discussion it has been assumed that the gang member who is appointed as leader acts "responsibly" (i.e. in the best interest of the group as a whole) when selecting quantity levels and that the rest of the gang remunerates the leader for his efforts. One of the key features of criminal organizations, however, is the wide latitude for opportunistic behavior. Whereas in legitimate markets, individuals can constrain their actions and the actions of others through the use of legally enforceable agreements, this type of credible third party enforcement is unavailable for participants in illegal activities. Given the covert nature of illegal transactions and the limitations on methods of enforcement, a variety of factors will influence the extent to which the leader is able to diverge from actions which are optimal for the gang as a whole. These include the visibility of the leader's actions, his ability to commit in advance to behave responsibly, the gains available from deviating and the probability and severity of punishment. The choice between vertical organization, in which the leader controls quantities, and horizontal organization, in which individuals control their own effort and quantity choices, must be reassessed in light of the ways in which the actions of the leader might diverge from those which would be in the best interest of the gang as a whole.

The Cost of Self-interest: A Model of Cheating by the Leader

Profitable opportunities for cheating arise when the leader has control over the purchase and allocation of quantities. Consider the base-line scenario presented in Model 1, with N identical gang members, quantity and effort chosen sequentially, and identical non-stochastic demand and cost conditions.

```
        Time 0                          Time 1                          Time 2
|------------------------|------------------------|------------------------|--------------------|
Choice of organization    Quantity Selected         Effort Selected          Profits earned
```

Gang members would like the leader to choose quantities that maximize group profits.

A "responsible" leader (LR) will solve the following problem:

$$\text{LR maximizes } \{q_1,q_2,q_3\} \sum_{i=1}^{N} \Pi_i \, [p_i(q,e)-c]q_i - r(e_i)$$

subject to, for i=1,2,3

$q_i \leq 0, e_i \leq 0$

i maximizes $\{e_i|q\}$ $\Pi_i = [p_i(q,e)-c]q_i - r(e_i)$

This yields a unique sequential equilibrium in which each gang member receives an identical profit of $\Pi_i^V(q_i^V,e_i^V)$. See Appendix Three for details.

In the absence of additional incentives or constraints, a self-interested leader will select quantities that maximize his own profit.[72] The leader, denoted as gang member 1, will maximize $\Pi_1^C(q_1^C,q_2,q_3,e_1^C,e_2,e_3)$, where C denotes the cheating outcome.[73] Gang members who know that their leader is self-interested will anticipate cheating at time 0 and will adjust their effort choices accordingly.[74] The leader solves the following problem:

$$\text{L maximizes } \{q_1,q_2,q_3\} \; \Pi_1^C = [p_1(q_1,q_2,q_3,e_1,e_2,e_3)-c]q_1 - r(e_1)$$

subject to, for i=1,2,3

$q_i \leq 0, e_i \leq 0$

i solves max$\{e_i|q_1^C,q_2^C,q_3^C\}$ $\Pi_i = [p_i(q,e)-c]q_i - r(e_i)$

Under sequential decision making, when $q_i^V < q_i^H$ it will be profitable for the leader to select $q_1^C > q_1^V$ for himself and $q_i^C \leq q_i^V$ for the other gang members. Where $q_i^V > q_i^H$, it will be profitable for the leader to select $q_1^C < q_1^V$ for himself and $q_i^C \geq q_i^V$ for the other gang members. In both cases $\Pi_1^C(q_1^C,e_1^C) > \Pi_1^V(q_1^V,e_1^V)$ for the leader and $\Pi_i^C(q_i^C,e_i^C) < \Pi_i^V(q_i^V,e_i^V)$ for the other gang members. Where gang members anticipate cheating in advance and the leader cannot commit in advance not to cheat, the result is a distortion in effort choices made by the gang members. Where the leader has an incentive to restrict the quantity allocated to other gang members, they will respond by exerting less effort, and this will lower the leader's profits. Where the leader has an incentive to increase quantity levels to free ride on the effort exerted by other gang members, they will respond in the same way, exerting less effort and lowering the leader's profits. It will be more profitable for the leader to cheat when market share externalities are large and externalities from investments in effort are small.

Proposition 5: The cost of cheating varies positively with the magnitude of the market share and positive effort externalities.

See Appendix Three for the proof. The distortionary effects of cheating will be larger under the simultaneous decision making scenario because of the leader's inability to constrain his opportunistic behavior. For any given level of effort the leader will have an incentive to reduce the quantities allocated to other gang members and is unable to commit not to act opportunistically where effort and quantity choices are made simultaneously. This generates the extreme result that under simultaneous decision making a self-interested leader who has sufficient retail selling capacity will end up acting as a monopolist, allocating zero quantities to all other gang members and supplying the full monopoly amount.

Proposition 6: The costs from cheating will be larger when quantity and effort choices are made simultaneously. If gang members anticipate cheating the leader will end up giving each gang member zero quantity and each gang member will exert zero effort.

See Appendix Three for the proof.

In a single period model in which cheating can only be observed after profits have been realized, the threat of punishment if cheating is observed will not be credible unless the punishment is costless to inflict. This is because implementing the punishment after the leader has cheated will have no further payoff for the other gang members and they will therefore choose not to punish. The same problem arises with respect to promises to pay the leader for services performed. Once profits are realized, gang members have no incentive to pay the leader since his services are no longer required. Where the gang members expect to engage in repeated transactions for an indefinite length of time, the gang members will be willing and able to punish the leader for observed wrong doing if they can observe deviations from the equilibrium outcome and the cost of punishing the leader is not too high. Similarly, gang members will have an incentive to pay the leader for services rendered in order to ensure continuing service. These types of problems make leadership easier to sustain in gangs with a longer expected life span and low membership turnover. To see this, consider the following example.

Suppose that the leader is permanently kicked out of the gang whenever deviations from the equilibrium outcome are observed and it is profitable for the other gang members to carry out the punishment. Let the discount rate for future profits be given by ∂, where $0<\partial<1$. The discount rate could be interpreted as the probability that the gang will still be functioning in the next period.[75] The gang members will kick out the leader when they observe deviations from equilibrium conditions if and only if the future benefit of higher profits outweighs the cost, and the leader will be deterred only if the threat to punish is credible and the future loss outweighs the short run gain. The cost of replacing the leader through new investments in supplier information is given by I.

Proposition 7: Cheating can be deterred at zero cost when deviations are observable, the leader can be replaced at reasonable cost and gang members care sufficiently about future profits. i.e. $I < (1/1-\partial)(\Pi_i^V-\Pi_i^C)$, $I<(1/1-\partial)(\Pi_i^V-\Pi_i^C)$ and $(1-\partial)\Pi_i^C<\Pi_i^V$.

Proposition 8: Horizontal organization will be more profitable than vertical organization when cheating cannot be deterred and quantity and effort are chosen simultaneously. It will also be more profitable when decisions are sequential and $\Pi_i^C(q_i^C,e_i^C)<\Pi_i^H(q_i^H,e_i^H)$ for $i\neq 1$.

See Appendix Three. Propositions 7 and 8 are based on the assumption that cheating can be detected with certainty. In this case, the threat of punishment is sufficient to deter cheating. Difficulties arise, however, once the assumptions of non-stochastic and identical (or observable) cost and demand conditions are relaxed, because cheating becomes more difficult to detect.[76] The greater the inference problem, and the more often changes in market conditions occur, the more costly it will be to sustain vertical organization where replacing leaders is costly.

Thus, cheating is more likely to pose a problem in markets where it is very costly to replace the leader and in markets where quantity and effort choices are made simultaneously. The benefits of leadership are likely to be lower and the turnover of leaders is likely to be higher in markets where demand and supply conditions are volatile and where there is a larger variation in cost and demand conditions across members. Gangs with a longer expected life span and a more stable leadership will be better able to deter cheating, and will thus find vertical organization relatively more advantageous. Larger gangs which are able to support a leadership that is removed from direct involvement in the retail trade will also be better able to prevent cheating by the leader, but may gain little if cheating is replaced by collusion.

Risk from Rival Gangs

One of the main distinguishing features of illegal markets is the high risk that market participants face. Risk of physical harm and profit loss are imposed by rival gangs and by rival members of the same gang, and gang members also face threats of arrest, imprisonment and profit loss from law enforcement. The nature and magnitude of risks and differences in risk attitudes will influence (and be influenced by) the organizational structure of the gang. One of the distinctive features of retail drug dealing by street gangs is the competition that exists between geographically distinct groups of drug sellers. This competition often takes the form of attempts by one gang to take over the market territory occupied by a rival gang through the use of force. While a number of papers have focused on different aspects of adversarial competition for control over productive resources, the analyses have not been extended to consider the implications of competition for organizational choice.[77] The strategic implications of gang organization can be illustrated in the context of a Cournot model with two identical gangs who compete for control of the market through effort choices. Where there is risk of market capture by a rival gang, and this risk is decreasing in the amount of effort (e) exerted by gang members as a group, a gang that adopts a vertical form of organization will be better able to withstand attack than a horizontally organized gang as long as quantity and effort decisions are made sequentially. Where decision making is simultaneous, however, the gang may be worse off.

Suppose that there are two identical rival gangs, denoted as gang a and gang b, competing for control of a given territory (or drug market) T. Only the gang who gains control of T can sell drugs in T. Let the probability that gang a will be able to expand its market to include territory T be given by the military technology $x(e_a,e_b,\alpha)$, where $(1-x(e_a,e_b,\alpha))$ equals the probability of successful capture by the rival gang. e_a is the vector of effort levels exerted by gang a and e_b is the vector of effort levels exerted by gang b, where effort can be interpreted as energy exerted in producing market safety through fighting and surveillance activities. α is a random variable which behaves in accordance with the standard probability density function $f(\alpha)$ and reflects the inherent uncertainty in outcome of gang conflicts. The military technology $x(e_a,e_b,\alpha)$ satisfies the following:

Assumption: $x(e_a,e_b,\alpha)$ is a continuous, differentiable function with the following properties: (i) $0 \leq x(e_a,e_b,\alpha) \leq 1$; (ii) $x(.)$ is linear in α; (iii) $dx/de_{ai}>0$, $dx/de_{bi}<0$, $dx/d\alpha>0$; (iv) $d^2x/de_{ai}^2<0$, $d^2(1-x)/de_{bi}^2<0$; (v) $x(.)$ is negative definite in the positive orthant.

Each individual within a gang chooses his effort level to maximize his own expected profit, taking the actions of the other members of his own gang and the rival gang as given. Gang members are risk neutral, and expected profit is linear in the probabilities. Gang member i solves:

$$\Pi_i = x(e_a,e_b,\alpha)p_i(q_1,q_2,q_3,e_1,e_2,e_3)q_i - cq_i - r(e_i)$$

The equilibrium must satisfy the conditions for a Nash Equilibrium both within the gang and between competing gangs. The outcome of the game will depend upon the nature of the military technology and the organizational structure adopted by each gang. See Appendix Four.

Proposition 9: In a Cournot model of competition where two gangs compete for control of the same market through "military investments"(i.e. effort choices), a vertically organized gang will have a strategic advantage over a horizontally organized gang where quantity and effort choices are made sequentially and a horizontally organized gang will have a strategic advantage where quantity and effort choices are made simultaneously.

See Appendix Four for the proof.

III. Applications of Results to Observed Variations in Gang Organization

The model developed in Part II suggests the kinds of economic factors which should influence choice of organizational structure by a profit maximizing drug dealing gang. The model highlights a small set of determinants of organization that can be mapped into a broader set of economic factors. The results suggest that markets which allow a separation between selection of quantity, which can be centrally controlled, and investment of effort, which cannot, and markets in which price is more sensitive to quantity than to quality variations, will tend to favor vertically organized gangs. The organization of rival gangs will also play a role. Larger and more mature markets, markets in strategic locations, and markets with low price volatility, concentrated market structure and high price elasticity will be most likely to evince the characteristics which favor vertical organization. Product markets that are relatively stable, with frequent repeat customers and moderated swings in product quality, will likewise be most conducive to vertical organization. Horizontal organization will predominate in markets with the opposite characteristics. This section compares predictions about organizational choice with observed variations in organizational structure in criminal street gangs operating in the U.S. illicit drug trade. It examines the ability of the model to explain differences in the organizational structure of criminal street gangs based on identifiable features of drug markets, providing support for the theory that gang structure is explainable as a rational economic response to market conditions.

A Comparison of Street Gang Organization in Major U.S. Cities

The largest and most sophisticated illegal drug markets have emerged in New York City, Miami, Los Angeles, Chicago and Houston. The cities are points of entry for large immigrant populations, many of whom end up settling, at least initially, in ethnically homogenous, relatively poor neighborhoods. The proliferation of segregated neighborhoods characterized by low financial resources and concentrated interaction between residents have provided enclaves for street gang activity. These cities are also points of entry and distribution hubs for large quantities of imported illegal drugs and operate as centers for large scale drug operations (domestic and foreign). These cities have had a relatively long history of gang activity, with some of the gangs spanning multiple generations. The illegal markets in these locations have a relatively well-developed infrastructure, with established producer and consumer networks. As the model would predict, the gangs which operate in these cities tend to be larger and more sophisticated, on average, than the gangs in other cities, and the incidence of vertically organized gangs is higher. The drug trade in New York City and Chicago in particular are dominated by large, vertically organized gangs. Miami and Los Angeles support vertically organized gangs, but the operations of even the larger gangs tend to be more decentralized, particularly where the control exercised by foreign organized crime groups (such as the Cali cartel in Miami) has been attenuated. Gang operations in mid-size markets like Detroit and Washington tend to be more decentralized in comparison, and smaller, lower crime cities like Boston are characterized by relatively small and loosely organized gangs whose members engage in independent illegal market activities.

Vertical Organization in New York

American branches of the Italian Mafia, known as La Cosa Nostra, have been dominant players in the American crime scene dating back to the

Prohibition era, and over time they have established power bases in legitimate markets and political circles. The "Commission", composed of the heads of the five leading Mafia families, has historically dominated the New York City crime scene. The Commission is charged with the responsibility of overseeing the operations of the organization, reducing friction and unprofitable competition between Mafia crime families, and addressing concerns about market entrants and changing market trends. New entrants into New York markets have had to adopt their organizational structures to coexist with the Mafia, identifying territorial and product market niches for themselves. This has created ethnic enclaves of affiliated vertically organized groups.

The maturity and size of illegal markets in New York have created conditions that are conducive to vertical forms of organization. Concentration and continuity of players facilitates informal credit arrangements, thus allowing for separation of wholesale (i.e. quantity based) and retail (i.e. effort intensive) transactions. Market control allows for greater policing of quality variations and greater gains from quantity restrictions. Repeated interaction in relatively stable markets makes cheating easier to identify and easier to deter, thus reducing the incentive problems associated with centralized control. The presence of centralized market control has preserved market conditions favorable to vertical organization. It is interesting to note that as the dominance of the Italian Mafia has declined, due in part to law enforcement activities and to an influx of new immigrant organized crime groups, the typical form of organization in the market has undergone a corresponding change.

Vertical Organization in Chicago

Organized crime in Chicago also dates back to the Prohibition era, and criminal networks and markets have had the opportunity to expand and mature. While the Mafia has traditionally exercised control over illegal markets, non-traditional criminal groups (i.e. criminal street gangs) began to establish strong power-holds over specific locations in the city and over specific markets (particularly drug markets) in the late 1960s and 1970s. The street level drug dealing activity in Chicago is now dominated by two large competing nations, or factions of African-American gangs, the Vice Lords and the Black Gangster Disciples. The Latin Kings, a constellation of gangs mainly of Hispanic ethnic origin, are aligned with the Vice Lords. Both the Vice Lords and the Disciples have emerged from an older generation of gangs, and many of their core members have a multi-generation history of gang activity. The gang "nations" in their current extensive forms have developed from a foundation of well-established gangs with an extended history and path of development. These gangs were able to establish oligopolistic control over certain types of drug markets at an early stage. By focusing on activities different from those of the Italian mob, and locating activities in a different geographical space, they were able to coexist with their powerful neighbors. Highly organized gangs such as the El Rukns laid a foundation for establishing larger and more sophisticated forms of gang organization. An additional layer of alliances developed in the mid-1970s when two major multiethnic gang coalitions, "the People" and "the Folks" emerged in Chicago and Illinois prisons, and these super alliances spread to the streets.[78] Estimates suggest that there are about thirty-one street gangs in Chicago that are affiliated with "the Folks" and twenty-seven that identify with "the People."

Chicago provided a sufficiently large drug market and a good base for moving into other mid-western cities, allowing the gangs to expand to their current size and economic power. The segregation of large groups of similarly situated African-Americans in highly concentrated and economically declining neighborhoods has facilitated the development of vertically organized gangs by reducing communication costs and increasing the ability to exert control over participants. The presence of vertically organized crime groups such as the Mafia, and the corresponding presence of an established criminal underground, contributed to the formation of a more vertically organized gang structure. The illegal drug markets in Chicago have not experienced the same influx of new organized crime groups that east coast cities such as New York and Miami have, and those gangs which have traditionally dominated central drug markets in the area continue to do so relatively unchallenged. The gangs in this location have therefore not faced the same pressure to alter their organizational structure.

Vertical and Horizontal Organization in Miami

Miami dominated the drug scene in the 1980s and continues to be a center for illegal drug market activity. Geography makes this an ideal point of entry for foreign distributors, and the Colombian drug cartels in particular had an established strong-old over the Miami drug market for a number of decades. In contrast to cities like Chicago, many of the gangs in Miami are either affiliated with or composed of foreign-born members, many from Colombia and other South American countries. While it was in the control of the Colombian cartels, the market was dominated by satellite operations established by the Cartels. These operations were vertically organized, and exercised substantial control over market conditions. Different ethnic enclaves developed their own organizations, generally vertical in nature and generally with strong ties to foreign countries involved in the drug trade.

The market has attracted foreign entrants from other Latin American countries as well, increasingly so as the previously dominant Medellin Cartel (now dismantled) and Cali Cartel have come under concentrated attack, and the influx of new foreign groups has made the Miami drug scene more chaotic and volatile than that experienced elsewhere. The decline of centralized control by a few key players has led to an increase in competition and market volatility. More active law enforcement activities have placed an added burden on large vertically organized criminal groups. Thus, the larger and more centralized gangs in the city are undergoing the same shift towards hybrid forms of organization as is evident in New York.

Horizontal Organization (Confederations) in Los Angeles

California has replaced Florida as a leading center of the national drug trade. Non-traditional groups (i.e. criminal street gangs) are now responsible for the vast majority of large-scale narcotics trafficking in California. African American gangs in Southern California are divided into two main groups of affiliated gangs, the Crips and the Bloods. These alliances take the form of loosely associated umbrella groups which have varying degrees of interaction with their affiliates. The Los Angeles based Crips and the Bloods each contain multiple "sets" of gangs. Different "sets", or affiliated gangs, have reached different levels of sophistication and are in varying degrees of contact with each other. The Bloods emerged in response to the threat posed by the Crips to independent gangs. The Crips are relatively less closely affiliated, with substantial rivalry between some of the Crips sets, which may be due in part to their greater size.[79] Southern California has a large number of Latino gangs. The Latino gangs tend to be more territory oriented and less business oriented. They pay less attention to "super alliances" than they do to local concerns, although some of the Latino gangs are affiliated with the Bloods and the Crips. Many of these groups have long traditions of gang activity, and have well-established gang structures and systems of status, respect and authority. The nature of the gang structure reduces the need for controlling externalities thorough a delegation of authority. Latino gangs are more likely to adopt horizontal forms of organization than are their African-American counterparts.

The Los Angeles drug market is more diffuse and fragmented than other major drug centers. The market is composed of sub-markets which are somewhat isolated. The sub-markets tend to be racially and ethnically homogenous, and interaction between gangs is predominantly inter-racial. The presence of numerous sub-groups tends to increase the level of competition. Coalition building is concentrated at the intra-gang level rather than at the inter-gang level. While there are well-established gangs in the Los Angeles area, no single group has achieved dominance, nor would they want to given the increased attention they would receive from law enforcement and rival groups. Indeed, perceived dominance by a single group often acts as a catalyst for cooperation between rival groups and has done so in the past.[80] The absence of a dominant set of players in the Los Angeles markets contributes to market volatility, and entry of criminal groups from Mexico and other foreign locations adds to this volatility. A relatively high rate of migration of Los Angeles based gangs to other states has been documented, suggesting the greater degree of competition and greater mobility of California based gangs. Taken as a whole, these characteristics have created a market environment that is more conducive to horizontal forms of organization. The drug markets in Los Angeles are characterized by a mix of horizontally and vertically organized gangs connected by a loose horizontal alliance structure.

Horizontally Structured, Organized Gangs in Detroit

Detroit is characterized by relatively small, horizontally organized gangs, some of which resemble small business enterprises in illegal markets. While the concentration of poor ethnic groups in very poor neighborhoods would facilitate vertical organization, the declining market and the high degree of competition for scarce resources has made vertical organization unfeasible in many instances. Moreover, rather than building on an established criminal structure, the gangs have emerged in reaction to poor economic opportunities. The depressed state of the city has not made it an attractive target for expansionist gangs from other cities. Gang ethnographers have commented on the transformation of loosely affiliated gangs into more highly structured "corporate" gangs, but these corporate gangs have for the most part remained fairly small and have not developed the same kind of vertical infrastructure as their counterparts in larger cities.

Horizontally and Loosely Structured Gangs in Boston

The Boston street gang criminal scene is composed primarily of small and fairly loosely organized African-American street gangs who operate in tandem with older affiliated drug dealers. This gang structure can be attributed in part to the small size of the Boston market, its close proximity to a much larger market, the absence of pre-existing well-established criminal gangs, the fragmentation of neighborhoods within the city, and the immediate attention which new sophisticated entrants attract from law enforcement. While Boston gangs typically lack the degree of sophistication found in larger cities, some of the gangs manifest corporate tendencies. The Intervale Posse, a Boston street gang responsible for distributing crack cocaine, provides a good example of the smaller teen-age run drug gangs which predominate. According to one Boston Police officer, "In their own ways, these kids are as organized as some small companies....that's the nature of the business. Even illegal activity takes some organization, or you'd never last as long as some of those people have. The product has to come from somewhere, be delivered and be cut up, sold and graded."[81] A previous Boston street gang known as the Capsule Boys operated with an even more corporate-like structure which included annual three-week paid vacations for its dealers.[82] The drug market and the gangs which operate in it have been increasing in sophistication as distribution channels have become better established. The fear of becoming the immediate target of law enforcement attention has acted as a limited on the expansion of established gangs. The premium placed on keeping information about more sophisticated criminal organizations hidden from law enforcement has hindered the development of vertically structured organizations. Concentration of activity has taken the form of geographic concentration in certain areas rather than domination by specific, easily identifiable street gangs.

Product Differences and Organizational Structure

Under simultaneous quantity and effort choices, vertical organization will be less prevalent in markets where product quality, advertising and investment in reputation and market protection are relatively important, and will be more prevalent where price is very sensitive to quantity changes. Differences in market conditions will interact with product differences to create variations in organizational structure. Both sequential and simultaneous decision making may occur in cocaine and heroin markets, for example, depending on local market conditions. On the one hand there is wide scope for adulteration or improvement of the product, transactions are conducted under risky conditions (e.g. on street corners), products are subject to swings in price, quality and availability, and there is a relatively high risk of confiscation and arrest, all of which are factors which support horizontal organization. On the other hand, concerns about reputation are important and consumer transactions are frequent and repeated relative to wholesale dealings, which support a choice of vertical organization.

Sequential decision making (and hence vertical organization) is more likely to occur in markets for manufactured drugs such as P.C.P., D.E.T. and L.S.D., and in the illicit trade in diverted substances, where markets tend to be more sophisticated, access to already existing modes of credit and distribution easier, and operations more covert. There is also a greater division between the wholesale and retail suppliers of these types of drugs, creating a natural separation between wholesale and retail activities. There is a higher incidence of vertical organization among gangs who engage in multiple activities. This can be explained in terms of the greater need for coordination of activities and sequential planning in situations in which the gang is involved in multiple product lines. Vertical organization facilitates a division of labor while maintaining some form of centralized control.

While the heroin addict population is small, the criminal activity surrounding heroin addiction has let to a focus of attention on the phenomenon. There was an estimated chronic user population of 420,000 in 1979, marking a sharp drop from the 523,000 users in 1976. The estimated 1,500,000 casual users account for only 10 percent of total consumption, meaning that most consumers are repeat consumers. The heroin market in the U.S. is worth from $7 to $9 billion annually. The cocaine market has a broader consumer base. Between 7.3 and 17.5 million Americans had used cocaine, and about 10 percent of these users were daily users accounting for approximately 50 percent of all cocaine users. By 1979 the largest increase in incidence of use was reported in the 18 to 25 age group, who then represented 80 percent of all users.[83] This trend has not been reversed. By 1980, the U.S. was importing between 40 and 48 metric tons of cocaine, worth an estimated $27 to $30 billion in retail sales. The cannabis trade is also voluminous. In 1979 it was believed that at least 55 million Americans had consumed marijuana at least once, and that the number of regular users had reached 23 million. The user population for drugs of this type has been relatively older, and while there are fewer new users there are more continuing users. The demand for cannabis products is much wider spread and diverse than that for other types of street drugs, and consumer transactions are less frequent. The use of psychotropic drugs is of growing concern. Diversion of amphetamines and methaqualone and other types of manufactured drugs produced for controlled sale was, according to the International Narcotics control Board, the major international control problem of the 1980s. In the U.S., methaqualone, a type of psychotropic drug, is the most widely used illegal drug next to marijuana and causes more injuries and trauma than heroin or cocaine. Most comes from chemical manufacturers who send the drug to legitimate brokers who in turn sell to fraudulent firms A decrease in the use of amphetamines and barbiturate-type drugs in North America has left firms with huge stocks of drugs, and production of psychotropics continues to increase. Developments in the illegal drug market which are worthy of future study include the emerging phenomenon of multiple drug abuse, where consumers have access to a variety of drugs and can switch from one to another according to variations in supply,[84]and the wide-spread abuse of prescription drugs and corresponding growth of illicit trade in controlled drugs.[85]

Recent Trends

The influx of immigrant gangs who maintain close ties to foreign based crime groups has had a substantial impact on American drug markets in recent times.[86] New York's new ethnic crime groups now include Russian counterfeiters, Albanian, Nigerian and Chinese heroin traffickers and Colombian cocaine traffickers.[87] New crime groups in Los Angeles include Colombian, Cuban, Israeli, Hungarian and Russian migrant groups, and there is a similar diversity of ethnic crime groups, or "nontraditional organized crime groups" in other major U.S. cities.[88] One scholar has argued that the transformation of U.S. gangs is a result of the decline of traditional groups such as the Italian Cosa Nostra in combination with new waves of immigration.[89] He suggests that the crime scene of the future will involve a large number of different ethnic operations who compete for control in contrast to the "old days of Mafia control." These new ethnic crime groups often begin by establishing criminal enterprises in their own ethnic enclaves, where they are able to capitalize on the distrust of American law-enforcement authorities by immigrants and on the support of extended families and fraternal organizations.[90] Many then expand into broader illegal market territories.

These ethnic gangs are typically ethnically and racially homogenous, and until recently there has been little collaboration between most of them. Their links with foreign wholesale suppliers and their connections to the international illegal crime scene make vertical organization profitable. While they maintain links with established foreign organized crime groups, however, these gangs have a measure of autonomy from centralized control. Asian gangs, some with domestic roots and some associated with Asian-based crime syndicates, have proven to be some of the most dangerous entrants into an increasingly diverse American crime scene. According to the FBI, Asian gangs currently operate in at least 17 different cities.[91] The emergence of some of the new unorganized Asian street gangs has been supported by Asian-based crime syndicates who wish to establish an American presence, and many of them maintain links with the syndicates.[92] There is a growing concern that these new Asian street gangs are poised for an expansion similar to that of Italian-led groups in the 1930s.[93] Unlike more established and sophisticated Asian crime groups such as the tongs, who operate primarily in their own ethnic enclaves and already have control over profitable legitimate and illegal enterprises, the new gangs are in a less secure environment and seem to have broader aspirations.[94] Chinese groups now control about 70 percent of New York's heroin-smuggling business.[95] It has been suggested that the new Vietnamese street gangs who appeared in Boston and other U.S. cities in the late 1980s are part of an emerging criminal enterprise similar to the centuries old Chinese crime syndicates, or "triads." The Boston-based gangs were linked to similar groups in California, New York, Virginia and Pennsylvania.[96] Although initially employed by Chinese organized crime groups, Vietnamese youth gangs have organized and are now beginning to challenge the dominance of their former employers.

The increasing lucrativeness of the illegal drug trade has fueled the organization of criminal street gangs. The Los Angeles based Bloods and Crips gang confederations are now reported as the top organized crime problem in the state of California and affiliated branches have appeared in numerous states.[97] According to the FBI, the Gangster Disciples, a Chicago based gang, has spread into 35 states in the Midwest and South, and has established working relationships with high level Colombian and Mexican drug cartels.[98] The increasing level of organization within street gangs has extended to include greater linkages between street gangs and prison gangs - hardly a surprising connection given the large number of gang members that either end up in prison or run the risk of doing so.[99] The emergence of a new prison group, the Consolidated Crips Organization, which is composed largely of incarcerated Los Angeles Crips street gang members provides evidence of the tightening connection.[100] These linkages allow incarcerated gang members to continue to play an active role in the operations of street gang activities and provides a mechanism for disciplining gang members who end up in jail. It also provides prison gang members with an expanded set of criminal opportunities. The Nuestra Familia prison gang, for example, which is one of the "big four" prison gangs, has exercised substantial control over drug trafficking and prostitution in many Northern California barrios. Prison gang activity involving parolees and their associates has also continued to grow.

The entry of new criminal groups and new types and forms of drugs into local American drug markets, coupled with concerted law enforcement attacks on traditional organized crime, have led to increasing market uncertainty and volatility. The increases in volatility and competition have induced a general streamlining of criminal organizations, with a trend towards decentralization of large-scale operations and greater interaction between small, independent units. Even traditional criminal organizations such as La Cosa Nostra and the Colombian and Mexican drug cartels have engaged in decentralization. The movement away from a highly centralized structure has been evidenced even in well-established and highly organized groups such as La Cosa Nostra (the American branch of the Italian Mafia) and the Mexican and Colombian drug cartels. According to one theorist, "Italian-American organized crime has actually moved from more bureaucratic forms to a structure that can best be portrayed as a franchise - the "McDonald's-ization" of the Mafia. This modern form of organization has allowed a small number of persons to retain a great deal of influence and amass considerable amounts of income with minimal effort."[101] Analysts at the Drug Enforcement Administration have recently "compared the loose structure of Mexican drug trafficking to a federation rather than a series of cartels.... About a dozen lower-ranking "division-heads"...may join different bosses for different deals. Division heads, in turn, contract with smuggling groups at different points along the border to move their shipments into the United States."[102] New non-traditional organized crime groups are increasingly adopting a mixed structure - small hierarchical units which are loosely affiliated with each other in horizontal groups. Entrants such as the Jamaican Posses, which operate as small semi-independent units, have been successful at breaking into drug markets in part because of their willingness to decentralize and to work in tandem with other drug gangs at different stages of the drug distribution chain. This type of organization has emerged in response to the more competitive environment and the constraints imposed by the use of large-scale investigations and organized crime tools that target large-scale organized crime groups.

IV. Conclusion

This chapter applies economic tools to explain observed differences in the organizational structure of criminal street gangs located in different markets. It suggests that important aspects of criminal street gangs can be understood and modeled in the same way as other business enterprises. The model draws a distinction between a vertical and a horizontal form of gang organization. In a horizontally organized gang there is no identifiable leadership and individuals have private information about and control over their own market transactions.[103] Individuals establish their own connections with high level drug distributors, make their own marketing decisions, and earn their own profits. In a vertically organized gang there is a vertical chain of command, an identifiable leadership, and centralized control over decision variables. Gang members are unable to acquire more than the quantities given to them by the leader because they do not know the identity or location of whole-sale drug suppliers.[104] The model examines the conditions under which a vertical form of organization would be more or less profitable than a horizontal form of organization in the sense of maximizing total gang welfare. as measured by the sum of expected profits. Selection between organizational structures is tantamount to allocation of control over choice variables and is enforced through strategic investment in information, in this case private information about suppliers.[105] Attention is focused on how organizational structure affects the trade-off that the drug selling group faces between reducing incentive problems and controlling market externalities, highlighting the coordination difficulties faced by a group of actors with partially overlapping and partially conflicting interests in a situation of imperfect information and enforcement. The relative efficiency of a specific form of organization depends upon the ability to observe and control quantity and effort choices and the costs associated with failing to do so. Assumptions made about the timing of decisions and the level of uncertainty can be mapped into a broader set of market characteristics, and the results can then be used to suggest the types of organizational forms which one would expect to observe in different types of markets.

The model also suggests ways in which law enforcement may impact upon organizational choice. Enforcement activities which force quantity and effort choices to be made simultaneously, increase the volatility of demand and supply, or restrict wholesale drug supplies will favor horizontally organized gangs, for example. A law enforcement strategy which increases the uncertainty of demand and supply will generally be more effective at reducing the profitability and stability of a vertically organized gang than a horizontally organized gang. Thus, the implications of enforcement policies for choice of gang organization should be taken into account when selecting between alternative strategies.[106] Examining organized crime within a law and economics framework can provide law enforcers with a greater understanding of the criminal organizations whose activities they seek to control.[107] Areas of further research include an expanded study of gang structure, a comparison of the organization of illegal enterprises involved in different criminal activities, and an exploration of the dynamics of interactions between rival gangs and law enforcers.

Appendix One

Model 1: Sequential Quantity and Effort Choices

First and Second Order Conditions for First Best

Under the first-best scenario, e_i and q_i are chosen to satisfy, respectively:

(1) $dp_i/de_i \times q_i - dr/de_i + dp_j/de_i \times q_j + dp_k/de_i \times q_k = 0$
(2) $dp_i/dq_i \times q_i + (p_i - c_i) + dp_j/dq_i \times q_j + dp_k/dq_i \times q_k = 0$

The second-order conditions (which are satisfied given assumption that p(.) is negative definite and r(.) is convex) are:

$q_i \times d^2p_i/de_i^2 - d^2r/de_i^2 + q_j \times d^2p_j/de_i^2 + q_k \times d^2p_k/de_i^2 < 0$
$2dp_i/dq_i + q_i \times d^2p_i/dq_i^2 + q_j \times d^2p_j/dq_i^2 + q_k \times d^2p_k/dq_i^2 < 0$
p(.) satisfies the conditions for negative definiteness in positive orthant

Note: This is a convex programming problem subject to non-negativity constraints with a non-empty feasible set, which implies that the first-order approach is appropriate.

This problem has a unique solution given by $\Pi_i^F(q_i^F, e_i^F)$ for i=1,2,3

First and Second Order Conditions For Horizontal Organization

Gang member i chooses e_i and q_i to satisfy, respectively:

(3) $q_i \times dp_i/de_i - dr/de_i = 0$
(4) $p_i - c + q_i \times dp_i/dq_i = 0$

Second-order conditions:

$2dp_i/dq_i + q_i \times d^2p_i/dq_i^2 < 0$
$q_i \times d^2p_i/de_i^2 - d^2r/de_i^2 < 0$
p(.) is negative definite, and thus objective function is strictly concave

This yields a unique Nash Equilibrium solution $\Pi_i^H(q_i^H, e_i^H)$ for i=1,2,3

First and Second Order Conditions for Vertical Organization

The gang member chooses $e_i(q)$ such that:

(5) $q_i \times dp_i/de_i - dr/de_i = 0$

The gang leader chooses q_i given $e_1(q)$, $e_2(q)$, $e_3(q)$:

(6) $q_i \times dp_i/dq_i + q_j \times dp_j/dq_i + q_k \times dp_k/dq_i + (p_i - c)$
$+ (q_i \times dp_i/de_i - dr/de_i + q_j \times dp_j/de_i + q_k \times dp_k/de_i) de_i/dq_i = 0$

From the first-order conditions of the gang member:

$$de_i/dq_i = -\ (dp_i/de_i)\ /\ (q_i \times d^2p_i/de_i^2 - d^2r/de_i^2) > 0$$

Second-order conditions for q_i and e_i respectively:

$[q_i \times d^2p_i/dq_i^2 + dp_i/dq_i + q_j \times d^2p_j/dq_i^2 + q_k \times d^2p_k/dq_i^2 + dp_i/dq_i] + [dp_i/de_i \times de_i/dq_i$
$+ (q_i \times dp_i/de_i - dr/de_i + dp_j/de_i + dp_k/de_i) d^2e_i/dq_i^2] < 0$
$-[q_i \times d^2p_i/dq_i^2 + dp_i/dq_i + q_j \times d^2p_j/dq_i^2 + q_k \times d^2p_k/dq_i^2 + dp_i/dq_i] q_i \times d^2p_i/de_i^2$
$- d^2r/de_i^2 < 0$
p(.) satisfies the conditions for negative definiteness in positive orthant

Note: We know that both the leader's objective function and the gang members' objective functions are concave since p(.) is negative definite and r(.) is convex. Thus, there will be a unique maximum given by $\Pi_i^V(q_i^V, e_i^V)$ for i=1,2,3.
For the proofs to Proposition 1-3, define:

$A = (p_i - c) + q_i \times dp_i/dq_i$
$B = [q_i \times dp_i/de_i + q_j \times dp_j/de_i + q_k \times dp_k/de_i - dr/de_i] de_i/dq_i = [D+E] de_i/dq_i$
$C = q_j \times dp_j/dq_i + q_k \times dp_k/dq_i$
$D = q_i \times dp_i/de_i - dr/de_i$
$E = dp_j/de_i \times q_j + dp_k/de_i \times q_k$

Proposition 1: When quantity and effort choices are sequential, vertical organization dominates horizontal organization. Vertical strictly dominates horizontal organization if gangs compete for market share and/or investments of effort benefit all sellers in the market. i.e. $\Pi_i^H(q_i^H, e_i^H) \leq \Pi_i^V(q_i^V, e_i^V)$, holding with strict inequality when B>0 and C<0 and B≠-C when evaluated at q_i^H, e_i^H.

Vertical organization does not yield the first best outcome where there are positive externalities arising from individual effort choices, and horizontal organization does not yield the first best outcome where there are market share and/or effort externalities. i.e. if $B>0$, $C<0$ and $B\neq -C$ at q_i^H, e_i^H, then $\Pi_i^H(q_i^H, e_i^H) < \Pi_i^V(q_i^V, e_i^V) < \Pi_i^F(q_i^F, e_i^F)$.

Proof:

(i) Show $\Pi_i^H(q_i^H, e_i^H) \leq \Pi_i^V(q_i^V, e_i^V)$

This is a simple Stackelberg problem. The leader can induce (e_1^H, e_2^H, e_3^H) by choosing (q_1^H, q_2^H, q_3^H), since the first-order conditions for effort choice are the same under both forms of organization. That is, since (3) and (5) are the same when evaluated at the same quantity level, it must be the case that $e_i^V(q_i^H)=e_i^H$. The leader can select $q_i^V=q_i^H$. Thus, the gang can do at least as well under vertical organization as it can under horizontal organization. Therefore, $\Pi_i^H(q_i^H, e_i^H) \leq \Pi_i^V(q_i^V, e_i^V)$.

(ii) Show that if both externalities are non-zero (i.e. B and C are non-zero) and $B\neq -C$ when evaluated at q_i^H, e_i^H, then $\Pi_i^H(q_i^H, e_i^H) < \Pi_i^V(q_i^V, e_i^V)$

We know from (i) that $\Pi_i^H(q_i^H, e_i^H) \leq \Pi_i^V(q_i^V, e_i^V)$.
Compare the first-order conditions for quantity under first best and horizontal organization, given by (2) $A_F+C_F=0$, (4) $A_H=d\Pi_i/dq_i=0$
For a given effort level, at quantity choices satisfying $A_H=d\Pi_i/dq_j=0$ we know that $\sum_{i=1}^{N} d\,\Pi_i/dq_j<0$. In order to satisfy (6), $A_H<A_F$, and since A is decreasing in q, this implies that $q_i^F<q_i^H$ for any given level of effort.

Compare the first-order conditions for effort under first best and horizontal organization, given by (1) $D_F+E_F=0$, (3) $D_H=0$. Evaluating the first-order conditions for a given quantity, at effort choices satisfying $d\Pi_i/de_i=0$, $\sum_{i=1}^{N} d\,\Pi_i/de_i>0$ (since $B>0$), which implies that $D_F<D_H$ and thus that $e_i^H<e_i^F$ when evaluated at same quantity since D is decreasing in e.

From above, we know that $q_i^F<q_i^H$ when evaluated at e_i^H and that $e_i^H<e_i^F$ when evaluated at q_i^H. Thus, starting from (e_i^H, q_i^H) it will be possible to

increase profits through marginal changes in q and e. If we increase q_i, then individual i will select higher effort e_i since:

$$de_i/dq_i == [-dp/de_i] / [d^2p/de_i^2 - d^2r/de_i^2] > 0$$

This increase in effort and quantity will have two competing effects on profits, given by B and C. When B>-C,

$$\sum_{j=1}^{N} dp_j/de_i \times de_i/dq_i - dr/de_i \times de_i/dq_i > - \sum_{j \neq 1}^{N} q_j \times dp_j/dq_i$$

If B<-C then starting from the non-cooperative equilibrium, profits can be increased by decreasing quantity and effort. Therefore, $\Pi_i^H(q_i^H, e_i^H) < \Pi_i^V(q_i^V, e_i^V)$ when there are non-zero externalities which do not offset each other.

(iii) Show $\Pi_i^H(q_i^H, e_i^H) < \Pi_i^F(q_i^F, e_i^F) = \Pi_i^V(q_i^V, e_i^V)$ when B=0 and C<0

When B=0 the first-order conditions for vertical organization become the same as the first-order conditions for the first best (i.e. (5) and (6) are identical to (1) and (2)). From the first-order conditions, $q_i^V = q_i^F$ and $e_i^V = e_i^F$, and so $\Pi_i^V(q_i^V, e_i^V) = \Pi_i^F(q_i^F, e_i^F)$. From the same first-order conditions, when B=0 and C≠0, the first-order conditions under horizontal organization diverge from the first-best, and $\Pi_i^H(q_i^H, e_i^H) < \Pi_i^F(q_i^F, e_i^F) = \Pi_i^V(q_i^V, e_i^V)$.

(iv) Show $\Pi_i^H(q_i^H, e_i^H) = \Pi_i^V(q_i^V, e_i^V) = \Pi_i^F(q_i^F, e_i^F)$ when B=C=0

When B=C=0 the first-order conditions under horizontal organization (1) & (2) are equivalent to the first-order conditions under the first best (5) & (6) . Therefore, $\Pi_i^H(q_i^H, e_i^H) = \Pi_i^V(q_i^V, e_i^V) = \Pi_i^F(q_i^F, e_i^F)$ when B=C=0.

(v) Show $\Pi_i^H(q_i^H, e_i^H) < \Pi_i^F(q_i^F, e_i^F) = \Pi_i^V(q_i^V, e_i^V)$ when B>0 ,C<0 and B≠-C.

Consider the quantity and effort levels which satisfy (1) and (2), given by (q_i^F, e_i^F). Under vertical organization, if the leader selects $q_i = q_i^F$, effort level e_i^V will be selected to satisfy $q_i^F \times dp_i/de_i - dr/de_i = D = 0$. But from the first-order conditions under the first best we know that $D_F + B_F = 0$.
Given that $B_F > 0$ it must be the case that $e_i^V \neq e_i^F$ when $q_i^V = q_i^F$.
Since $q_i \times dp_i/de_i - dr/de_i$ is decreasing in e_i, $e_i^V < e_i^F$ when $q_i^V = q_i^F$.

But (q^F, e^F) yields the unique profit maximizing outcome, so it must be the case that $\Pi_i^V(q_i^V, e_i^V) < \Pi_i^F(q_i^F, e_i^F)$. Thus, $\Pi_i^V(q_i^V, e_i^V) < \Pi_i^F(q_i^F, e_i^F)$ when $B>0$.

Proposition 2: When the negative market share externalities have a larger effect on the gang's total profit than the positive effort externalities, quantity and effort choices will be restricted under vertical organization, and where the reverse conditions obtain quantity and effort choices will be higher than they would under horizontal organization.

Proof:

(i) Given the same level of effort, the first-order condition for quantity choice under horizontal and vertical organization are given, respectively, by (2) $A_H=0$ and (4) $A_V+B_V+C_V=0$.

When evaluated at the same effort level, if $B_V+C_V<0$ then $A_V>A_H$.
Since $dA/dq_i<0$, this implies that $q_i^V<q_i^H$ when $A_V>A_H$. From the first-order conditions, this implies that effort will also be lower under vertical organization i.e. $e_i^V<e_i^H$. Likewise, when $B_V+C_V\geq 0$, then $A_V\geq A_H$ and $q_i^V\geq q_i^H$. Effort will be higher, i.e. $e_i^V>e_i^H$.

(ii) Show $e_i^V\leq e_i^H$ when $q_i^V\leq q_i^H$ and $e_i^V> e_i^H$ when $q_i^V>q_i^H$

Fully differentiating the first-order conditions for effort choice of gang member i with respect to quantity:

$$de_i/dq_i = dp_i/de_i \,/\, [q_i \times d^2p_i/de_i^2 - d^2r_i/de_i^2]>0$$

Given that $e_i^V=e_i^H$ when $q_i^V= q_i^H$, this implies that $e_i^V< e_i^H$ when $q_i^V<q_i^H$ and that $e_i^V> e_i^H$ when $q_i^V>q_i^H$.

Corollary 1: Law enforcement policies which increase the risk of consumer transactions may have the perverse effect of increasing the level of criminal activity in vertically organized gangs if choice of quantity and effort is sequential.

Proof:

Consider a policy which has the effect of increasing B. Where B>-C, the optimal response of a leader under vertical organization will be to increase q in order to induce higher effort, since the relative return on higher effort has been increased. This type of effect will not occur under horizontal organization, since quantities are not linked in the same way to higher effort.

Corollary 2: Law enforcement policies which restrict the quantity of drugs sold may improve the profitability of horizontally organized gangs.

Proof:

Under horizontal organization, quantities are chosen to satisfy $d\Pi_i/dq_i=0$. For a given effort level, at quantity choices satisfying $d\Pi_i/dq_j=0$ we know that $\sum_{i=1}^{N} d\,\Pi_i/dq_j<0$. Where B>-C when evaluated at e_i^H, q_i^H, profits can be increased by restricting q_i.

To see this, let the policy induced restriction be given by q_i^{Hc}. Under horizontal organization, individuals who do not face a constraint on their ability to obtain the desired quantity of drugs will purchase and sell q_i^H. The first-order condition for quantity selections made by an individual gang member, given by (i), is increasing in q_i when evaluated at q_i^{Hc}. Since profits are increasing in q_i up to q_i^H, if individual gang members are constrained in their ability to obtain drugs to a level below q_i^H, denoted by q_i^{Hc}, they will purchase q_i^{Hc}. If $q_i^{Hc} \geq q_i^V$ then profits for each gang member will be higher since $\Pi_i^V \geq \Pi_i^H$. If $q_i^{Hc}<q_i^V$ then profits may be lower.

Under vertical organization, if $q_i^{Hc} \geq q_i^V$ then there will be no change in outcome since the constraint is not binding. If $q_i^{Hc}<q_i^V$, then profits will be lower than they would in an unconstrained situation.

Appendix Two

Model 2: Simultaneous Quantity and Effort Choices

First-order Conditions under First Best and Horizontal Organization -- same as Model 1

First-order Conditions for Vertical Organization

Each gang member chooses e_i to satisfy:

(5') $dp_i/de_i \times q_i - dr/de_i = 0$

The leader selects q_i to satisfy the following:

(6') $dp_i/dq_i \times q_i + (p_i - c) + dp_j/dq_i \times q_j + dp_k/dq_i \times q_k = 0$

The result is a nash equilibrium in effort and quantity choices where the leader and gang members make their selections taking the actions of others as given. The equilibrium satisfies the following conditions, for i=1,2,3:

$\Pi_i(q^{V'}, e^{V'}) \geq \Pi_i(q^{V'}, e_i', e_{-i}^{V'})$ for all $e_i \geq 0$
$\Pi_L(q^{V'}, e^{V'}) \geq \Pi_L(q_i', q_{-i}^{V'}, e^{V'})$ for the gang leader and all $q_i \geq 0$

This yields a Nash-Equilibrium profit of $\Pi_i(q^{V'}, e^{V'})$ for i=1,2,3.

Proposition 3: Where investments in quantity and effort are made simultaneously, quantity and effort levels will be lower under vertical organization than under horizontal organization. They will be strictly lower where there are externalities associated with both choices. i.e. $q_i^V \leq q_i^H$ and $e_i^V \leq e_i^H$ and $q_i^V < q_i^H$ and $e_i^V < e_i^H$ when $d\Pi_i/dq_j < 0$ &/or $d\Pi_i/de_j > 0$.

Proof:

(i) Compare first-order conditions for effort choices under horizontal and vertical organization. The conditions, given by (1) and (3') are the same when evaluated at the same quantity levels. The first-order conditions for quantity under horizontal and vertical organization are given by, respectively, (2) $A_H=0$ and (4') $A_V+C_V=0$. Since $C_v<0$, it must be the case that $A_V>A_H$. But $dA/dq_i<0$ and $dA/de_i>0$, which implies that for $e_i^V \le e_i^H$, $q_i^V<q_i^H$.

(ii) Suppose $q_i^V=q_i^H$. Then from the first-order conditions for effort, which are given by (1) and (3'), it would have to be the case that $e_i^V=e_i^H$. But at the same or lower effort level we know from above that $q_i^V<q_i^H$. Therefore, $q_i^V \neq q_i^H$.

Suppose $q_i^V>q_i^H$. The first-order conditions for effort choice under vertical and horizontal organization will both satisfied only if $e_i^V>e_i^H$. Compare first-order conditions for quantity, given by (2) and (4'). When $e_i^V=e_i^H$, we know that $q_i^V<q_i^H$. Where $e_i^V>e_i^H$, $A_V > A_H$ at $q_i^V=q_i^H$ since $dA/de_i>0$ and $dC/de_i=0$. Thus, when $e_i^V>e_i^H$ the first-order conditions are both satisfied only when $q_i^V<q_i^H$. But this contradicts the original assumption that $q_i^V>q_i^H$. Thus, $q_i^V<q_i^H$.

(iii) Suppose $q_i^V<q_i^H$ Then from the first-order conditions for effort choice, $e_i^V<e_i^H$. Likewise, when $e_i^V<e_i^H$, it must be the case from the first-order conditions that $q_i^V<q_i^H$.

Proposition 4: When quantity and effort choices are made simultaneously, horizontal organization will be more profitable than vertical organization if positive effort externalities dominate negative market share effects and vertical organization will be more profitable where the opposite conditions obtain.

Proof:

(i) Show that (q^H,e^H) is not obtainable under vertical organization.

The leader chooses q_i^V to satisfy (4'), which is given by $A_V+C_V=0$. Under horizontal organization, quantities are chosen to satisfy $A_H=0$. At this quantity, the leader's first-order condition is not satisfied. Since $C_V<0$ it must be the case that $A_V>A_H$, which requires that $q_i^V< q_i^H$ when $e_i^V=e_i^H$. If gang members each select effort levels e_i^H, it can be seen from a comparison of (2) and (4') that the leader's best response is not given by $q_i^V=q_i^H$. Similarly, it can be shown from the first-order conditions that $e_i^V<e_i^H$ when $q_i=q_i^V$, where (q_i^V,e_i^V) solve the vertical problem.

(ii) Show that (q^V,e^V) is not obtainable under horizontal organization.

Under horizontal organization there is a unique non-cooperative Nash Equilibrium given by $(q_1^H,q_2^H,q_3^H,e_1^H,e_2^H,e_3^H)$, and as showing in (i) this diverges from the outcome obtained under vertical organization.

(iii) Find the conditions under which
$\Pi_i(q_i^H, q_j^H, q_k^H, e_i^H, e_j^H, e_k^H) > \Pi_i(q_i^V, q_j^V, q_k^V, e_i^V, e_j^V, e_k^V)$

Choice of quantity and effort levels will necessarily be lower under vertical organization, as shown in Proposition 1, so $ei^H > ei^V$ and $qi^H > qi^V$ for all i. Effort will be too low, and quantity levels too high, under horizontal organization, i.e. $e_i^H < e_i^F$ and $q_i^H > q_i^F$. Effort will be still lower under vertical organization, but quantity will also be lower. Starting from the first best position (q_i^F, e_i^F), horizontal organization will be more profitable where marginal changes in effort have a larger effect on profits than downward changes in quantity i.e. when $-\sum_{i=1}^{N} d\,\Pi_i/dq_i < \sum_{i=1}^{N} d\,\Pi_i/de_i\; de_i/dq_i$.

The first-order conditions for effort under horizontal and vertical organization and the first best are given by (1), (3') and (5). At effort choices satisfying $d\Pi_i/de_i=0$, $\sum_{i=1}^{N} d\,\Pi_i/de_i>0$ when evaluated at the same quantity Since $e_i^V < e_i^H$, the divergence from first best effort will be larger under vertical organization. The divergence will be increasing in B and decreasing in C.

Compare first-order conditions for quantity under horizontal and vertical organization and the first-best, given by (2), (4') and (6).

(2) $A_H=0$; (4') $A_V+C_V=0$; (6) $A_F+C_F=0$

When evaluated at the same effort level, there is no divergence in optimal quantity choices between vertical organization and first best. For $e_i^V < e_i^F$, however, $q_i^V < q_i^F < q_i^H$. If -C is large and B is small, then the divergence from first best quantity will be smaller and less costly under vertical organization, and this will offset the larger divergence of effort choices from first best levels under vertical organization.

Rationale: Under vertical organization the leader is unable to commit to choice of a higher quantity level in return for higher effort choices by gang members. At higher output levels he will always have an incentive to restrict quantity.

Appendix Three

Model of Leadership and Incentive Problems

1. A Static Model of Cheating

Gang members would like the leader to choose quantities which maximize group profits. A "responsible" leader (L_R) will solve the following problem:

$$L_R \text{ maximizes } \{q_1,q_2,q_3\} \sum_{i=1}^{N} \Pi_i \, [p_i(q,e)-c]q_i - r(e_i)$$

Subject to, for i=1,2,3

$q_i \leq 0, e_i \leq 0$

i maximizes $\{e_i|q\}$ $\Pi_i = [p_i(q,e)-c]q_i - r(e_i)$

Under this scenario, the gang member chooses $e_i(q)$ such that:

(1) $q_i \times dp_i/de_i - dr/de_i = 0$

The gang leader chooses q_i given $e_1(q)$, $e_2(q)$, $e_3(q)$:

(2) $q_i \times dp_i/dq_i + q_j \times dp_j/dq_i + q_k \times dp_k/dq_i + (p_i - c)$
$+ (q_i \times dp_i/de_i - dr/de_i + q_j \times dp_j/de_i + q_k \times dp_k/de_i) de_i/dq_i = 0$

From the first-order conditions of the gang member:

$$de_i/dq_i = -\,(dp_i/de_i) \,/\, (q_i \times d^2p_i/de_i^2 - d^2r/de_i^2) > 0$$

This problem yields a unique sequential equilibrium in which each gang member receives the same profit, given by $\Pi_i^V(q_i^V, e_i^V)$.

A self-interested gang leader (denoted as gang member 1) will choose quantities and his own effort level to maximize $\Pi_1^C(q_1^C, q_2^C, q_3^C, e_1^C, e_2^C, e_3^C)$, where C denotes the cheating outcome. The effect of cheating on gang member behavior will depend upon whether gang members anticipate it and, if not, when they observe it. The leader (denoted as gang member 1) will solve the following problem when he is dealing with gang members who anticipate cheating:

L maximizes $\{q_1,q_2,q_3\}$ $\Pi_1^C=[p_1(q_1,q_2,q_3,e_1,e_2,e_3)-c]q_1-r(e_1)$

subject to, for i=1,2,3

$q_i\leq 0, e_i\leq 0$

i solves max $\{e_i|q_1^C,q_2^C,q_3^C\}$ $\Pi_i=[p_i(q,e)-c]q_i-r(e_i)$

Under sequential decision making, when $q_i^V<q_i^H$ it will be profitable for the leader to select $q_1^C>q_1^V$ for himself and $q_i^C\leq q_i^V$ for the other gang members. Where $q_i^V>q_i^H$, it will be profitable for the leader to select $q_1^C<q_1^V$ for himself and $q_i^C\geq q_i^V$ for the other gang members. In both cases $\Pi_1^C(q_1^C,e_1^C)>\Pi_1^V(q_1^V,e_1^V)$ for the leader and $\Pi_i^C(q_i^C,e_i^C)<\Pi_i^V(q_i^V,e_i^V)$ for the other gang members.

Note: If gang members did not expect the leader to cheat, then each $i\neq 1$ would solve the following problem based on the assumption that $q_i=q_j$ for all i,j, and the result would be a smaller distortion of effort and a larger gain from cheating.

i maximizes $\{e_i|q\}$ $\Pi_i=[p_i(q,e)-c]q_i-r(e_i)$ i=2,3

Under this scenario, each gang member chooses $e_i(q_i)$ such that:

(3) $q_i\times dp_i/de_i-dr/de_i=0$

The gang leader chooses q_1 to solve:

(4.1) $q_1\times dp_1/dq_1+(p_1-c)+(q_1\times dp_1/de_1-dr/de_1)de_1/dq_1$

The gang leader chooses q_j, $j\neq 1$, to solve:

(4.2) $q_1\times dp_1/dq_j+(q_1\times dp_1/de_j)de_j/dq_j=0$

where $de_j/dq_j=-\ (dp_j/de_j)\ /\ (q_j\times d^2p_j/de_j^2-d^2r/de_j^2)>0$

Proposition 5: The cost of cheating varies positively with the magnitude of the market share and positive effort externalities.

Proof:

Consider the first-order conditions for q_1 where the leader is "responsible" and chooses quantities to maximize group profits, as given by

(2) $A_R+B_R+C_R=0$

where $A= q_1 \times dp_1/dq_1+(p_1-c)+(q_1 \times dp_1/de_1-dr/de_1)de_1/dq_1$

$B=(q_2 \times dp_2/de_1+q_3 \times dp_3/de_1)de_1/dq_1$

$C= q_2 \times dp_2/dq_1+q_3 \times dp_3/dq_1$

Compare this to the first-order conditions for q_1 where the leader chooses quantities to maximize his own profit, which is given by $A_C=0$.

(i) If B=C=0 then the outcome is the same under either scenario and there is no cost from cheating.

(ii) Where B and C are not zero, $\Pi_1^C(q_1^C,e_1^C)>\Pi_1^V(q_1^V,e_1^V)$ for the leader and $\Pi_i^C(q_i^C,e_i^C)<\Pi_i^V(q_i^V,e_i^V)$ for the other gang members. Where $q_i^V<q_i^H$, leader will select $q_1^C>ql^V$ and $q_i^C<q_i^V$. Evaluated at q^V , i's profit is increasing in i's quantity and decreasing in j's and k's quantities since $d\Pi_i/dq_i>0$ when $\sum_{i=1}^{N}[\, d\Pi_j/dq_i+d\Pi_j/de_i \times de_i/dq_i]=0$. The reverse holds where $q_i^V<q_i^H$, and the leader gains from free riding on the effort exerted by other gang members.

The divergence between the cheating and non-cheating outcome (i.e. distortions in quantity and effort choices) will depend on the magnitude of B and C. For a given level of effort, when -C>B (which, as shown in Appendix 1, implies that $q_1^V<q_1^H$) then $A_R>A_C$ and therefore since $dA/dq_1<0$ it must be the case that $q_1^C>q_1^V$. Likewise, when -C<B then $q_1^V>q_1^H$ and $q_1^C<q_1^V$. Since effort moves in the same direction as quantity in the relevant range of quantity choices, $e_1^C< e_1^V$.

Proposition 6: The costs from cheating will be larger when quantity and effort choices are made simultaneously. If gang members anticipate cheating the leader will end up giving each gang member zero quantity and each gang member will exert zero effort.

Proof:

Under simultaneous decision making the leader's problem is given by:

Maximize $\{q_1,q_2,q_3\}$ $\Pi_1^C=[p_1(q_1^C,q_2^C,q_3^C,e_1^C,e_2^C,e_3^C)-c]q_1-r(e_1)$

subject to

$q_i \geq 0$, $e_i \geq 0$

The gang members solve:

$$i \text{ maximizes } \{e_i\}\ \Pi_i=[p_i(q,e)-c]q_i-r(e_i) \quad I=1,2,3$$

First-order conditions for quantities are given by:

$$dp_1/dq_1 \times q_1+(p_1-c)=0$$
$$dp_1/dq_i \times q_1=0 \text{ for } i\neq 1 \text{ ---> } q_i=0 \text{ for } i\neq 1$$

Each gang member chooses e_i to satisfy:

$$dp_i/de_i \times q_i-dr/de_i=0 \text{ ---> } e_i=0 \text{ when } q_i=0$$

Suppose that the gang leader is not capacity constrained. The result in this case is for the gang leader to select $q_1=q_m$ (monopoly output) and $q_i=0$ for all $i\geq 0$. Given $q_i=0$, $e_i=0$. Where the leader is capacity constrained this extreme result can be avoided.

2. Model of Cheating in Repeated Game

Suppose the leader is permanently kicked out of the gang whenever deviations from the equilibrium outcome are observed and it is profitable to carry out the punishment. Let the discount rate for future profits be given by ∂, where $0<\partial<1$.

Proposition 7: Cheating can be deterred at zero cost when deviations are observable, the leader can be replaced at reasonable cost i.e. $I < (1/1-\partial)(\Pi_i^V-\Pi_i^C)$; and gang members care sufficiently about future profits i.e. satisfies $I<(1/1-\partial)(\Pi_i^V-\Pi_i^C)$ and $(1-\partial)\Pi_i^C<\Pi_i^V$.

Proof:

The gang members will find it profitable to kick out the leader upon observed deviations from equilibrium conditions, given cost I of replacing the leader through new investments in supplier information, iff:

(i) $(\partial/1-\partial)\Pi_i^V(q^V,e^V)-\partial I>(\partial/1-\partial)\Pi_i^C(q^C, e^C)$ for $i\neq l$ (l=leader)

The leader will not cheat iff (i) is satisfied and:

(ii) $\Pi_l^C(q^C, e^C)<(1/1-\partial)\Pi_l^V(q^V,e^V)$

Cheating will not occur as long as I is sufficiently small and is sufficiently large, ie. when (1) $(1/1-\partial)(\Pi_i^V-\Pi_i^C)>I$ and (2) $(1-\partial)\Pi_l^C<\Pi_l^V$.

As long as the threat to punish the leader is credible (i.e. (i) is satisfied) and sufficiently large (i.e. (ii) is satisfied), there will be no need to punish in equilibrium and cheating can be costlessly deterred.

Proposition 8: Horizontal organization will be more profitable than vertical organization when cheating cannot be deterred and quantity and effort are chosen simultaneously or are sequential and $\Pi_i^C(q_i^C,e_i^C)<\Pi_i^H(q_i^H,e_i^H)$ for $i\neq l$.

Proof:

From Proposition 1 in Appendix One, we know the vertical organization will be more profitable than horizontal organization under sequential decision making when there is no cheating, and the result will continue to hold where cheating can be costlessly deterred. If cheating cannot be deterred, then all of the gang members apart from the gang leader will receive $\Pi_i^C(q_i^C,e_i^C)$ if they adopt a vertical form of organization. Since there is no scope for cheating under horizontal organization, they must compare the cheating outcome under vertical organization, given by $\Pi_i^C(q_i^C,e_i^C)$, to $\Pi_i^H(q_i^H,e_i^H)$ when deciding which form of organization to adopt. The cost of cheating will depend upon B and C, as shown in Proposition 5. From Proposition 6, it follows that when B and C are non-zero, and the leader is not capacity constrained, other gang members earn zero profits and will therefore be better off under horizontal organization.

Appendix Four

Model of Two Competing Gangs

Suppose there are two identical gangs (a and b) competing for control over market territory T. Let the probability that gang a will capture the market be given by $x(e_a,e_b,\alpha)$ and the probability that gang b will capture the market is given by $(1-x(e_a,e_b,\alpha))$. e_a is the vector of effort levels exerted by the incumbent gang and eb is the vector of effort levels exerted by the other gang. Effort can be interpreted as energy exerted in producing market safety through fighting and surveillance activities.

α is a random variable which behaves in accordance with the probability density function $f(\alpha)$, reflecting the stochastic nature of military conflicts. $x(.)$ is the military technology, where $x(e_a,e_b,\alpha)$ satisfies the following properties:

Assumption: $x(e_a,e_b,\alpha)$ satisfies the following properties: (i) $0 \leq x(e_a,e_b,\alpha) \leq 1$; (ii) $x(.)$ is linear in α; (iii) $dx/de_{ai}>0$, $dx/de_{bi}<0$, $dx/d\alpha>0$; (iv) $d^2x/de_{ai}^2<0$, $d^2(1-x)/de_{bi}^2<0$; (v) $x(.)$ is negative definite in the positive orthant.

Gang member i seeks to maximize his expected profit, which is given by:

$$\Pi_i = x(e_a,e_b,\alpha)\, p_i(q,e)q_i - cq_i - r(e_i)$$

Each individual within the gang chooses his individual effort level to maximize his own profit, taking the actions of the others as given. But now the equilibrium must also satisfy the conditions for a Nash Equilibrium between the gangs.

Stage 1: Internal Nash Equilibrium

Look at Nash Equilibrium within gang a taking gang b's effort choices as fixed.

1. Horizontal Organization

Under horizontal organization, gang member i selects quantity and effort levels to maximize expected profits, solving:

$$\text{Maximize } \{q_i,e_i\}\ \Pi_i = x(e_a,e_b,\alpha)p_i(q,e)q_i - cq_i - r(e_i)$$
st
$$q_i \geq 0,\ ei \geq 0$$

Each gang member selects (q_i^H, e_i^H) to satisfy:

$$\Pi_i(q_i^H,q_j^H,q_k^H,e_i^H,e_j^H,e_k^H,eb) \geq \Pi_i(q_i,q_j^H,q_k^H,e_i^H,e_j^H,e_k^H,eb) \text{ for } q_i \neq q_i^H \ \&\ e_i \neq e_i^H$$

From the first-order conditions, q_i^H and e_i^H are chosen to satisfy their respective first-order conditions, taking e_b as given:

(i) $x\, p_i - c + x\, q_i \times dp_i/dq_i = 0$
(ii) $x\, q_i \times dp_i/de_i + dx/de_i \times q_i - dr/de_i = 0$

This yields profit for gang member i equal to $\Pi_i^H(q_i^H, e_i^H)$.

2. Vertical Organization

The leader now solves the following problem:

$$\text{Maximize } \{q_1,q_2,q_3\}\ \ x(e_a,e_b,\alpha)p_i(q,e)q_i - cq_i - r(e_i)$$
subject to
$$q_i \geq 0,\ e_i \geq 0$$
$$i \text{ solves } \max\{e_i|q_i\}\ E\Pi_i = x(e_a,e_b,\alpha)p_i(q,e)q_i - cq_i - r(e_i)$$

Solving this problem yields a unique sequential Nash Equilibrium $(q_1^V,q_2^V,q_3^V,e_1^V,e_2^V,e_3^V,e_b)$ in which the leader selects quantities which, together with the effort levels they induce, maximize expected joint profits and each gang member chooses his own profit maximizing level of effort given the quantity he is allocated and the effort and quantity levels of the other gang member and the effort exerted by the rival gang. From the first-order conditions, the leader chooses q_i to satisfy (ii) based on the first-order conditions for the gang member's choice of effort given in (i).

(i) $x \times dp_i/de_i + dx/de_i \times q_i - dr/de_i = 0$
(ii) $x \times dp_i/dq_i + x \times dp_j/dq_i + x \times dp_k/dq_i + x \times p_i - c + x \times dp_i/de_i$
$- dr/de_i + q_j \times dp_j/de_i + q_k \times dp_k/de_i)de_i/dq_i + dx/de_i \times de_i/dq_i \times q_i = 0$

This yields a profit for gang member i given by $\Pi_i^V(q_i^V, e_i^V)$.

3. First-best Outcome

The first-best outcome is obtained by selecting quantity and effort levels to maximize total expected profits. Quantity and effort are chosen to solve:

$$\text{Maximize}\{\{q_1,q_2,q_3,e_1,e_2,e_3\}\ x(e_a,e_b,\alpha)p_i(q,e)q_i-cq_i-r(e_i)$$
$$\text{st}$$
$$q_i\geq 0,\ e_i\geq 0\ i=1,2,3$$

This yields the solution $(\{q_1^F,q_2^F,q_3^F,e_1^F,e_2^F,e_3^F,e_b)$, where q_i and e_i are chosen to satisfy their respective first-order conditions:

(i) $x\times dp_i/dq_i\times p_i-c+x\times dp_j/dq_i\times q_j=0$

(ii) $x\times dp_i/de_i\times q_i+dx/de_i\times q_i-dr/de_i+x\times dp_j/de_i\times dp_k/de_i\times q_k=0$

The profit for each gang member is given by $\Pi_i^F(q_i^F, e_i^F)$.

Stage 2: Nash Equilibrium Between Gangs

Each gang chooses its aggregate effort level taking the effort of the other as given, and the equilibrium satisfies the conditions for a Nash Equilibrium.

$$e_a \text{ is chosen to maximize } E\Pi_I=\sum_{i=1}^{N} x\,(e_a,e_b,\alpha)[p_i(q,e)-c]q_i-r(e_i)$$

$$e_b \text{ is chosen to maximize } E\Pi o=\sum_{i=1}^{N} (\,1-x(e_a,e_b,\alpha))p_i(q,e)q_i-cq_i-r(e_i)$$

Proposition 9: In a Cournot-type model of competition where two gangs compete for control of the same market through "military investments"(i.e. effort choices), a vertically organized gang will have a strategic advantage over a horizontally organized gang where quantity and effort choices are made sequentially and a horizontally organized gang will have a strategic advantage where quantity and effort choices are made simultaneously.

Proof:

Consider a Cournot model with two identical gangs who compete for control of the market through effort choices. Given that the gangs are identical, symmetry implies that gang members will exert the same positive level of effort in equilibrium, and the two rival gangs will face equal probabilities of capturing the market.

Under vertical organization and sequential decision making, the total loss of profits for all gang members from failing to capture the market will be taken into account by the leader, and quantity decisions will be adjusted to induce higher effort levels from the gang members. From Proposition 2, we know that effort choices will be higher under vertical organization where the net benefit to the gang is positive. A shift from horizontal to vertical organization by gang a has the effect of shifting the gang's reaction curve, given by $e_a(e_b)$, out. Where gang b is horizontally organized, the result will be $x>(1-x)$.

Where decision making is simultaneous, however, the gang may be worse off because the leader is constrained in his ability to increase effort levels. Under simultaneous decision making, $e^V<e^H$. In this case, a switch from vertical to horizontal organization by gang a, but not gang b, had the effect of an outward shift in the reaction curve $e_a(e_b)$, out. Where gang b is vertically organized, the result will be $x>(1-x)$.

Notes

[1] For example, attempts to eliminate the Jamaican Posses, drug gangs distinguished by their capacity for violence and their high degree of centralized organization, had the effect of inducing these groups to become less centralized and more willing to delegate certain tasks to other groups. Rather than eliminate these groups, the measures taken may have actually reduced police control over them by increasing the dispersion of their operations. An understanding of the organizational structure of the gang might have aided law enforcers in selecting a more effective enforcement strategy.

[2] Hagedorn, J.M. (1994), 'Neighborhoods, Markets, and Gang Drug Organization', *Journal of Research in Crime and Delinquency*, vol. 31, pp. 264-294.

[3] Prominent researchers in this debate have included Taylor (1990), Skolnick (1990), Jankowski (1991) and Hagedorn (1994).

[4] Gang units within the Cambridge and Boston City Police Departments claim that gang activity in these areas is disorganized, with a large number of small and informal groups engaged in street level drug trafficking. Yet in 1995 it was suggested by interviewed gang members who were active in the street level drug trade that a few leading participants in the Boston drug market have been able to restrict the supply of high quality cocaine in the market in order to drive up its price, implying a relatively high level of organization at the top end of the local drug market.

[5] Sanchez-Jankowski, M. (1991), *Islands in the Street: Gangs and American Urban Society*, University of California, Berkley.

[6] Hagedorn, J.M. (1994), 'Neighborhoods, Markets, and Gang Drug Organization', *Journal of Research in Crime and Delinquency*, vol. 31, pp. 264-294.

[7] Id.

[8] Hagedorn, J.M. (1996), 'Gang Violence in the Post-Industrial Era', Working Draft, University of Illinois, Chicago.

[9] According to Hagedorn "(t)he turbulent environment of drug dealing is probably not a good fit for rational drug-selling organizations." Id. at p. 289...Hagedorn suggests that his study "points out that gang drug organization is probably not simply a matter of rational choice by career criminals. Rather, environmental conditions may exercise considerable influence on complexity of drug organization....Gang drug dealing today can be best understood as a semi-organized response of young people to decreased opportunities in the postindustrial era." Id. at p. 291.

[10] Padilla, F.M. (1992), 'The Gangs as an American Enterprise', Rutgers University Press, NJ.

[11] Hagedorn, J.M. (1994), 'Neighborhoods, Markets, and Gang Drug Organization', *Journal of Research in Crime and Delinquency*, vol. 31, pp. 264-294.

[12] Sullivan, M.L. (1989), *Getting Paid. Youth Crime and Work in the Inner City*, Conrell University Press, Conrell. See also Taylor, C.S. (1988), 'Youth Gangs

Organize for Power, Money', *School Safety*, Spring, 26-27; and Taylor, A.C. (1990), *Dangerous Society*, MI, East Lansing: Michigan State University Press.

[13] Although a number of researchers have focuses on the connection between gangs and employment, they have not paid as much attention to the interaction between socio-economic organization and criminal activities.

[14] Block, C.R. and R. Block (1993), 'Street Gang Crime in Chicago', *Research in Brief: National Institute of Justice*, U.S., DOJ.

[15] Taylor, C.S. (1990), *Dangerous Society*, East Lansing, MI, Michigan State University Press.

[16] Id. at p.98. "Corporate gangs...are part of organized crime in America. Drugs, as a commodity, have become the same unifying economic force for gangs today (adult and juvenile) as alcohol during prohibition....Detroit gangs are using drugs as this vehicle for social mobility...". Id at p.97.

[17] Id. at p.97.

[18] Spergel, I. A. (1995), *The Youth Gang Problem: A Community Approach*, Oxford University Press, Oxford.

[19] Id. at p. 89.

[20] Wilson, W.J. (1987), *The Truly Disadvantaged*, University of Chicago, Chicago.

[21] In 1980 ten large U.S. cities had black isolation indices in excess of 80 (Atlanta, Baltimore, Chicago, Cleveland, Detroit, Gary, Neward, Philadelphia, St. Louis, and Washington, D.C.), meaning that the average black person in these cities lived in a neighborhood that was at least 80% black. A large number of other cities are characterized by similar patterns of residential segregation. See Massey, D. S. and N. Denton. (1993), *American Apartheid: Segregation and the Making of the Underclass,* Harvard University Press, Cambridge, p.160.

[22] "The isolation of Negro from white communities is increasing rather than decreasing...Negro poverty is not white poverty. Many of its causes...are the same. But there are differences-deep, corrosive, obstinate differences-radiating painful roots into the community, the family, and the nature of the individual." President Lyndon Johnson, address to Howard University, June 4,1965.

[23] Fagan, J. (1989), 'The Social Organization of Drug Use and Drug Dealing Among Urban Gangs', *Criminology*, vol. 27, pp. 633-667.

[24] Vigil, J.D. and Yun, S.C. (1996), 'Southern California Gangs: Comparative Ethnicity and Social Control', in Huff, R.C. (ed.) *Gangs In America*, Second ed. Sage, Thousand Oaks, CA, pp.139-156.

[25] See Klein, M.W. (1990), 'Having an investment in violence: Some thoughts about the American street gang', Sutherland Award address to American Society of Criminology.; Klein, M. W. (1993), 'Attempting gang control by suppression', *Studies in Crime and Crime Prevention: Annual Review*, Stockholm. Klein, M.C. and Maxson, C.L. (1994), 'Gangs and Crack Cocaine Trafficking', in Mackenzie, D.L. and Uchida, C. *Drugs and Crime*, Sage Publishing, London. Klein, M.W. (1995a), 'Street Gang Cycles', in Wilson, J.Q. and Petersilia, J. (eds.) *Crime*, Institute for Contemporary Studies, San Francisco: Klein, M. W. (1995b) *The American Street Gang: Its Nature, Prevalence, and Control*, Oxford University Press, New York.

[26] Klein cites a number of studies which indicate that joining gangs leads to more criminal involvement, and he argues that the group identity of a gang is shaped in part by the criminal focus.
[27] The increase in what is perceived as gang migration has prompted some interesting studies in gang migration and proliferation. Maxson, Klein and Woods (1995) study the pattern of gang migration in the United States in some detail.
[28] See Klein, M. (1995), *The American Street Gang*, Oxford University Press, Oxford, p.29.
[29] See Kleiman, M. (1995), *Against Excess: Drug Policy For Results*, HarperCollin Publishers, U.S.; Moore, M.H. (1990), 'Drugs: Getting A Fix On The Problem and the Solution', *Yale Law and Policy Review*, vol. 8, no.1 p. 86.
[30] Moore points out that heroin costs sixty times more than the equivalent dosage of morphine, and cocaine is fifteen times more expensive in illegal markets than in legal markets. Moore, M.H. (1990), 'Drugs: Getting A Fix On The Problem and the Solution', *Yale Law and Policy Review*, vol. 8, no.1, p. 28.
[31] Figures are taken from Reuter and Kleiman (1986) in Table 3, Structure of Drug Prices, Moore, M. H. (1990), *Supply Reduction and Drug Law Enforcement*, p.129.
[32] Kleiman, M A. (1995), *Against Excess: Drug Policy For Results*, HarperCollin Publishers, U.S., p.109.
[33] Id. at 110.
[34] Kleiman, Mark A. (1995), *Against Excess: Drug Policy for Results*, HarperCollin Publisher, p.129.
[35] Mollen Commission (1994*), Mollen Commission to Investigate Allegations of Police Corruption*, Mollen Commission, The City of New York.
[36] Becker, G. (1968), 'Crime and Punishment: An Economic Analysis', *Journal of Political Economy*, vol. 76, pp. 169-217.
[37] Fiorentini, G. and Peltzman, S. (eds.) (1995), *The Economics of Organized Crime*, Cambridge University Press, Cambridge.
[38] This view is popular with prosecutors of organized crime. It was clearly the view adopted by the Italian prosecutors who started the "maxi-trial" against the heads of the Sicilian Mafia. They argued that a committee composed of the Mafia heads acted as a centralized decision-making unit for a large range of economic activities. See Savona, E. (ed.) (1993), *Mafia Issues: Analysis and Proposals for Combating the Mafia Today*, International Scientific and Professional Advisory Council of the United Nations Crime Prevention and Criminal Justice Program, Milan.
[39] Skaperdas, S. and Syropoulos, C. (1995), 'Gangs as primitive states', in Fiorentini, G. and Peltzman, S. (eds.) *The Economics of Organized Crime*, Cambridge University Press, Cambridge.
[40] Polo, M. (1995), 'Internal Cohesion and Competition Among Criminal Organizations', in Fiorentini, G. and Peltzman, S. (eds.) *The Economics of Organized Crime*, Cambridge University Press, Cambridge.
[41] Fiorentini, G. and Peltzman, S, 'Introduction', in Fiorentini, G. and Peltzman, S (eds.), *The Economics of Organized Crime*, Cambridge University Press, Cambridge
[42] Advantages from centralization include (a) economies of scale in some basic

services; (b) exploitation of monopolistic prices in some markets less open to external competition; (c) internalization of negative externalities due to oversupply of violence; (d) avoidance of resource dissipation through competitive lobbying and corruption; (e) better management of a portfolio or risky activities; and (f) easier access to financial markets. Strong forces which reduce the degree of central coordination include: (a) the risks involved in illegal transactions decrease more than proportionately with their size since it is impossible to make contracts binding; (b) the property rights over the commodities are not well defined and can be subjected to seizure by enforcement agencies, thus discouraging large investments; (c) risk of detection increases with the number of people involved; and (d) problems in keeping financial markets efficient as they are thin markets. See Fiorintini, G. and S. Peltzman (eds.) (1995), *The Economics of Organized Crime*, Cambridge University Press, Cambridge, p. 6.

[43] Becker, G. (1968), 'Crime and Punishment: An Economic Analysis', *Journal of Political Economy*, vol. 76, pp. 169-217.

[44] Focusing on group activities also allows for an examination of the interaction between internal and external incentive systems and a study of coordination problems and the potential for multiple equilibria. For example, given the protective and retaliatory nature of much of the violence engaged in by street gangs, and the importance to gangs of relative positioning, it is plausible to assume that increases in violence will generate further increases and decreases in violence could engender further decreases, generating the possibility of state of high and low level violence, leading to multiple possible outcomes.

[45] Rather than treating organizational design as a rational ex ante decision made by group members, one could instead adopt an evolutionary approach based on a study of dominant strategies. Analogies could also be drawn to the predator-prey type modeling utilized in biology. Fiorentini and Peltzman (1995) suggest that the significant increase observed in the share of transactions which are directly or indirectly under the control of highly-structured and highly-diversified organizations signals "a trend towards greater efficiency in the allocation of resources used in the production of illegal commodities and a growing need for the agents involved to adopt management schemes which minimize organizational costs in order not to disappear in the course of competition".Fiorintini, G. and S. Peltzman (eds.) (1995), *The Economics of Organized Crime*, Cambridge University Press, Cambridge, p.3.

[46] This is analogous to a situation in which the presence of external producers can facilitate cooperation between member producers of a trade block. The presence of a threat to absolute gain can be used to undermine concerns about relative gains.

[47] In many cases threats of violence and the importance of maintaining a reputation for fulfilling obligations will operate as effective checks on opportunistic behavior even in the absence of legally enforceable agreements. An interesting question for future study concerns the extent to which threats of violence can be used as a replacement for legal enforcement of agreements.

[48] See Macaulay, S. (1963), 'Non-Contractual Relations in Business: A Preliminary Study', *American Sociological Review*, vol. 28, p. 28.

[49] See Bernstein, L. (1992), 'Opting Out of the Legal System: Extralegal Contractual Relations in the Diamond Industry', *Journal of Legal Studies*, vol.XXI. A possible explanation for this type of reliance on non-legal sanctions lies in the strategic use of private information and the corresponding "personalization" of transactions. The trade-off between incentives and market externalities in an environment of imperfect and costly information also arises in the context of exclusive dealing and franchise arrangements. While there has been much discussion in the anti-trust literature on the relative merits of these types of business arrangements, there has been little in the way of formal modeling of the trade-offs involved.

[50] There is evidence of the growing importance of economic motivation in gang membership, particularly for black-American gangs, and they are increasingly viewed by their members as business organizations designed to generate income.

[51] Private information about suppliers or about market conditions specific to the gang's territory can be used as an effective source of control in much the same way as control over physical assets, particularly where the high risks involved make acquisition of this information by other gang members difficult and costly.

[52] Rabin (1993) focuses on the organizational implications of private information, looking at its role in determining the control of physical assets, although he focuses on how agency problems could lead to less efficient ownership structures due to problems in conveying private information.

[53] Moreover, wholesale suppliers will not want to engage in side deals with other gang members because the benefits of obtaining additional business will be smaller than the costs imposed by the increase in risk.

[54] See Holmstrom, B. and P. Milgrom. (1991), 'Multitask Principal-Agent Analyses: Incentive Contracts, Asset Ownership, and Job Design', *The Journal of Law, Economics and Organization*, vol. 7, pp. 24-52. Holmstrom and Milgrom provide an analysis of the contractual problems arising when some variables can be verified while others cannot, suggesting this as an explanation for the prevalence of muted incentives within firms. They do not extend their analysis to examine the implications of having both observable and non-observable variables for the structuring of group activities, however.

[55] Effort level could be interpreted as a measure of product quality. The easiest way of making a profit is to take the amount of drugs that has been purchased and increase the quantity by diluting the drugs with cheaper ingredients. This is known as "cutting" the drugs. Consumers will not always be able to detect dilution, at least not until after their purchase, and this introduces monitoring problems in the market. Individuals will have an incentive to free ride on the gang's reputation for quality products by selling a lower quality product for a higher price.

[56] Where an individual gang member increases the quantity he sells, this will decrease the demand facing the other gang members. Where an individual gang member exerts effort in creating a safe market, sells a high quality product, or recruits new drug users, this will have a positive effect on the demand facing other gang members.

[57] One of the most important features of an illicit market is the absence of feasible methods of sharing and verifying market information. The need to keep transactions hidden and to minimize the number of participants and the number of transactions place severe constraints on the methods by which sellers and buyers can advertise their needs and monitor the actions of their competitors.
[58] A useful analogy can be drawn to multi-national trade blocks composed of states which benefit from cooperation but have conflicting interests. The types of risks imposed on the block will have an important effect on the ability of members to cooperate and coordinate their actions.
[59] Although there may be some pooling of financial resources and information, such arrangements are voluntary and decisions are made by the members as a group based on self-reported information rather than by delegation of authority.
[60] This assumption is designed to reflect and to capture the effects of personalizing transactions (i.e. of structuring transactions in such a way that the identities of the parties who are involved is an important feature of the transaction). It is interesting to note that many of the deals that take place within legitimate markets also involve personalized transactions . Developing industry norms of behavior and implicit understandings not encapsulated in formal contracts have been found to be an efficient way to organize business dealings in legitimate markets and will be even more useful in illegitimate markets.
[61] The high turnover rate and fairly rapid replacement of leadership in most gangs supports the notion that leaders are replaceable, although the turbulence which accompanies such transitions suggests that the transition is costly. While there would be no replacement of the leader in the equilibrium of this model, a positive turnover in leadership could arise within this framework once the assumptions of non-stochastic demand and supply conditions are relaxed.
[62] The results generated in this section do not depend upon the size of N.
[63] It is assumed that this cycle is repeated continuously until the gang is forced out of its market or until the market becomes unprofitable.
[64] The cost of administrative activities (drug purchase and allocation) becomes important once the assumptions of responsible leadership (i.e. no shirking or cheating) and compensation for services rendered (i.e. no incentive problems with respect to compensating leader) are relaxed.
[65] One of the interesting features of the sale of addictive goods is the possibility that demand, and therefore price, may actually be increasing in quantity sold over certain quantity levels.
[66] Given that q_i is determined by the best response function $R_{iq}(q_j,e_j)$ and e_i by the best response function $R_{ie}(q_j,e_j)$, both quantity and effort choices are strategic substitutes if $d^2R_iq/dq_idq_j<0$ and $d^2R_ie/de_ide_j<0$. The results of the model do not hinge on whether the variables are strategic complements or substitutes, however, but rather on the presence of external effects of decisions by one gang member on other gang members.
[67] In reality one would expect cost to fall with the quantity purchased given the fixed costs associated with each transaction and given larger bargaining power.

[68] When individuals cannot observe the actions taken by others, the sequential problem in which each gang member chooses quantity and then effort is equivalent to the problem in which quantity and effort levels are chosen simultaneously.
[69] This conclusion holds as long as the additional costs associated with appointing and supporting a leader are not too large and do not depend upon gang size.
[70] The best response functions are given by $q_i=R_{il}(e_i,e_j)$ and $e_i=R_{if}(e_j,q_i,q_j)$.
[71] The same result occurs in the context of strategic delegation, where the gains from delegation stem primarily from the ability to shift best response functions so as to take advantage of a stackelberg point. See Vickers, J. (1983), 'Delegation and the Theory of the Firm', *The Economic Journal*, vol. 29, p. 138.
[72] The cost of cheating will vary positively with the degree to which cheating is anticipated and negatively with the leader's ability to constrain his own behavior in advance.
[73] Cheating could also take the form of the leader providing other gang members with the quantities they expect (q_i^V), inducing them to choose the same effort levels as before, but choosing a higher output for himself.
[74] Expectations about cheating and commitment opportunities will depend upon factors such as the expected life-span of the gang, the rate of turnover of gang members and gang leaders, and the personal reputation that the leader either already has or plans to develop. If gang members do not know in advance what quantity they would receive from a responsible leader (e.g. due to uncertain cost conditions) the gang leader will be able to allocate quantities without the fear of being detected until profits are realized, and gang members will select their effort levels based on the assumption that quantity allocations are identical. Cost will be less in this case.
[75] The discount rate will depend on factors such as the chance of attack from rival gangs and the risk of arrest and/or confiscation of goods by law enforcers.It would be interesting to consider the implications of allowing for differences in discount rates for different gang members, perhaps reflecting differences in risk attitudes or variations in risks
[76] Punishing the leader in periods where profits fall below a certain "trigger" level could be one way of minimizing the incentive to cheat, although it would sometimes result in punishing the leader for exogenous drops in demand. This type of trigger price strategy in the presence of stochastic demand parallels that employed by Green and Porter in the context of price wars in the gasoline market. In their model trigger price strategies lead to price wars along the equilibrium path even though no individual seller has an incentive to cheat. See Green, E. and Porter, R. (1984), 'Non cooperative collusion Under Imperfect Price Information', *Econometrica*, vol. 52, no.1, p. 87. Imperfect information about market conditions could also be addressed by employing a system of rotating leadership. If there is a positive probability of a change in leadership during each period, then the leader knows that he faces a positive risk of discovery and punishment if he cheats.
[77] See Skaperdas, S. and Syropoulos, C. (1995), 'Competing For Claims to Property', Working Paper, University of California. Skaperdas and Syropoulos focus on some of the costs of insecure resources generated by competing groups

who must divide their endowments between production and appropriation. While Skaperdas and Syropoulos do focus on the effects of competition for control over a productive input and pay some attention to the role of characteristics such as wealth in determining the outcome of the struggle, they do not look at the role that organizational structure can play in influencing the division of the coveted resource. See also Garfinkel, M.R. (1990), 'Arming as a Strategic Investment in a Cooperative Equilibrium', American Economic Review, vol. 80, pp. 50-68; and Rider, R. (1993), 'War, Pillage, and Markets', *Public Choice*, vol. 75, pp. 149-56.

[78] Spergel, I. (1995), *The Youth Gang Problem: A Community Approach*, Oxford University Press, New York, p. 80.

[79] Spergel, I. (1995), *The Youth Gang Problem: A Community Approach*, Oxford University Press, New York, p. 81.

[80] It has been suggested that the emergence of the Bloods was largely in response to the perceived threat of the Crips, for example.

[81] Lupo, A. (1996), 'Gang bust-ups reveal their business side', *Boston Globe*, Sept.22, at p.1.

[82] Id.

[83] McNicoll, A. (1983), *Drug Trafficking: A North-South Perspective*, North-South Institute, Ottawa, pp. 41-46.

[84] Id.

[85] As early as 1979, the then chief of the Drug Enforcement Administration commmented that prescription drugs "present a much greater health hazard to the general populace than drugs wholly illegal in nature", adding that at least 30 to 250 million dosage units of controlled drugs manufactured each year in the U.S. were diverted into illegal markets. Id.

[86] A number of organizational differences between ethnic groups can be identified. Asian groups, for example, tend to adopt a very hierarchical organizational form, with a clear chain of authority and division of functions. Jamaican Posses, known for their ruthlessness, operate in small, private and tightly knit groups, preferring to minimize interactions with outside groups. Latin American street gangs tend to be larger and more loosely organized, with more attention given to the social aspects of gang membership. Differences may be due in part to factors such as product type, stage of development and the skills and resources which gang members and their communities have available.

[87] See DeStefano, A.M. (1986), 'New Ethnic Mobs Rival Cosa Nostra', *Newsday*, Nov.30,1986, at p.7.

[88] See William O. (1988), 'Street Gang Networks Called State's Greatest Crime Danger', *Los Angeles Times*, Sept. 7 at p.3. The 1987 Organized Crime Report included reports of 150 members of the Medellin group had set up half a dozen separate cocaine distribution and money laundering rings in the state, while two Cuban groups totaling 400 members specialized in narcotics dealing and a 350-member "Israeli Mafia" in Los Angeles was linked to arson, fraud and drugs.

[89] Kleinknecht, W. (1996), The New Ethnic Mobs. Free Press, U.S.

[90] Id.

[91] Black, C. (1996), 'Senate proposals target street gangs', *Boston Globe*, April 25 at p.14.
[92] The Japanese Yakuza, the Taiwan-based United Bamboo Organized Crime Syndicate and the Chinese "triads" are involved in narcotics trafficking, extortion, prostitution, gambling and money laundering in the American underworld. See Harris,S. (1986), 'Study cites menace of drug-crime networks', *L.A. Times*, July 23, at p. 3.
[93] Dao, J. (1992), 'Unorganized Asian gangs poised for criminal takeover', *Fort Worth Star-Telegram*, April 5 at p.11.
[94] The recent exposure of a nationally orchestrated Asian criminal organization involved in heroin distribution and armed robberies of computer micro chips provides one of a series of recent examples of the growing sophistication and versatility of many new ethnic criminal groups. Arrests were made in California, New York, Oregon, Minnesota and Virginia following an 18-month investigation named "Bytes Dust". The organization worked by stealing and selling computer chips to finance heroin imports from Southeast Asia, also engaging in illegal gambling, firearms trafficking and extortion. Hunt, K. (1996), 'Feds bust major Asian drug-trafficking, high-tech robbery ring', *The Fresno Bee*, April 12, p. B3.
[95] Id.
[96] Cullen, K. (1987), 'Gangs seen as carefully organized', *Boston Globe*, Jan.7, p.17.
[97] Overend, W. (1988), 'Street Gang Networks Called State's Greatest Crime Danges', *Los Angeles Times*, Sept. 7, p.3.
[98] Black, C. (1996), 'Senate proposals target street gangs', *Boston Globe*, April 25, p.14.
[99] The big four prison gangs are the Black Guerrilla Family, the Mexican Mafia, the Aryan Brotherhood and the Nuestra Family. Newer groups such as the Consolidated Crips Organization have emerged to challenge them.
[100] Harris, S. (1986), 'Study Cites Menace of Drug-Crime Networks', *Los Angeles Times,* July 23, p. 3.
[101] Abadinsky, H. (1987), 'The McDonald's-ization of the Mafia', in Bynum, T.S. (ed), *Organized Crime in America*, Criminal Justice Press, New York, p.43.
[102] Drug Enforcement Agency, Report (1997).
[103] While there may be some degree of role differentiation in a horizontally organized gang, role assignments are flexible and impermanent and are defined largely along functional lines. The model developed in this chapter deliberately ignores functional differences in order to focus on the role of information in shaping group activities.
[104] This assumption is designed to reflect and to capture the cost and importance of personalizing transactions. It is interesting to compare this with the importance of "contacts" and informal understandings in legitimate business relationships.
[105] This is a plausible assumption to make given the tremendous risks associated with participating in illegal transaactions and the need for secrecy. Much of the mark-up of price in illegal drug markets can be attributed to the risk premium required by retail –level transactors.
[106] Four different types of strategies for attacking illegal market activity,

particularly illegal drug sales, can be identified: (1) supply reduction at the producer level (through destruction of illegal crops, for example); (2) supply reduction at the retail level (such as direct intervention in retail selling through arrests and confiscation of assets); (3) supply reduction at the wholesale level (such as interdiction and other such measures to reduce wholesale supply); and (4) demand reduction (such as measures aimed at market disruption, risk enhancement for consumers, or drug abuse prevention and treatment programs). Each of these types of strategies would reduce the profitability of illegal drug selling (and other illegal market activities) in a different way.

[107] While the United States government has focused it's anti-drug efforts on broad, macro-level measures such as interdiction, countries such as Japan have focused instead on altering the incentives of criminal organizations in order to induce substitution into less socially harmful modes of operation. Japanese law enforcers often overlook the activities of organized crime groups, for example, as long as the activities of these groups remain within tacitly understood boundaries, and in some European countries such as Amsterdam, areas have been designated within which certain "illegal" activities are (unofficially) tolerated. See, for example, 'The Mob's Truly Sorry: Killing Upsets the Police', *New York Times*, Wed.Sept. 6,1995, p. A4. "As with almost everyone else in Japanese society, organized-crime figures know their boundaries. As long as they stay within those boundaries...they are within what people here call limits of tolerance....The police adamantly deny any hint of collusion with the mob, or Yakuza, because it is obviously unacceptable to condone criminal activity in public. But almost everyone else readily acknowledges a rough social contract, which until recently at least has been a source of comfort to all sides."